Morgans' Brewery Yard, c1900

Norwich Pubs and Breweries Past and Present

Norwich Pubs and Breweries is published by Norwich Heritage Projects, an independent non-profit-making organisation which simply aims to encourage an appreciation of the heritage of a wonderful city.

Norwich Pubs and Breweries: Past and Present
Published by Norwich Heritage Projects
Norwich Heritage Projects
5, Cringleford Chase
Norwich
NR4 7RS
www.norwich-heritage.co.uk

Norwich Heritage Projects is an independent
non-profit-making organisation which simply aims
to encourage an appreciation of the heritage of a
wonderful city.

First edition 2011
Second edition (revised) 2015
ISBN 978-0-9566272-5-4

Edited, designed and brought to production by
Norwich Heritage Projects.
Printed and bound in the UK by
Barnwell Print Ltd, Dunkirk Industrial Estate,
Aylsham, Norfolk, NR11 6SU

Every reasonable effort has been made to establish
the copyright holders of all the photographs and
information sources used in this book. Any errors
or omissions are inadvertent. Anyone who has not
been contacted is invited to write to the publisher so
that a proper acknowledgement can be included in
subsequent editions.

Front cover (top to bottom and left to right) :
Ribs of Beef (Mike Dixon), Jolly Butchers (Albert
Cooper), Fat Cat sign (Cass Hooton), Orford Arms
(Ollie Potter), Bullards' 'landlord' (Pat Burrows),
Ship Inn (George Plunkett), Ferry Boat (Dick
Hudson), Phyllis Burgess (Gloria King), Star
Brewery dray (Peter and Carol Turner)

Back cover: Little Bethel Street (NCC Library and
Information Service), Drinkers outside the Golden
Star (Peter and Carol Turner)

Image Credits.
We are very grateful to all of the following for their
kind permission to reproduce images. Subjects have
only been specified where more than one person's
work appears on the page. In cases where the photographer or artist is unknown the image is accredited
to the donor. All 'Photo Gallery' images have been
accredited in the text.

Albert Cooper: 63 (Albert Cooper), 64 (Black Anna
and Albert Cooper), 148, 212 (Black Anna), 214
Andy Field: 63 (Continentals),164
Antony Murray: 57 (Prince of Denmark images)
Arthur Houlston: 21
Arthur Pank's family: 48, 49 (sign), 51 (Rose &
Crown), 52 (sign), 53 (Lord Nelson and Mariners'
Tavern), 59, 84,189 (Plough Inn sign), 206, 217
(sign)
Barry Berwick: 17, 18
Barry Lambert: 211 (Harry and Ethel Lambert)
Basil Gowan: 114, 136 (Great Hospital), 139, 158
(Elizabethan room), 167 (postcard), 212 (Billy)
Carol and Peter Turner: 45, 118, 119
Cass Hooton: 61
Chris and Glynis Higgins: 202 (exterior), 203
Derek McDonald: 19, 23 (emblem), 41 and 158
(Backs' bar), 72, 73 (St Faith's Tavern), 75 (Little
John), 97(exteriors), 107 (Leopard building, John W
Stokes), 137 (Goodsons),140 (Prince of Wales), 144
(exterior), 145 (Turkey Cock), 146 (Wild Man), 157
(Coach & Horses, 2003), 158 (exterior), 170 (Vine),
200 (Coachmakers), 201 (exteriors), 211 (exterior)
Derek Spanton: 34, 35
Dick Hudson: 107 (sign), 218 (Ferry Boat)
E. H Butt: 157 (Coach & Horses, 2003)
Gary Freeman: 65 (Contours), 124 (Wellington),
165 (Contours)
**George Plunkett (permission from Jonathan
Plunkett):** viii, 14, 49 (exterior), 64 (Jolly
Butchers),70, 81(Clarence Harbour)85, 90 (Cat &
Fiddle), 92, 93 (1935 exterior), 95 (Rose), 96 (Royal
Oak), 98, 101, 104, 105 (churches), 106 (Cellar
House), 107 (Horse Barracks), 108 (exterior), 116,
120, 121 (Morning Star), 123 (buildings), 124
(Woolpack), 137 (Bishop Bridge Inn and Briton
Arms), 156 (photo), 159 (George & Dragon),
162, 166, 168 (Arcade Stores), 169 (photo), 171
(photo),182 (Bell, 1936), Cock (182), 184 (Nag's
Head), 187, 189 (Plough), 190 (Shirehall), 191
(exteriors), 192 (exteriors), 195, 199 (hospital), 204
(Trumpet), 207, 213, 216 (photo), 220
Gloria King: 16
Janet Hope: 74, 75 (fishing club)
Jarrold & Sons: 181
John Hutson: 12
Jon Tydeman: 179
Leonard Thompson: 54 (sign), 94 (sign), 171
(White Swan)

Steward & Patteson workers checking the brew, c1950

Revise or Reprint?

It was in 2011 that we published the first edition of 'Norwich Pubs and Breweries: Past and Present'. We were somewhat surprised that it sold out very quickly and we were left with the quandary of whether to reprint immediately or wait a while and revise it. Since completing the original publication we have researched and written 'The Story of the Norwich Boot and Shoe Trade' and 'The Courts and Yards of Norwich'. Time has passed and we now find ourselves some four years out of date.

As the book is mainly about the City's heritage rather than a modern pub and brewery guide much of the content remains unchanged, but of course the industry continues to evolve. In the last four years a few premises have closed, a few have reopened many more have been renovated, refurbished and renamed. Long gone are the days when simply providing pub grub is enough to keep a premises open, now customers demand a high-quality offering.

On the brewery front an interesting development since the last edition is the resurrection of old brands, and so City drinkers can once more enjoy a pint of S&P and Bullards. The old brewery buildings have gone, but their names live on.

We hope the book will satisfy your curiosity, but it will not quaff your thirst...however, we know a number of establishments that will.

Cheers

Frances and Michael Holmes

July 2015

Contents

Introduction

In 1925 Walter Wicks wrote the 'Inns and Taverns of Old Norwich', followed in 1947 by Leonard Thompson's 'Norwich Inns'. More recently, in 1975, John Riddington Young produced his own version of Walter Wicks' work. All of theses books contain wonderful stories, and give brilliant insights into the pub scene and the characters that inhabited it at the time. They also share another feature . . . they are all out of print. Therefore, with some trepidation, we decided that it was time to make another foray into a subject that has contributed so much to Norwich's heritage.

When we first proposed the book a number of people raised the question of combining the story of the pubs with that of Norwich's breweries. It made sense to do this, after all for the majority of the 20th century they owned around 95% of the pubs.

In all of our projects we try to bring history to life by including personal stories and photographs. In this respect we owe many thanks to the numerous people who have contributed. Additionally we are particularly grateful to both Richard Bristow (www.norfolkpubs.co.uk) and Derek McDonald, experts in this field, for so generously sharing their material with us.

Structuring the book has been a challenge. We had so much material! In the section on breweries we have been able to include the memories of people who worked at all of the major breweries. These give a real insight into a world long since gone. We were also able to come right up to date by including a section on Woodforde's, which originated in Norwich. The pub section tested our ingenuity more. Eventually we decided to have an in-depth look at general topics all linked with pub culture e.g. names, artists and entertainers, and then to research some establishments in more detail. But which ones? In the end we based our selection around the 1884/5 OS map of Norwich, which highlights all of the pubs and inns in the centre of the City which were open at the time. We have included extra information on many of the pubs which are still open, together with interviews given by City landlords.

Finally this is not a beer guide. We leave advice on this subject to the authorities at CAMRA. Our goal is quite simple. We aim to show the outstanding contribution that pubs and breweries have made, and indeed continue to make, to Norwich's culture in an informative but light-hearted manner.

Cheers

Frances and Michael Holmes

Blue Bell, Lower Goat Lane, 1935

Section 1 - Norwich Breweries

Steward & Patteson brewery workers, c1900

1

Brewing in Norwich

Early Days

Ale, which can be dated back to 3,000 years BC, is believed to be the world's oldest form of alcohol. When ancient nomadic civilisations such as Babylonia settled down to grow grain they were able to produce the two staple elements of their diets, namely bread and ale. At a time when water was often contaminated, ale was the healthy option. As soon as farming became established in the British Isles, tribes started to brew their own varieties of ale. It has been a common drink in England for about 1500 years, in fact until the early 15th century it was the principal drink.

The very early brewers produced malt by first soaking barley (or wheat) in water and then burying it in the ground to allow it to germinate. The malted cereal would then be dried, crushed and baked into large flat cakes which would be brewed by the simple process of being soaked in warm water and pressed through a sieve. The resulting liquid (or wort) was than fermented in large earthenware vessels. As can be imagined the resultant ale would not meet today's standards being somewhat cloudy, furthermore it was often so thick, with unfiltered barley husks, it had to be drunk through a hollow reed to enable it to be filtered.

For many years the Church exercised control over both brewing and the supply of ales. Monks were some of the earliest brewers in Norwich. Their breweries can be traced back to around the 11th century and were situated in their priories. For example the Benedictine monks had their brewery in the Cathedral Close whilst the Austin friars produced ale between Mountergate and St Anne's Staithe in King Street. It was also brewed in homes and on farms.

To produce ale the early brewers used herbs and spices to balance the sweetness of the malt. However, in the 15th century beer was introduced to this country from the Low Countries. Unlike English ales, beer was brewed with the addition of hops which added bitterness to the beer and extended its life.

Later in the same century, during the reign of Henry VI, the hop vine was first grown in England. At the time it was considered an adulterant and its use for brewing was banned by the monarch. It was more than a century before Henry VIII repealed the prohibition after which it became universally used and the terms 'ale' and 'beer' became largely synonymous.

At this time 'small beer' (of around 2% alcohol) was an important source of nutrition. Unlike the higher alcohol beers, which were served for recreational purposes, this weaker alternative contained just enough alcohol to act as a preservative. It provided hydration without causing intoxication.

During the Middle Ages brewing was mainly carried out in the home or by innkeepers, who produced beer solely to be drunk on their own premises. It was only during the 17th century that 'common breweries' (i.e. breweries which distributed products to a number of outlets) were established.

Until 1750, in terms of population, Norwich was the third largest city in England. However, by the end of the 18th century Norwich was in decline. Quite simply it did not have the natural resources that were essential in the new industrial age. As such the Industrial Revolution largely by-passed the region. Manufacturers were pushed towards industries based on agriculture, one of which was brewing.

Norwich was a natural site for the brewing industry being situated at the centre of an area which grew some of the best malting barley in the country. It also had the advantage of having access to good quality water, essential to the brewing process, from the chalk that underlies much of the City.

Barley + Hops + Water + Yeast + TLC = Beer

Growth and Expansion

In 1783 there were nine breweries in Norwich serving a population of about 35,000. Most would have been small. Additionally, publicans continued to brew beers for their own establishments.

As major brewers came to dominate production a new phenomenon emerged, namely the 'tied house'. This development played a huge part in the subsequent expansion and eventual demise of the Norwich breweries. It would appear that the early growth of the tie, whereby a publican agreed to take the product of a particular brewery and came under its control, was not a deliberate strategy. It often arose because the publican became indebted to the brewer, or a future landlord with insufficient capital may have sought financial help from the brewery. As it became more expensive for licensees to enter the trade it was seen as a sensible marketing strategy for the brewers to offer credit since it secured an outlet for their beer. Eventually the majority of houses were either owned, or leased, by the breweries. Subsequently a trend developed whereby the dominant producers took over their smaller competitors not for their breweries, which were often subsequently closed down, but as a means of getting their hands on the tied estate. One wonders if the 19th-century industrialists were aware that this strategy, which gave them early dominance, would eventually lead to their own downfall.

By 1836 there were 27 breweries in the City. However, new production methods were beginning to give significant advantages to the larger producers. In particular:

- Technological developments, e.g. the increased use of the steam engine, benefitted the larger companies who further gained from economies of scale
- An increase in popularity of porter (a malt liquor) which required longer, and hence more, storage. Steward & Patteson began producing it in 1840
- Greater control of the brewing process produced beer of a more consistent quality
- The growth of tied houses.

In Norwich there was a relatively high level of production and control by 'common brewers' such that in 1841 the industry was highly concentrated. By then over 75% of Norwich's 558 public houses were in the hands of seven firms, with Steward & Patteson controlling 33% of them. This concentration was probably linked to the relatively early growth of the larger brewers, indeed it is believed that Norwich had a lower proportion of pubs brewing their own beer than anywhere else in England. In fact the 1830 excise returns indicate that in the country as a whole one

Steward & Patteson's Pockthorpe Brewery, c1900

public house in three was brewing its own beer, whilst in Norwich less than 5% of all victuallers brewed their own beers.

All of the above required a substantial capital outlay and resulted in the larger profitable brewers expanding whilst the smaller were either taken over or collapsed. Thus by 1858 the number of breweries operating within Norwich had fallen to 12. By 1875 there were seven and by the 1920s there were just the 'big four', i.e. Steward & Patteson, Bullards, Morgans and Youngs, Crawshay & Youngs. Sadly as the breweries were taken over many local beers disappeared.

Although the number of breweries fell, overall output rose as a result of two main factors. Firstly, during the 19th century Norwich's population rose from 38,500 to 111,700, resulting in an increase in demand. Secondly, as rail and river transport improved, the City breweries were able to extend their activities to rural areas where they could easily compete with, and often ruin, small country breweries.

By the end of the 19th century the 'big four' had become limited companies which enabled them to raise capital through share issues. The breweries were attractive to investors so that when Steward & Patteson floated in 1895, the £150,000 share capital offered to the public was oversubscribed sevenfold.

What made the brewers appealing was the financial strength they had amassed in their tied estates. In fact in 1895 Steward & Patteson and Bullards held 930 pubs between them (split 489 and 441 respectively). The majority of the premises were in Norwich and rural Norfolk although significant portions were in Yarmouth and Ipswich. It is estimated that the tied estates amounted to some 80% of the assets of the breweries.

During the early part of the 20th century expansion of the Norwich breweries was further helped by the growth of motorised transport, which allowed the industry to expand further than was possible with horse-drawn drays, river and rail. Although production declined in the interwar years during WWII it rose. It is reputed this was driven by sales to the USAAF Seventh Air Force which had 18 airfields in the surrounding countryside.

Morgans' brewery, c1900

4

Decline

By the early 1960s the British brewing industry was in a highly volatile state which was epitomised by aggressive mergers. At the same time marketing was being transformed, keg beers were being introduced and lagers (such as Carlsberg and Harp) were growing in popularity. All these trends contributed to the demise of large-scale brewing in Norwich.

The old family firms did not respond well. There is some speculation that new generations did not have the flair or drive of the founders. Despite this for some time they had been protected by a production process which was not subject to dramatic technological change. They were further cushioned by the value of their tied estates. Both enabled them to survive without displaying outstanding management flair. Nevertheless they eventually succumbed to tempting bids for their empires.

The first of the 'big four' to close was Youngs, Crawshay & Youngs' Crown Brewery on King Street. In 1958 the company was bought out by Bullard & Sons who took over their 50 tied houses but had no need of the brewery which was closed in 1958.

In 1961 Morgans' brewery was acquired jointly by Steward & Patteson and Bullards. The acquisition was valuable in that Morgans not only had a tied estate of over 400 pubs but they also had the most modern brewery in the City. The division of the public houses proceeded amicably, if somewhat unprofessionally. With Gerald Bullard (Bullards' chairman) later recalling: 'These were shared out one morning between us after John Morse [Steward & Patteson's chairman] and I had cut cards to see who should have first pick.' Despite assurances to the contrary it was clear that the purchasers were only interested in the estate and almost immediately sold the brewery on King Street to Watney Mann. The decision was based on the fact that the two boards believed that the extended 'public house empire' was too small for three breweries but too large for two. Hence Steward & Patteson and Bullards entered into an agreement with Watney Mann whereby the latter was allowed to supply the Norwich breweries' tied houses with some Watney Mann lines e.g. Red Barrel and bottled Brown Ale. Unfortunately the boards at Steward & Patteson and Bullards had totally underestimated the power of the Watney Mann products and national advertising campaign, which was so strong that by July 1962 Watney Mann keg beers were responsible for over half of their total bitter sales.

With the increased competition from Watney Mann, net profits at Steward & Patteson faltered after 1961. There is some indication that the latter's directors had no appetite to compete. Watney Mann began to purchase shares in both Bullards and Steward & Patteson, their finances having been stretched by the Morgans' purchase. By 1963 Watney Mann owned over 17% of Steward & Patteson's ordinary shares and around 18% of Bullards' equity. Both boards accepted the takeover although the sale of Steward & Patteson was not fully completed until 1967 when the company's breweries and 1064 licensed properties were finally sold to Watneys for £7.67m. In the meantime Bullards' 530 licensed houses and brewery had also been taken over.

Thus it came to pass that Watneys acquired a huge tied estate in Norfolk which gave them monopoly power and inspired huge public criticism. Indeed the description of Norfolk as a 'beer desert' was one of the early rallying cries of the Campaign for Real Ale (CAMRA).

Management accounts to September 1968 reveal that the Pockthorpe Brewery (previously Steward & Patteson) was the major brewer in Norwich making some 131,000 barrels annually. At the Old Brewery, King Street (previously Morgans), 79,000 barrels were produced annually, whilst at Bullards' Anchor Brewery 55,000 barrels were made. By the end of 1970 only the Old Brewery remained in production. Here Watney Mann invested in a new £2.2 million keg beer production plant which many hoped would secure its ongoing viability. Links with Norwich were further strengthened when in 1976/7 the local production company Watney Mann (East Anglia) Ltd (which had been taken over by Grand Metropolitan Hotels Ltd) was renamed the Norwich Brewery Company. In subsequent years attempts were made to reproduce some of the cask conditioned ales that had disappeared with the demise of the local breweries. For example, in 1981 Bullards' Mild was launched.

Then, on Friday 11th January 1985, it was announced that with countrywide lager sales increasing, the Old Brewery site was superfluous to requirements and was to be closed with the loss of around 160 jobs. Despite protestations that advertising campaigns had created an inflated demand for lager at the expense of traditional ales, production ceased at the end of April 1985, bringing 'a tragic end to an historic tradition of brewing in Norwich' (Norfolk & Norwich Branch of CAMRA).

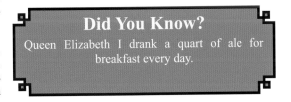

Did You Know?
Queen Elizabeth I drank a quart of ale for breakfast every day.

Recovery

Across the country a similar pattern was emerging. In 1960 there were 360 breweries in Britain. Over the following decade 40% of British breweries were closed down and the industry was increasingly dominated by six national groups: Allied Breweries, Bass Charrington, Courage, Scottish & Newcastle, Watneys and Whitbread. The processed keg beers produced by these firms, such as Watneys' Red Barrel, often replaced traditional local bitter. Additionally with the majority of the pubs tied to these corporates it became increasingly difficult for drinkers to buy traditional local bitters. Then in the 1970s a revolution began.

In 1971 The Campaign for Real Ale was formed, initially as 'The Campaign for the Revitalisation of Ale'. In the early days its campaign persuaded national firms to reintroduce cask beers and in so doing promoted both the popularity of drinking and making traditional beers. In 1972, when the Selby Brewery opened in Yorkshire, it was remarkable for being the first new independent brewery launched in Britain for 50 years. It was not until 1981 that a new brewery opened in Norfolk when, somewhat like waiting for a bus, two arrived together. Thus in

March of that year the Star Brewery opened on Duke Street (in Norwich City-centre) followed in April by Woodforde's in Drayton (Norwich outskirts). At the time one of their biggest challenges was the fact that so many of Norwich's pubs were owned and tied to Watneys or Courage.

Now operating at Woodbastwick, Woodforde's has gone from strength to strength. Unfortunately the Star only shone for a short period. Nevertheless, a number of other breweries still operate in Norwich today. These include the Chalk Hill Brewery, attached to the Coach & Horses on Thorpe Road, which has been trading since 1993, and the Fat Cat Brewery on Lawson Road which started brewing in 2005.

Although brewing is no longer a major industry in Norwich local companies have risen to the challenge and are building excellent reputations. Maybe the position was best summed up in the programme of Norwich's 33rd CAMRA Beer Festival which described the closure of Norwich's last major brewery as '…a sad loss, maybe, but now we can enjoy a huge range of local beers from new small brewers. Brewers who brew, often with local malt, quality ales and who listen to what local drinkers want.'

A Norfolk Nip, clockwise from top: John Strickland, Ray Ashworth, Bram Lowe, David Winter, Colin Keatley, 1994

The Breweries and their Workers: Past

Until the 1960s brewing was one of Norwich's foremost industries.

This chapter not only tells the tale of the dramatic rise and fall of the individual breweries but also recounts anecdotes of the people who worked there. From office workers to draymen and from engineers to coopers, they all have tales to tell of an industry that was once a staple employer in Norwich, but which died in a dramatically short time.

Bullards' brewery workers, c1900

The job of 'ale taster' was introduced in the early 15th century. One of the taster's tasks was to determine the alcohol content in the ales, which in turn established the level of duty that would be charged. There was no scientific method of doing this. However, it was known that the level of sugar in the wort (the ale in its pre-fermented state) correlated to both its stickiness and the brew's final alcoholic strength. Thus the ale taster would pour the wort on a stool and then sit on it. Its strength was determined by how much stuck to his leather breeches.

Youngs, Crawshay & Youngs' Crown Brewery, undated

History of the Crown Brewery

Some time after 1807 John Youngs set up his Crown Brewery on King Street. He was a dapper figure who on Saturdays wandered the local streets dressed in a waistcoat with half guinea gold buttons. He was later joined at the brewery by his son, also called John.

By 1845 the brewery had over 70 tied houses in Norwich. In 1851 the pub estate grew when John Crawshay joined in partnership. Charles had been associated with a brewery at St Stephen's Gate which provided some 25 tied houses to the Youngs' portfolio before it closed. Initially the partnership was known as Crawshay & Youngs, but when Robert Youngs (the founder's son) joined the business Youngs, Crawshay & Youngs was formed.

In 1865 the brewery on King Street expanded when the firm purchased the adjacent Music House together with further property to the east and south, covering in all some three acres of land. Underneath the brewery were huge cellars which had the appearance of 'ancient catacombs' and the capacity to store 1,500 barrels of beer. In 1897 the firm became a limited company.

Although part of the Music House was given over to the brewery tap i.e. its home pub (until 1932) and as the residence of the chief brewer, it was mainly used as offices. It was here that the architects and surveyors department was set up in 1900. This department spearheaded Youngs' pioneering approach to the modernisation of its public houses. As reported in their Coronation Souvenir Brochure (1937): 'At that time brick floors were common, sprinkled with sea sand. There were spittoons, and counter fronts were provided with a narrow trench at floor level to confine a layer of sawdust for those indulging in the objectionable habit of spitting.' Youngs removed spittoons and introduced lino, carpets and rugs to their houses even going so far as to advise their tenants that a clean floor would be respected by their customers.

Between 1923 and 1937 Youngs, Crawshay and Youngs were awarded seven first prize medals at the London Brewers' Exhibition. Over the same period their tied estate continued to expand so that immediately before WWII the brewery's estate extended to 250 tied houses. However, despite their size and the quality of their brews, in 1958 the company was taken over by Bullards and the Crown Brewery was closed.

Memories of Working at the Crown Brewery

John Beaumont (pictured below) worked as the architects' clerk for Youngs, Crawshay and Youngs for two years from 1956, and here he shares his memories:

'As the clerk I also acted as a receptionist and did odd jobs. The offices for the architects' department were in the Music House which was a lovely old building with a fantastic atmosphere. The office I had was the one that you can see from the road with steps up into it. It was huge, about 25ft square, and there was just my desk in the middle. I was too junior to have a telephone and had to write with a dip pen.

'The directors were very good to the publicans and everyone who worked there. When I went for my job interview one of the directors said to me: "If you ever carry a knapsack always make sure it contains a field marshal's baton." I wasn't quite sure what he meant at the time. Later I discovered that it was a saying used by Napoleon who believed that every soldier in his army had the potential to be a general. It rather amused me.

'Beneath the Music House was an undercroft (pictured right). The temperature was cool and constant, providing perfect conditions for the barrels of wine that were stored there. There was a chap who worked in there who bottled the wine and banged the corks in with a hammer. It was amazing to watch. One swipe and the cork was in.

'The brewery had a counting house, today it would be a cashiers' department. It was totally staffed by men who sat there with pens behind their ears and ink pots on their desks. As the draymen returned from their deliveries they handed cash over and the details were entered into huge ledgers. It was very Dickensian.

'The staff who worked in the bottling department were all women. It was very relaxed and had a great atmosphere. There were always rumours that they smuggled the odd bottle home. I don't know how they did it as they were always checked when they walked out.

'Most of the draymen drank during their rounds but the only accident I can remember occurred one Christmas Eve when a lorry was returning from the north Norfolk coast. Normally on the return trip they piled the drays ten crates high, all were filled with empty bottles. On this occasion it was 12 crates high, too tall for the garage entrance. The dray crashed into it and took out the door. There was glass everywhere. The driver was disciplined, that was all. Mind you it took a long time for him to live it down with his mates.

'Lou Lockwood and Charlie Graver were our two full-time maintenance men. Lou had a sideline in chimney cleaning. I can still picture his sidecar which carried the slogan: "Let Lou clean your flue."

'I was allowed to rent 169a King Street, which used to be Major Crawshay's house, for the grand sum of 17 shillings a week. It was four stories high with both an attic and a wine cellar. My daughter was a little girl then and she spent a lot of time outside in the yard. The men always greeted her. It was a very friendly place to work.

'Morale really fell when we found out that we were going to be taken over by Bullards. The men thought they'd get jobs there, but of course that rarely happened. I lived in a tied house and couldn't afford to hang on. I got a job and left before the brewery officially closed. I missed it afterwards. We were expected to work hard but I really enjoyed working and living there.'

The Crown Brewery Site Today

In 1961 the Norfolk Education Committee purchased the brewery site. It is now home to the Wensum Lodge Adult Education Centre. Though much of the brewery was destroyed in 1965 some buildings remain. These include the stables, which have been converted into a conference hall called the Crown Room, whilst the riverside coffee bar is housed in an old malting. The Music House also remains and appropriately a bar still operates in its cellars. We are sure John Youngs would have approved!

Bullards' coopers, 1920

History of the Anchor Brewery

In 1837 Richard Bullard, in partnership with James Watts, founded the Anchor Brewery in premises near St Miles' Bridge. Richard had previously been a publican brewer and had run the Excise Coffee House (Lower Goat Lane) which despite its name was a tavern.

Although the partnership with Watts was dissolved in 1847 Richard Bullard presided over the business until his death in 1864. At this time his son Harry (who was knighted in 1886) took over with brothers Charley and Fred as partners.

Around 1868 a new brewery building was constructed on the same site adjacent to the River Wensum. Ten years later the building was under water when the river overflowed its banks and wreaked havoc across the City. At the time Harry Bullard, who was mayor, oversaw the establishment of food distribution centres and shelters for victims of the flood. He was particularly lauded for both his calming influence and organisational abilities. The same skills had contributed to the prosperity of the brewery such that in 1895, when the business was registered as a limited company, the tied estate amounted to some 441 public houses (280 owned and 161 leased). At the time of incorporation Sir Harry Bullard was chairman supported by directors John Boyce and George Coller.

By the end of the 19th century the Anchor Brewery had been further extended to occupy substantial red-brick buildings covering a seven-acre site. Richard had chosen an excellent position for the brewery. Not only was it adjacent to the river (which as noted previously was a mixed blessing) it was also built over an artesian well dug deep in the chalk under the brewery. The water from the well was of a very high quality which gave the beer its excellent flavour. It was pumped to water cisterns at the top of the brewery which amazingly had an aggregate capacity of some 15,000 gallons. They were also able to dig huge cellars into the chalk which were capable of accommodating 6,000 barrels.

Following the death of Sir Harry Bullard in 1903 family members, including his son Edward and nephew Ernest, continued to be actively involved. By 1914 Bullards had 133 tied houses in Norwich, seven more than their nearest rival, Steward & Patteson.

In 1957 they enlarged their brewing capacity and erected an extension to their bottling store. Then in 1958 they purchased Youngs, Crawshay & Youngs' brewery in King Street. Despite the fact that Bullards was apparently flourishing, in a remarkable turn of fortunes, within eight years the famed Anchor Brewery closed.

It was in 1961 that John Morse (Chairman of Steward & Patteson) and Gerald Bullard joined resources to buy Morgans. At the time they were very clear that they did not want an additional brewery. As Gerald said: 'We were of course largely interested in the properties. There were about 400 of them, mainly in Norfolk and Norwich, and they were shared out one morning between us. We cut cards to see who should have first pick.'

The two chairmen made a disastrous mistake in selling the Morgans' brewery to Watney Mann, who ostensibly wanted a brewery to supply their free trade outlets in the area. Watneys now had a foothold in Norfolk and Bullards, with their huge tied estate, were very attractive to them. By 1963 Watneys had acquired around 18% of Bullards' shares and the company passed across to them.

On 18th October 1966 the Eastern Evening News announced that brewing was to stop at the Anchor Brewery. Instead Bullards' beers would be produced at the Watney Mann Brewery at King Street and the Anchor site would be merely used for racking and bottling. However, by 1969 even the bottling plant was declared superfluous to requirements and closed.

Bullards' Anchor Brewery, c1960

Memories of Working at the Anchor Brewery

John Hutson recalls his time with Bullards:

'In 1949 I started my apprenticeship at F.W. Hall on Pitt Street, which had been set up in 1893 as a firm of coppersmiths and brewery engineers. We worked for all of the major Norwich breweries. I was on loan to Bullards, from 1956 to 1966 during which time I never returned to the workshop. Eventually I was taken on by the brewery in 1966. When Bullards were taken over by Watneys I was transferred over to King Street.

'Bullards was a family firm, very patriarchal. In my day Gerald Bullard was the Chairman. He wasn't a brewer, but would often wander around and speak to us. I remember one day one of my mates called him "sir" to which he responded: "It's either Mr Gerald or Mr Bullard . . . I haven't been knighted yet." The social club was in Westwick Street and they ran loads of activities such as football and fishing. Our children particularly remember attending the firm's Christmas parties and being visited by Father Christmas.

'At Bullards we undertook both building and repair work. When I worked there we could weld all the vessels we made, such as fermenters, but before this they had to be riveted and soldered and earlier still brown paper was placed between the layers which were then riveted together.

'When I was there all metal goods were made out of copper, even the buckets they used for cleaning. I suppose it was because it was a cheap material. I used to make fermenting vessels which were enclosed tanks 12ft cubed and also skimming vessels which measured around 16ft square and were 4ft 6ins tall. It was here that yeast was manually skimmed off the top of the beer. Two men with a big board would walk down either side of the tank scraping off the yeast which would be pushed ahead and eventually down the parachute, which was like a big funnel. It was than caught in a huge barrel which was over 6ft tall and called a jumbo. The good yeast was than sorted out to be reused whilst the surplus was sold for the production of Marmite.

'Stories about ways to get an illicit drink were rife. Some of the labourers used to drink three gallons of beer, that's 24 pints, over an eight-hour shift. In the brewery we used a piece of copper tube with a non-return valve which if pushed into a barrel was a good way of extracting beer. It made a very peculiar bubbling noise and hence was nick-named "uggle guggle". Once the beer was ready it was put in barrels with temporary bungs in the top store where it waited to be put on lorries. When the workers replaced the temporary bungs I would often hear "uggle guggle" coming from that store! When I worked at Bullards it was really easy to get a drink if you wanted one 'cos the vessels were all open, but using the modern techniques that were employed at King Street the beer never saw the light from the day it went into the copper until the day it was put into the barrel.

'There were some really heavy manual jobs, such as emptying the unwanted waste from the mash tun, which was done daily. When the barley was put in it was dry but than a sparge arm went around and sprayed it with boiling water. Subsequently the liquid would be extracted leaving a tub of something resembling porridge. The workers would then put on their thigh boots and open the top of the mash tun. They knew there was one plate on the base of the tun which could be lifted so they jumped into the steaming mash up to their thighs around that point, lifted the plate and swept the waste through it into to a lorry below. Farmers used to come and collect it to feed their pigs. When I walked by the vessels I could really feel the heat, so goodness knows what it was like inside.

'Cleaning the fermenting and skimming vessels was a hard job. Before the liquid went in they were gleaming, not polished, but gleaming a lovely matt coloured copper and then three or four days later they'd be all gooey and yeasty. The men would climb into the vats with a mixture of cleaning materials and scrub them by hand.

'Then there were the girls in the bottling plant. When I started they wore clogs and sacking aprons. I think the clogs were for safety. In the 1970s, when I worked at the Norwich Brewery on King Street, we had to wear heavy boots if we worked with glass bottles because they were always breaking.

'In 1966 Harry Lubbock, Bullards' engineer, retired at the age of 70 and I was offered the job. I was already working there on behalf of F.W. Hall and as the change meant a very large pay rise, I leapt at the chance. In 1968 when Watneys took over Bullards there wasn't any resentment towards the Bullard family. Us workers weren't concerned about our jobs, we just assumed that we would be moved across to King Street. We didn't all go at once, it was in dribs and drabs, but I don't think any of us in the engineering department lost our jobs.'

The Anchor Brewery Site Today

In 1972 the brewery site was sold to a private developer and for a number of years the site was allowed to fall into disrepair until Norwich City Council agreed a scheme for a residential development known today as Anchor Quay.

Although some of the original buildings have been retained it is regrettable that the old chimney, which dominated the skyline for so many years, has been lost. It was destroyed in 1982 despite being described in a report to Norwich City Council as being 'the best surviving example of an industrial chimney in Norwich'. Unfortunately it was deemed too expensive to repair and maintain and in July 1982 it came down. All that now remains is a panel, embedded into a wall, which was rescued from the base of the once majestic chimney picturing an anchor flanked by the words 'Bullard and Sons' Brewery, 1868'. It is a fitting memorial to a company which played such an important role in Norwich's industrial heritage.

Bullards' chimney demolished, 1982

Did You Know?

Bullards had the motto 'Full to the Bung'.

Did You Know

In 2015 the Bullards' brand was revived at the Redwell Brewery, located on Braccondale, after they acquired the rights to the name.

The brewery was set up by a group of beer lovers in 2013 with the aim of re-igniting the City's brewing heritage.

Bullards' Anchor Brewery site, 2011

The Pockthorpe Brewery, 1974

History of the Pockthorpe Brewery

In 1793 John Patteson bought Charles Greeves' brewery at Pockthorpe with a view to finding an occupation for his son. These innocuous beginnings laid the foundations for the firm of Steward & Patteson which by 1961 was one of the largest non metropolitan breweries in the country.

John was very involved in City politics, being sheriff in 1785, mayor in 1788 and the City's elected MP in 1806 and 1807. From the beginning he was interested in expansion by acquisition, with early purchases including Beevor's brewery on Magdalen Street and Postle's brewery on Cowgate. In 1820 when he retired from the business John was succeeded by his son John Staniforth Patteson. He was joined by William Steward and his brothers Ambrose and Timothy together with the latter's son Timothy Jnr and the brewery became Steward Patteson & Stewards. Subsequently in 1831, following the amalgamation of George Morse's brewery, together with its estate of 77 pubs, the firm became Steward, Patteson & Co.

By the time of John Staniforth Patteson's death in 1832 the brewery controlled some 120 pubs (both owned and leased) of which 80 were in Norwich. In September 1837 expansion continued when Peter Finch's brewery, also in the St Martin at Oak area, was taken over together with its 55 pubs (40 in Norwich).

At this time the firm's name changed again to: Steward, Patteson, Finch & Co. The Brewery itself also underwent a name change. Confusingly it had been known as the Anchor Brewery but by the end of the 1850s it had been rechristened as the Pockthorpe Brewery.

By 1845 the brewery had control of 183 tied houses within Norwich. Although Steward, Patteson, Finch & Co continued to take over breweries in subsequent years they concentrated on businesses whose estates were mainly (often entirely) outside the City. In 1895, the firm was registered as Steward & Patteson Ltd, when they controlled 489 public houses.

In the following decades they did not sit on their laurels and continued to expand by acquisition. In particular in the late 1950s and early 1960s Steward & Patteson were involved in a series of aggressive mergers which culminated in August 1957 with the acquisition of East Anglian Breweries of Ely and Huntingdon. This deal alone added 400 pubs to the Steward & Patteson empire, bringing their estate to a massive 1250 houses. Then in 1961 Steward & Patteson and Bullards each bought a half share in Morgans' brewery with its 400 tied pubs.

Did You Know?

In 1797 HRH Prince William Frederick, nephew of George III, had lunch at the Pockthorpe Brewery in a large new vat.

It is claimed that Sir Robert Bignold, Chairman of Morgans, had been trying to bring the three breweries together to secure the independence of Norwich brewing, but if that had been the aim of the merger it was spectacularly unsuccessful. The new owners believed that Morgans' brewery was superfluous to requirements and sold it to Watney Mann. Additionally they entered into a trading agreement whereby Watney's undertook to supply the Bullards' and Steward & Patteson tied houses with such lines as 'Red Barrel'.

Steward & Patteson were now financially stretched and, after years of being the hunter, in November 1963 the tables were turned when the firm was on the receiving end of an aggressive bid by Watney Mann. By this time Watney's owned 17% of Steward & Patteson's ordinary shares and in February 1967 they completed on the purchase, which included a staggering 1064 licensed properties, for £7,666,270.

The assurances by Watney Mann about the preservation of the Pockthorpe Brewery proved as genuine as those made by Steward & Patteson when they themselves took over brewing minnows, and on 27th January 1970 the last brew in Pockthorpe was made.

The brewery was largely demolished between 1972 and 1974. However, the old brewery offices on Barrack Street have recently been renovated and restored.

Steward & Patteson directors. Back: H T Patteson, Don Stevens, C Finch. Front: G H Morse, H S Patteson, c1895

Memories of working at the Pockthorpe Brewery

Pauline Smith joined Steward & Patteson in 1939:

'I went there when I was 17, straight from the Blyth School, and stayed for two years until I reached call up age. I worked in the office on the corner of Silver Road and Barrack Street. It's still there.

'I worked in the ledger room and upstairs on the switchboard. The latter was on the same level as the directors' offices and was in the same room as their secretary. It was all rather old-fashioned. The furniture was very solid, similar to what you'd have found in a bank. When the War started the main brewery workers had an air raid shelter but the "ladies in the office", we were always referred to as "the ladies", had to go into the second-floor safe. It was a big room but also contained ledgers and I found it very claustrophobic.

'One of the directors, old Colonel Morse, lived at "The Mead" at Coltishall which became the Norfolk Mead Hotel. He was very tall, with a handlebar moustache, and very nice. I remember when our home on Greenhills Road was bombed. He called me into his office, which really worried me. But he said to me: "Miss Payne, do you have anywhere to live?" So I told him that we were going to move in with my aunt and he said: "Otherwise I can tell you now that we've plenty of room at the Mead and you can bring your family with you." His heart was in the right place.'

Gloria King's mother, Phyllis Colman (née Burgess), also worked there around the same time:

'The photos of my mother (below) were taken with her workmates at the beginning of WWII. She was one of 11 children of whom only eight survived to adulthood. At the time that the pictures were taken she lived in Supple Close (not far from Harvey Lane) and she married the boy next door (Harry Colman) in April 1941 when she was just 20.

'I think that the photographs were taken in the summer as my mother appears to be wearing a gingham dress. All the girls have an overall and some of them like my mother were wearing clogs.

'She told me that she got a job at the brewery because the pay was good and on another occasion that she had wanted to get married to avoid going into the ATS as her older sister had done. I think that she wanted the extra pay so that she could save up to get married. She said that the work at the brewery was hard and that there was a lot of heavy lifting; I think this was of cases and barrels of beer. Presumably the girls were employed doing this as the men were in the services.'

Phyllis Burgess, left, c1940

Phyllis Burgess, front left, c1940

Barry Berwick was a cooper at the Pockthorpe Brewery:

'In 1958 I was taken on at Steward & Patteson as an apprentice cooper. I was 15 when I started. Not only did my family live in Anchor Street, next to the brewery, but my grandad, father and nine uncles (six of them Berwicks) all worked there. The photo (right) was taken in the brewery yard. In it you can see various members of the Berwick family: Grandad Billy, who was a foreman; my dad, Ernest, and Uncle Alfred who all worked in the fermenting department; Uncle Leonard who was an engineer; Uncles Albert and George who were in transport; Uncle Billy who was in the boiler room. All of them worked there for over 40 years and my grandad and Uncle Billy made it to 52 years apiece.

'My dad worked shifts. When I was young me and my sister took him up his sandwiches. In the room where he worked there were big open vessels containing fermenting beer. He used to say "put your nose over there and take a big sniff", it really smelt strongly of yeast and quite took your breath away. He also gave me a little glass of beer!

'My dad put me forward for the apprenticeship. I never had a formal interview. At the time a family recommendation was enough to get you in. My job mostly consisted of repairing barrels. I used to take out broken staves, which are the narrow strips of wood forming part of the sides of a barrel, and put in new ones. It was all done by eye, there were no measurements. Though I never made one from scratch, when bigger barrels were worn out I used to take out the staves and saw them down to make a good smaller one.

'If a pub had a problem with a full barrel we used to go there to mend them. In those days you had hops in the barrels and the beer would be cloudy and it needed to stand and settle so if the landlords returned the leaking barrels to us the beer would've been shaken up and ruined. We repaired the full barrels with tow, which

Berwick family in the Steward and Patteson yard, c1950
Back Row (l to r): Ernest (dad), Leonard, Albert, Alfred.
Middle Row (l to r) Billy (jnr), George.
Front row: Billy (Snr).

was like coarse cotton wool, that we forced down to where it was leaking with a little instrument a bit like a screwdriver.

'When the barrels were returned to the brewery for refilling they were washed. A bloke used to smell them to make sure they were clean. There were two holes in the barrel, one for the tap the other at the top for the bung. He'd look inside the barrels from the top hole and insert a gas lamp through the bottom one so that he could see inside and check that they weren't damaged. He often found bits of wood inside that he'd take out. He put a big cross on the side of damaged barrels which came over to us in the coopers' shop.

'When I joined there were four coopers but it was only about three years later we got the "Coopers Journal" and saw an article about the London breweries using kegs. We all knew then that the writing was on the wall, although I worked as a cooper until 1970 when the last brew was made at Pockthorpe.'

Did You Know?

In 2013 Andy and Tom Keeley resurrected the S&P brewery name. Based in Horsford on land once owned by Steward & Patteson, they produce beers made with water drawn from their own bore well and locally malted Marris Otter barley.

Did You Know?

Beer is made up of 93% water. Brewers call brewing water 'liquor' to distinguish it from tap water. The flinty water of Burton-upon-Trent in the East Midlands is the benchmark for brewing liquor in Britain. Today brewers 'Burtonise' the liquor in order to give the final brew the best flavour.

Steward & Patteson coopers' workroom: front left Barry Berwick front right Leonard (Alfred) Savage, c1960

Steward & Patteson lorry, George Berwick second from left, c1920

Morgans Ltd – The Old Brewery

Morgans' brewery proudly displays its new transport, c1920

History of the Old Brewery

The Conisford Brewery, which later became known as the Old Brewery, was established on King Street as early as 1563 by a John Barnard. By 1660 it had passed into the hands of the Thompson family who owned it for almost 200 years.

Around 1844 Charles and Henry Thompson sold the brewery, along with its estate of 54 public houses, to brothers John and Walter Morgan. By 1879 the business was renamed Morgan & Co and in March 1887, when it was registered as a limited company, the firm controlled 188 pubs (106 owned and 82 leased) and the brewery occupied a two-and-a-quarter-acre site. Over the coming years the firm took over a number of breweries in Norfolk, including Elijah Eyre's Lady Bridge Brewery in King's Lynn. Takeovers were used to build the tied estate which by 1904 had increased to some 600 houses, both owned and leased, of which over 80% were outside Norwich. Although the breweries associated with the tied estates were normally closed, luckily for Morgans, they continued to brew at the Lady Bridge Brewery. As a result, in June 1942, when the Old Brewery suffered severe bomb damage, Morgans were able to temporarily transfer their brewing operation there.

Around 1946, as they started to rebuild the Norwich site, Sir Robert Bignold (chairman), expressed his intention to construct a brewery that was big enough to brew for Norfolk and Norwich. Despite being in competition, the other Norwich brewers helped their rival at this difficult time. Michael Falcon who was employed at the brewery in 1951, when Guy Green was head brewer, remembers that: 'The "big four" breweries in Norwich were competitors, however, it was friendly competition and there was little, if no, animosity.'

The Old Brewery was back in production by 1950, but Morgans were unable to maintain their profitability and in September 1961 they went into voluntary liquidation. By prior arrangement they were taken over by Bullards and Steward & Patteson who shared the tied estate, amounting to over 400 premises, between them and sold the brewery to Watney Mann Ltd.

Did You Know?

Morgans had an unfortunate early history when in May 1845 Walter Morgan, who with his brother had just bought the Thompson's Brewery in King Street, was found drowned in the fermenting vat there.

Memories of working at the Old Brewery

Arthur Houlston, 2011

Arthur Houlston recalls his time at the brewery:

'I joined Morgans as a learner driver in 1947 when I was 22. Four other members of my family worked there. My dad George was there for 35 years. He worked shifts cleaning out the vats. He and the other vat cleaners always wore clogs with wooden soles and leather uppers and steel rims to keep their feet dry. My Uncle Walter, who's in the front row of the 1948 photograph (opposite) worked in transport, Uncle Eddie was in charge of loading the lorries with bottles and barrels, and even my mum Edith worked in the bottling department before she was married.

'Although motorised transport was widely used the brewery still employed two draymen, Charles Curl and Jack Murrell, they're both in the photograph as well. The draymen and lorry drivers all got along well but being a lorry driver I thought using horse-drawn transport was quaint. But all the breweries did it. At Morgans the horse and drays were used for deliveries to pubs in the vicinity of the brewery. The horses were stabled in the yards at Howard House, on the corner of Mountergate and King Street whilst the brewery offices were in the house itself.

'When I started I drove a tug (cab) which pulled an old petrol bowser (mobile tanker) which had been cleaned and sterilised and filled with beer. I took it to our bottling plant in King's Lynn. Around 1950 a new Leyland Octopus was added to the fleet. Until then Morgans' largest vehicles were three-tonners, but this was a 20-ton lorry. At the time I think I was the youngest driver but I was chosen to drive it. I was really chuffed, not least because my pay went up from £7 to £7 10s a week.

'The lorries were loaded at the brewery from a staging that was at the same height, so it was easy to roll the barrels onto the vehicle, which were then stacked upright for the journey. It was the driver's and mate's responsibility to unload at the other end and believe you me we came across some very funny cellars. The barrels were unloaded upright from the lorry on a skid (a ramp) onto a rope cushion, you couldn't roll them or you wouldn't have been able to stop them. That said we rolled them into the cellar using a sort of rope pully system. We'd upend an empty barrel and lay a rope around it on the floor which would then be looped around the full barrel. The driver would than stand in front of the empty barrel (which would take some of the weight) and use the ropes to control the speed as the full barrel was rolled down into the cellar. The mate was at the bottom ready to catch it! I particularly remember delivering to the Sheringham Crown where we unloaded full barrels each weighing a quarter of a ton. The cellar was no more than half an inch wider than the barrel, so unloading was really tricky. Once in the cellar the barrels needed to be lifted onto stands. To do this the driver and mate would face each other and lift the barrels with their heads together, which gave them extra leverage.

'All employees had an allowance of a pint a day drunk at around ten, it was part of your morning break. A barrel of beer was kept in a cubby hole and you'd just draw it off. If you wanted a soft drink you'd just go up the road to the café. The drivers were normally out so they missed it but they were always offered a complimentary pint at pubs after deliveries had been made. So you can imagine what some drivers were like after their tenth pub. The story goes that some had no problem driving their lorries back to the yard but couldn't get on their bikes to cycle home!'

Morgans' transport department, Arthur is circled, 1948

Arthur Houlston's new 'Octopus' lorry, c1950

When Watneys bought Morgans' 'Old Brewery' they acquired a modern brewery capable of producing pasteurised beers, in particular Red Barrel, which was the forerunner of todays mass-produced keg beers.

Many talk of the golden era before Watneys took over the Norwich brewing industry, yet what many forget is that although the 'big four' produced great cask ales, they were perishable. The quality of a pint bought in a pub depended upon the cellar skills of landlords. Ted Williams, joint organiser of Norwich's first beer festival at the Bystanders' Club, recalls: 'Although the pubs at the time sold cask beers, either through lack of turnover or because the landlords didn't look after their pumps, the beer served was often below par. Obviously there were some excellent pubs, such as the Compasses on Upper King Street or the Beaufort Hotel on Prince of Wales Road, but they were few and far between. The Bystanders' Club used to run beer races. On one route we started at the Compasses, went up Magdalen Street and finished at the Artichoke. On another we started around St Andrews, went along St Benedicts and finished at the Barn, which was at the bottom of Grapes Hill. On both routes we took in 16 or 17 pubs and had to drink a half in each and you were lucky to get more than one decent drink.'

So in fact a keg beer, such as Red Barrel, was not necessarily bad. It all started well but production soon went downhill as explained by Ray Ashworth, founder of Woodforde's: 'Watneys started to produce keg beer in the 1950s and 1960s. In principle it was a brilliant idea because it removed the perishability of the product. The beer was well packaged and sterile and basically you didn't get problems with the beer. I think that people forget that prior to the keg beers there was a lot of horrible-tasting stuff out there. The quality often depended on the ability of the landlord to manage his stock. The problem at Watneys was that it seemed the accountants took over and they were more concerned with costs than the taste of the final product. As a result it became emasculated. I remember visiting the brewery and, in the grain store, I saw a sack and wasn't sure what the product was. It was actually the worst quality of "crystal" malt that I had ever seen. The death knell was when CAMRA called them "Grotneys". It was soon after that they changed their name locally to the Norwich Brewery.'

The other problem ensued from the fact that when Watneys took over Steward & Patteson and Bullards they effectively became the owners of around 95% of Norwich's pubs. This meant that for a time the vast majority of Norwich drinkers had no choice as to what beer they drank. Again the position is summed up neatly by Ted Williams: 'When Watneys' "Red Revolution" came at first it was acceptable because we had consistency. However, as the monopoly grew and quality fell they became an object of derision.'

By 1970 the Old Brewery was the only Norwich brewery in production. Subsequently in 1972 Watneys itself was taken over by Grand Metropolitan Hotels, essentially a property company. In 1976/7 the business was renamed as the Norwich Brewery Company and efforts were made to reproduce the cask-conditioned ales that had disappeared with the demise of the local breweries, these included Bullards' Mild (launched in 1981) and S&P Best Bitter (launched in 1984).

Despite investment in new plant, at 2pm on Friday 11th January 1985 it was announced that the Norwich Brewery was to close with the loss of around 160 jobs. Local workers were told that the closure had been forced by the increased popularity of lager and the fall in demand for beer. By the end of April brewing had ceased, although the distribution, commercial and administration departments remained on the site. By 2005 the site had been totally demolished.

Last days at the Norwich Brewery Co.

John Hutson, who had previously worked for Bullards, recalls what happened:

'On 11th January 1985 I was due to finish work at 2pm but phoned home to let my wife Vanessa know that I'd be late because there was going to be a union meeting. That's when we were told the brewery was closing. There was huge resentment amongst the workforce because we all knew that we were losing our jobs. I was over 50 and couldn't get another job so I used my redundancy money to buy equipment and decided to go self-employed. Watney's were very good and sold me tools from the engineer shop at a very good price.'

Despite the closure of Norwich's 'big four' breweries John's expertise was not lost to the industry:

'Whilst at Watneys one of my mates, Arthur Betts, had got to know Ray Ashworth who started Woodforde's. Arthur knew that Ray needed a maintenance man so he introduced us and I did work for Ray on a self-employed basis until 1999 when he sold the business. I helped set up the new brewery when it moved from Erpingham to Woodbastwick. I didn't make any of the vessels but adapted equipment that was brought in. I've also done work at the Chalk Hill Brewery on Rosary Road, again mostly pipework and adapting vessels. Now everything is stainless steel rather than the copper I worked with at Bullards. I've seen a huge change in the set up and size of the Norwich breweries . . . but I can honestly say that although all the jobs were different, I've always loved my work.'

Lacons – The 'Falcon' Brewery (Great Yarmouth)

Although technically outside the scope of this book, part of Lacons' tied estate was in Norwich so it seems appropriate to briefly look at its history, which has marked similarities with its Norwich rivals.

The brewery was originally founded around 1640 by Jeffery Ward in George Street, in the Fullers' Hill district of Great Yarmouth. In 1725 a John Laycon married into the Ward family and in 1741 he became a partner with his mother-in-law in the brewery business which was now known as Mrs Caroline Ward & Co. The business prospered and by 1742 the company stock had a net value of around £8,100. Its assets included the brewery, maltings, two malthouses in the broadland village of Ranworth and five horses.

Following Caroline Ward's death c1760 the business became known as Mr Laycon's brewery. Following his death it passed to his son Edmund who became mayor and was eventually knighted. It was Edmund who dropped the 'y' from the family name: thus Lacons was born.

As with Norwich's 'big four' the firm grew its assets by expanding its tied estate which in turn increased the demand for its beers. In 1894 the business became a private limited company. In April 1902 the company gained a foothold in Norwich when it purchased the St Margaret's Brewery from the Arnold family. The purchase included 32 tied pubs, most of which were located in Norwich. By 1914 they owned over 30 public houses in Norwich including the Ten Bells (St Benedict's Street), the Champion (Chapelfield Road) and the Duke of Wellington, previously known as the Iron Duke (Waterloo Road).

Lacons' emblem, which was taken from the family crest

From 1957, when Whitbread & Co acquired a 20% share holding, the brewery was living on borrowed time. On 19th November 1965 Whitbread took over Lacons, together with its 354 tied houses, for a reported purchase price of £3.2m. The brewery was closed on 28th February 1968. Although the brewery store was the last building to survive it was finally demolished in 1997 to make way for a supermarket.

All seemed lost, then in 2013 Lacons' Brewery returned to Great Yarmouth. Amazingly the firm produces ales using the original Lacons' yeast which had been preserved in the National Yeast Bank. They are proud of their rich heritage but are conscious of the need to move with the times and have the simple aim to 'craft a contemporary range of ales for today's drinkers and palate'.

Lacons' Duke of Wellington, Waterloo Road

Did You Know?

Michael Falcon (Lacons' director) recalls 'On the night of 24th June 1942, Yarmouth was badly bombed and St Nicholas Church and Lacons' brewery were burning. With limited resources the fire brigade had to decide which they would save…the church burnt to the ground.'

Woodforde's – The Broadland Brewery

History of the Woodforde's Breweries

In 1981 Ray Ashworth and Dr David Crease, both enthusiastic members of the Norwich Home Brewers' Club, set up Woodforde's Brewery on Drayton industrial estate on the outskirts of Norwich. Ray, recalls how he started brewing:

'I well remember making my first ever brew. It was 1963 and I was 19. Reginald Maudling, the Chancellor of the Exchequer, made it legal for anyone to brew beer in their own home and for their own consumption without the need to obtain a licence. The following weekend one of the Sunday newspapers ran an article showing its readers how to make beer. Well I just had to do it. So I got together with a mate, bought the ingredients, and as instructed boiled everything up for two hours in two big black enamel pans. We put the liquid into a bucket, allowed it to cool and bunged in the yeast, and sure enough it started to ferment. After a week the fermentation was complete, so we bottled it up. A couple of weeks later with much excitement we tasted our first beer…imagine our disappointment when we found that it was awful. In the end we just left it in a cupboard and forgot about it. We went back to it two to three months later and by now it was crystal clear and poured with a beautiful head!

It really wasn't bad, and from that day making beer really did fascinate me.

'Subsequently I became involved in a wine-making guild which had a home-brew section. I entered a pale ale in their beer competition. It came out rather dark in colour and I ended up winning the brown ale section!'

David Crease's experiences were somewhat similar:

'I've been interested in brewing since the early 1960s when, as a chemist, I was doing research at a lab in London. One of my colleagues had a friend called Trog who made beer at a time when home brewing was largely unheard of. As chemists we all thought we could make anything, so armed with Trog's instructions, which fitted onto a 3-inch square piece of paper, we embarked on making our first brew. To do this we bought and modified a dustbin, purchased malt extract from Boots, hops from a herbalist and used brewer's yeast. The resultant brew, which was 6% proof wasn't terribly palatable. Undeterred we decanted it into lemonade bottles and took it to parties where it was drunk at two in the morning when nothing else was left.

Ray Ashworth, 1992

Dr David Crease, 2011

'I persevered and by the late 1960s I started to make brews which were quite drinkable but had a distinct "home-brew twang". My breakthrough came in the mid 1970s when I read a book which advised home brewers not to use malt extract but to purchase a sack of malt and crack it in a coffee grinder. This allowed me to produce the type of beers I'd always wanted to make.'

Bram Lowe, first local chairman of CAMRA, recollects tasting Ray's home brew in the late 1970s:

'Both Ray Ashworth and myself were involved with Norwich CAMRA. On one occasion we were going to Yarmouth to inspect pubs for the Good Beer Guide. I called for Ray at his home in Acle and before leaving he asked if I wanted to try his home brew. I said yes more out of politeness and discovered it was wonderful, in fact it was the best I tasted all night. It was a prototype of "Wherry" and I told him that night he should be marketing it.'

By now David and Ray were both members of the Norwich and District Home Brewers' Club. One evening Ray's wife Isobel saw a television programme on the Blackawton microbrewery in Devon and said to Ray: 'You should do that.' So with the support of family members he swapped his Institute of Banking books for brewing literature and started to look for premises. At the time David was a teacher

and he joined Ray as a minor partner who could give scientific support and provide holiday relief.

Ray's first challenge was to find suitable premises, which proved somewhat difficult: 'Unfortunately I was unable to find suitable old buildings but I did locate a unit on the Frost industrial estate at Drayton (north Norwich). Whilst fitting out the unit I continued to work at Barclays and finally took up full-time brewing on the 6th April 1981. My first beer was Wherry, which is still being produced today.'

There was also the challenge of fitting out the brewery as explained by David:

'We built our first brewery from a variety of second-hand, and not always appropriate, pieces of equipment. The mash tuns came from the Bass experimental brewery at Burton-upon-Trent, the copper was adapted from a stainless steel tank, whilst the fermenters were 300-gallon plastic orange juice vessels which we bought from Colman's. The pipework was made up of large bore domestic copper piping and we soon found out why breweries used stainless steel! The latter being vastly superior for a number of reasons, not least of which is the fact that it can be easily cleaned. One of our major learning points was that we were trying to reinvent the wheel. In general the technical challenges had been solved but you needed the money to buy the professional solution.'

At this time the business faced a number of challenges:

'Our motivation was to make good-quality beer. We liked what we made and had the confidence to know that we could make reasonable beers that were better than the mass-produced stuff that was on the market. However, we quickly found out how difficult it was to achieve a consistent brew when we were working on a small scale. A very small variation in any one input made a huge variation in the final product. As you can imagine the fact that our water supply could come from any one of three different sources added to the problem. As home brewers we liked variations, but as commercial brewers we soon discovered that our customers wanted consistency, which was an area we had to work on. But the real eye-opener was when we realised that the market was very much a closed shop. Most of the local pubs were formally tied to breweries and even the free houses were often restricted as to who they bought from as they had entered into "soft loan agreements" with suppliers whereby they were obliged to purchase their products.

'At that time the market leaders in real ale were Adnams and Greene King. We were a very small niche producer and we knew that the only way we could grow was for our name and quality to be recognised.'

Faced with the above challenges very few microbreweries survived, let alone flourished. Ray is very clear as to why Woodforde's was an early success:

'I think that we succeeded where others failed because of my banking background and training. I realised from the beginning that making good beer was not enough to create a flourishing business. So I tried to cover what I couldn't do, albeit on a very small budget. I found selling difficult, but fortunately I had a very good friend in Bramwell Lowe. He was quite a character when it came to selling and with his help the company grew. It was impossible for us to do our own distribution so for this I mainly used Rusts of Cromer (now Waverley TBS) who had outlets across Norfolk. I did do one or two direct deliveries but we couldn't

Erpingham Brewery, c1983

have reached the markets we did without their help. It was also very useful to have Dr David Crease as a partner in those early days; David was a chemist so very good technically.

'At the beginning we had two important direct customers. In Norwich Jim and Hazel Johnson at the Ten Bells were hugely supportive whilst at Reedham we supplied the Railway Tavern. Then at Christmas 1981 we had a lucky break. At the time we were known to the Hotel Wroxham who got all their products from Courage. Luckily for us Courage had a delivery problem and we were asked to supply three kilderkins of beer, equivalent to 54 gallons, which was an enormous amount. At the time I went over to meet David Lamprell, the hotel partner in charge of the bar, who was really helpful. We subsequently supplied them for the duration. At this point I realised that to really sell we needed to get direct sales and at this point my friend Bram Lowe came on board full time.

'During the first year we made a loss of £6,000 which was a lot of money then. But after that sales gradually increased and we reached the magic break-even level.'

Because of large temperature fluctuations and a mains water supply of varying quality the unit at Drayton had never been totally suitable for the brewing of traditional ale. So in 1983 the brewery moved to a converted stable block behind the Spread Eagle at Erpingham which, with the enthusiastic support of the landlord John Marjoram, became the brewery tap. At the same time David made the decision to sell out his share of the company and concentrate on his teaching career. He did, however, keep his hand in and continued to be a dedicated home brewer.

In August 1983, within a month of opening, disaster struck when an electrical fault triggered a fire at the brewery. At the time Ray was on holiday and when he returned he found that it had been burnt to the ground. With the help of Peter Mauldon, an independent brewer, production was temporarily transferred to Sudbury. Within three months the brewery had been rebuilt. Once they had 'risen from the ashes' Ray and his team created a new brew to celebrate called Phoenix XXX, which was launched at the CAMRA Norwich Beer Festival in October 1983, and that's when the business really took off.

Erpingham Brewery after the fire, 1983

Ray Ashworth (centre) and Bram Lowe (right), receive the 'Champion Beer of Britain' award from CAMRA, 1992

In 1988 Ray moved Woodforde's from Erpingham to Woodbastwick. This gave the opportunity to invest in plant which had a much larger capacity and put the business in an ideal position to take advantage of the Draught Beer Orders that were introduced in 1989. The story is taken up by Ray:

'It was really quite a revolution because it gave landlords of tied houses the right to buy one guest beer from whomever they liked. Suddenly all of the pubs in Norfolk, the majority of which were owned by Watneys or Courage, were potential customers and our sales literally doubled. The big brewers didn't like losing sales to tiddlers like me and over the next few years they found ways around the Orders. Nevertheless getting Woodforde's name in their bars gave us a terrific boost as drinkers started demanding our beers.'

Major awards soon followed for Ray:

'In 1992 our Norfolk Nog was voted "Champion Beer of Britain" by CAMRA. We'd started producing Nog in 1985 after I'd been approached by James Ruddy, a reporter at the Evening Eastern News. Nog was a dark beer common to Norfolk and Suffolk and he wanted to run an article on it. Sensing the opportunity for good publicity I offered to research and produce a brew, which I did. I was absolutely amazed when we won. At the time we only produced five barrels of it a week and I remember Roger Cawdron at the Ribs of Beef, and other local supporters, being concerned

that there wouldn't be enough to go around. We won many awards but the real accolade came four years later when Norfolk Wherry, which you remember was my first-ever brew, was also voted "Champion Beer of Britain". We were the first brewery ever to win the accolade twice and demand absolutely exploded.'

Bram Lowe, sales director for Woodforde's, remembers receiving the second award:

'Roger Cawdron, Mike Betts and myself were travelling to the National Beer Festival in London at Olympia when Roger realised he'd lost his ticket. When we arrived there was a huge queue, so we went around to a back door to sort out how to get him in. Luckily I saw someone I knew who said that we might as well go in straight away, which was great. We had a walk around and saw a cluster of TV cameras and were asked if they could have a chat with us. As Mike was our PR man he went to do an interview and just before he started a CAMRA official let us know that Wherry had been voted the Champion Beer of Britain. Well we were absolutely shocked and over the moon. As for Mike he nearly fainted.

'It was a far cry from early festivals we'd attended at the Metropole Centre in Brighton. At the time we were all organised alphabetically and the "Ws" came right at the end down a little turning. Some evenings I stood there all night and was lucky to see more than a handful of people.'

Woodforde's Brewery Today

Mike Betts and Dennis Nudd, 2009

In 1999 Ray sold the brewery to a consortium led by local businessmen Dennis Nudd and Mike Betts, a previous director of Woodforde's. Mike Betts had long been an ardent supporter of Woodforde's:

'I first came across Woodforde's in 1981. I lived in the village of Drayton and heard that a new brewery had opened there in Bidewell Close, so I soon organised a visit to the brewery together with a group of friends and work colleagues. It had only been open a few months and I can distinctly remember knocking on the door and it being opened by a chap in a white coat, who turned out to be Ray Ashworth. Ray made us very welcome and showed us around the brewery which was extremely impressive. But the real icing on the cake was at the end of the tour when we had the chance to sample this wonderful new beer which was absolutely fantastic.

'At the time the beers we were drinking in Norwich lacked flavour. But Wherry, which was Woodforde's first beer, was made with quality local ingredients and had a fabulous flavour. From that moment on the 15 of us on that tour became unofficial members of the brewery sales team! Every time we went out drinking, often after a hot-air balloon flight, we'd ask the barman if he stocked Woodforde's beers and if not, which was generally the case, we sang its praises. At the time I never imagined that I would become a part owner of this impressive brewery!

'After that first meeting with Ray we built quite a friendship. At the time I worked in a marketing capacity in Norwich. Ray was great at producing beer but needed a bit of help advertising the beer, so I produced a few leaflets for him to promote and create awareness of Woodforde's Norfolk Ales.

'Moving forward to 1996 I had the opportunity to take early retirement from my job at Her Majesty's Stationery Office and I approached Ray about the possibility of a part-time job. He offered me the role of marketing manager, which I jumped at. A year later I was made a director and then in 1999 Ray decided he would like to sell the business. I put my head together with a great friend, Dennis Nudd, who also has a love of real ale, and we considered the possibility of being able to buy the brewery. I really didn't think we'd be able to do it, but as Dennis said: "If you're determined to do something you can always find a way." So we did! The 21st July 1999 was the big day when we took over the brewery.'

Dennis and Mike had very clear ideas on how they wanted to grow the brewery:

'At the time we knew that we had a fantastic brewery and brewing team, together with a superb product. Woodforde's beers were very special and we realised that we needed to put together a plan to expand production capacity and, at the same time, to step up our sales and marketing strategy. We needed to

expand the brewery and were fortunate to be able to retain the original brewery, and alongside we built a completely new brewery with the mash tun, copper and hop back supplied by Briggs Engineering of Burton-upon-Trent, generally regarded as the "Rolls Royce" of brewery engineers. This enabled us to more than double our production capacity. We made the big decision to continue brewing with whole hops, despite the extra cost implications, because we were not prepared to compromise on flavour. We did not become fully automated because we are, and wish to remain, a craft brewery. It is therefore important that our brewers are "hands on" at every stage of the brewing process.

'Woodforde's was well known for brewing real ales with flavour, that's what we've always been about. From its beginning Woodforde's has used the best possible ingredients to produce the best possible flavours. The recipes have obviously always been special and they've all used the main ingredients of water, yeast, malted barley and hops. But it's the blends you use and the way that you combine them which determines the flavours that you achieve. Norfolk barley is some of the best in the world,

especially the Maris Otter variety, so that's what we use. We work with Simpsons Malt and the Crisps Malting Group, both based in Norfolk, who are two of the best maltsters in the country. We also ensure that we buy the best hops available for each variety that we use each year. We don't have a limit on our budget for buying ingredients: our top priority is to buy the best.'

Woodforde's continues to win many prizes. In 2015 Kett's Rebellion and Norfolk Wherry were awarded overall Gold and Silver in the CAMRA Champion Beer of Norfolk Awards leaving Bruce Ash, brewery manager, 'chuffed'. But maybe even more pleasing was to be given the accolade 'Brewery of the Year' by *The Good Pub Guide*. The award is determined by nominations from beer lovers and so based completely on feedback from readers who obviously recognise the company's passion for brewing great beer.

But what of the future. Mike has very clear ideas: 'In ten years time we'd like to think that we'll still have the great team of dedicated and enthusiastic people we have working here. We don't want large-scale expansion, but would like to grow modestly each year whilst still being known as a craft brewery that produces quality beers with a great flavour.'

Working at the Broadland Brewery

Dr David Crease maintained his links with the brewery and eventually took on the role of head brewer in 1996 with a view to developing the scientific aspect of the brewing:

'My first task was to review the "rule of thumb" practices which had been instigated over the years and introduce more stringent scientific processes.

'I knew as we expanded the brewery would eventually reach a size which was beyond my level of expertise and we would need to employ a commercially trained head brewer. In the same way that you bring up children who grow up and make their own way in the world Woodforde's outgrew us. However, I do believe that it has achieved success because it had a sound foundation.'

Today scientific testing is an essential part of the brewing process. Maxine Moody is responsible for maintaining standards:

'In the laboratory we quality control every beer that is brewed here. Throughout the beer's shelf life I sample and test it every seven days. Then before any beer is racked a sample is bought into the lab and I test it for colour, bitterness, ph and yeast content. It's also put through the alcoliser which determines the gravity and alcohol content.

'In the microbiology lab I test samples from every stage of every brew to make sure there are no infections in the beer. I also regularly swab the pipes and the vessels to make sure they are clean.

'At around 12 o'clock each day I'm involved in the daily beer tasting. Samples of different beers are brought up to be tasted. We're looking for clarity and of course we have to taste it … I have read that I have the best job in the world, I can't think why!'

Neil Bain took over as head brewer in 2008. Neil's predecessors had built on their skills as home brewers. However, Neil is professionally trained but still has the same passion and drive to produce excellent brews as Ray and David before him:

'I've been involved in the brewing industry since 1977. Previously I worked in the Midlands. Unfortunately the industry went into decline and I was forced to look further afield. I'm glad I did because I found Woodforde's. Here the scale is much smaller. When I worked at Bass we packaged 20,000 barrels a week, whereas I'm now involved with brewing 20,000 barrels a year.

'In different parts of the country drinkers have developed different palates. In Norfolk people like a well balanced, fully fermented beer without a head, whilst Midlanders have a very sweet palate and definitely like a head on their beer. So if you produced a pint as we drink it in Norfolk for a Midlander, he'd hand it straight back to the barman and say "this pint is flat".

'Since I've arrived I've introduced quality standards at each stage of the production process. Such processes were second nature when I worked for Bass and they have enabled us to maintain consistency in the quality and tastes of our beers.

'At 12 o'clock every day we gather for a tasting. There's always at least two of us, although I like to see three or four people, as everybody's palate is slightly different. We first taste the water, both hot and cold, just to make sure we're starting with a good raw material and then we taste the beers at 1, 2, 7, 14, 28 and 42 days into their shelf life. We need to make sure that every beer we produce will be perfect right up to its "best before date".

Maxine Moody, working in the laboratory, 2011

Neil Bain, Director of Brewing, 2011

'The beers at Woodforde's are brewed using the best quality raw materials, which means that you always get a great result. We always want to produce well-balanced beers which have mass appeal. When we introduce a new beer we're obviously looking for something totally different. We know roughly what works in terms of how much of each different type of malt to add to give a particular flavour. With the hops it's like using herbs in cooking, they just give that extra dimension. So, for example, the last time we produced a new beer we sourced some of our hops from New Zealand, and there are only about 37 tons of this particular hop to go around the whole world! It introduced a nice gingery character which was well received first of all in "Game On", which was brewed for the 2010 football World Cup, after which the recipe was tweaked to produce "Once Bittern".

'Everyone here loves the beer and wants to see an excellent product going to trade. For me that's the best part of this brewery.'

But let's give the final word to brewery manager Bruce Ash:

'I first became involved in Woodforde's in 1987. My friend had a summer job here and he told me there was a vacancy on the Youth Training Scheme. They never told me I had the job, but I've been here so long now I think I've got it!

'I started off washing the barrels, then I moved on to filling them and looking after the storage side of things. I then became a brewer, and now I'm the brewery manager.

'Every beer I make I'm proud of. Just seeing people drinking the beer in pubs is fantastic, but obviously getting awards is also very special. We've won a number of high-profile awards, including the accolade of CAMRA's Supreme Champion Beer of Britain for both Nog and Wherry, whilst recently Nelson's Revenge got the silver medal in the International Brewing Awards competition.

'My favourite beer is Nelson's Revenge . . . it's just a proper English beer. Its 4.5% and has plenty of malt and hop character coming through. A fantastic decent pint.'

Bruce Ash, brewery manager, 2011

The Fur & Feather at Woodbastwick, the brewery tap, 2011

Horses and Drays

Steward and Patteson dray advertising Honeysuckle Ale in Norwich, c1960

Horses and drays were essential to the efficient running of the breweries. They were responsible for delivering the beer to pubs. However, they were more than just a form of transport. Because they bore a company's livery and often the name of its most popular brands they also served as advertisements.

In the early 1900s the average wage for a brewery worker was 16 shillings (80p) per week, for a drayman it was a low as 10 shillings (50p). Nevertheless there were perks to the job as the draymen received free beer from the public houses they visited on their rounds. Despite been somewhat inebriated at the end of a hard day they had no problems getting home as they could rely on their horses to return them safely to the brewery. Joe Soames was a drayman at Youngs, Crawshay & Youngs in the early 1900s. On Sunday mornings his son used to help his father feed the horses. He particularly remembers joining his father and a three-horse team on trips to the country, although he recalls being treated to a bottle a pop rather than a stronger tipple!

Although horses were still the principal source of motive power for breweries at the outbreak of the WWI many were commandeered by the army and few returned. In the 1920s motor vehicles became more readily available and the switch to motorised transport was made. Often the two sources of transport ran in tandem.

Barry Berwick recalls the Steward & Patteson horses:

'When I joined Steward & Patteson in 1958 they still had four horses pulling drays. They were named after the directors. I remember one was called Donald after Mr Steward and another John after Mr Morse. By then horse and drays were only used to supply some of the local pubs and they also pulled the lord mayor's coach in the carnival procession. They were mainly used to advertise brewery products. In the early 1960s they were taken to Yarmouth by train and walked up and down the front pulling a cart carrying a huge honey pot to promote Honeysuckle Ale.'

Today if you visit the Crown Room at Wensum Lodge on King Street you can still see the old stable block which housed Youngs, Crawshay & Youngs' shire and Suffolk punch carthorses. On the walls are the tethering rings and plaques which bear the names of some of these splendid animals, including: Nelson (named after head brewer, Nelson Tyrrell), Dick (after brewery manager, Dick Richards), Churchill (known as Winston), Callboy (after a famous racehorse) and Neville (after Neville Chamberlain).

In 1985 the Friends of Wensum Lodge gathered the memories of people who could remember the horses. These were recounted by Ken Davies, Chris Barringer and Joyce Gurney Read: 'One elderly lady talks of Sunday school treats to Bramerton. The girls, in their white pinafores, sat in the freshly scrubbed brewery cart with seating borrowed from the local school, which tipped over when the horses started off and some of the boys fell off the back.'

Derek Spanton: A 21st-century Drayman

Derek Spanton and HRH Prince Charles, c2003

'My family have worked with horses and drays for over 100 years. My granddad lived in Sloley [Norfolk village]. He worked for the Council. Every Monday morning he travelled with his horse and dray to the north Norfolk coast to places like Mundesley and Bacton and loaded up with gravel from the beaches which was used to make up roads. My father used to do a milk round with a cart and pony, so as a boy I enjoyed helping both my dad and granddad with their horses.

'My Uncle Oscar used to display his horses at local shows. I remember going with him to the Norfolk Show when I was 11. When the local Sunday school went on their summer outings to Yarmouth he used to take all the children to the train station on his dray. The girls all dressed up in their posh frocks. It was a great day for them. When my uncle died he left me land at Sloley and when I was going through his outbuildings I found an old harness in a trunk. At the time I worked as a lorry driver for the Electricity Board, but when I saw that harness I couldn't let it go. I had the land, I had a harness . . . all I needed was a horse!

'In 1988 I bought my first shire horse who I call Jim, after my father. Dad would've loved to have seen him. I've since bought Herbie and Bob. They're all shire horses and stand over 18 hands [6ft] and weigh over a ton. At first I just appeared in shows and worked with a harrow and a plough. But then I bought a dray which I found in an old barn at Worstead which used to belong to my uncle. It was in quite a state but I did it up.

'In 1994 I was approached by Ray Ashworth, from Woodforde's Brewery, to take Jim and the dray over to the opening of the Billy Bluelight in Norwich, which they'd just taken over. Ray was obviously pleased with what I did because he phoned me afterwards and asked if Woodforde's could sponsor me. I still work with them today.

'We've done some great events with Woodforde's. When Nelson's Revenge was first brewed we toured around 14 north Norfolk pubs in three days. Then in 2005 Herbie was one of six brewery horses invited to meet the Queen at Windsor . . . they let me go too!'

Derek recounts the work of a brewery drayman:

'They had a hard life in the breweries. In the mornings they'd be in by around five to feed and prepare the horses so that they were ready to leave and do their rounds by about nine. In the afternoons they'd be back by say four then they'd have to bed down the horses. They'd finish at around five.

'The draymen were responsible for the horses and the care of their harnesses. They'd have to clean the harnesses with oil to stop the stitches from rotting. But the drays were looked after by the brewery carpenters who would've maintained the wood and paintwork. They really had to keep an eye on them 'cos a typical load on a dray would be 15 barrels, each containing about 80 pints. Don't forget in those days the barrels were made out of wood so if it rained they got even heavier.

'The drays had spoked wheels with an iron rim. Even today if you take the wheel off, you can see the year the dray was made stamped on the stub of the axle.

'The barrels were loaded at the breweries from a platform which was at the same level as the dray, but the draymen had to unload the barrels onto the ground when they arrived at the breweries. They used to carry a skid under the base of the dray, which was basically a ramp which could be pulled out when you had to unload. The skids where made of wood but reinforced with metal. They were bowed in the middle so you could slide the barrels down and when they hit the bottom they'd stand up. You'd put a coconut mat at the bottom of the skid so that when the barrels hit the ground they didn't split. You couldn't roll them down the skid 'cos if you did you'd never be able to stop them, they'd have just carried on rolling down the street.

'The horses used to be reshod every two to three weeks. Generally breweries didn't have a farrier but they did have a forge, which was heated by coal, so the farrier would visit every week to shoe the horses.

'The local breweries tended to use either shires, whose lower legs are 'feathered' and white, or percherons, a clean-legged horse, i.e. no feathering. Steward and Patteson always had percherons, but Bullards used a mixture.

'The horses worked hard for the breweries but they'd usually have an annual holiday and be sent out to the fields. Old horses would be taken out with the young to help train them. When they came to the end of their working life some may have been kept by their grooms as a pet, but normally they were sent for slaughter.

'The draymen weren't paid much, but they got a pint at every stop. Luckily the horses knew their way home!'

Derek Spanton showing Herbie and his dray c2007

The Beer Festival

The Norwich and Norfolk CAMRA Beer Festival, which takes place during October in the magnificent St Andrew's and Blackfriars' Halls, has become one of Norwich's major annual fixtures.

Early Festivals

The festival evolved from a small event run by enthusiastic members of a club called the Bystanders. The story is taken up by member Ted Williams:

'The Bystanders' Society was founded in 1959 as a club for the "non-clubbable". We were non-political, non-commercial and non-sectarian. We attracted a vibrant mix of people. Although we weren't serious about much, we were serious about beer.

'In 1968 we moved to our own premises at 5, Thorpe Road where we met until 1995. It was great because we had a cellar which started our interest in serving our own beers. We were helped in this quest by both Adnams and Greene King, in fact we bought up a lot of old hand pumps that had been taken out of Greene King pubs. At the time the City's pubs were almost all owned by Watney's and we were one of the few outlets serving cask beers. In 1969, when the Volunteer (Chapelfield Road) was demolished to make way for the St Giles' roundabout, we were given permission to salvage a lot of the shelving from its Victorian bar which, together with two mirrors etched with pictures of volunteer soldiers, were used to create our own Volunteer Bar. It was named in both memory of the old pub and in recognition of our voluntary staff.

'We became quite popular for serving real ales. In 1970 a number of us, including myself, Ray Ashworth (who later founded Woodforde's), Bram Lowe and Charles Chaplin decided to promote our bar by holding an event where we brought in beers from other parts of the country. We called it a 'beer festival', which was borrowed from the German 'bierfest' and translated. This hadn't been done before, so we had to start from scratch. In particular we had to decide what we were going to serve. We selected beers from across the country of which we'd had good reports and ordered one or two firkins. The breweries were always happy to supply us as long as we picked them up ourselves. So we literally had a number of volunteers from the club who travelled the country picking up barrels. On one memorable occasion I set off from Norwich with a colleague in a hired Luton van at 2.30am. On this single journey we collected firkins from Border Ales at Wrexham, JW Lees in Manchester, Thwaites' Brewery at Blackburn, Hartley's Brewery at Ulverston and finally Sam Smith's in Tadcaster. We finally arrived back in Norwich to a welcoming committee 23 hours later.

'In October 1973 the festival received national recognition when the journalist Richard Boston, who was also a campaigner for real ale, wrote an article in the Guardian newspaper. In it he talks of visiting our cellar during the event and seeing "a collection of living beer the like of which I (had) not previously encountered". He went on to describe our festival as "unique". So I do think we can say that the Bystanders contributed to the idea of British beer festivals which then evolved into the National Festival. After the article was published we were flooded with letters from enthusiasts asking for advice on how to run their own events. We ran our last festival in 1978 when we offered 35 beers from 24 outlets. By then CAMRA had started to run their own beer festival, so we in effect passed the baton over to them.'

Bram Lowe, first chairman of the local branch of CAMRA, has no doubt as to the importance of the Bystanders' festivals: 'I always point out that the idea of a beer festival was first mooted at the Bystanders' Society in Norwich.'

Ray Ashworth, 1992

Bram Lowe, 1992

Ted Williams, 2011

Charles Chaplin, c1970

The Norwich Beer Festival

Bram recalls that:

'The first CAMRA beer festival in Norwich almost took place on the spur of the moment. I was chairing a branch meeting of CAMRA in August 1977, at the Beehive on Leopold Road, when Mick Betts, one of our members, put forward a strong proposal for a festival and we all basically said OK. We couldn't get St Andrew's Hall so we had to take Blackfriars'. This didn't particularly bother us, because we thought it would be plenty big enough. We soon learnt our error, because the place was heaving.

'We had portable tills in those days and on the final day some ne'er do well grabbed the till and started making for the exit. As he left he had to go down some steps and luckily one of our members on the door put out his foot and tripped him up, he went flying and we got our money back.'

The Norwich & Norfolk CAMRA beer festival is still going strong. Festival goers have the opportunity to buy over 200 cask-conditioned real ales from Britain's independent brewers, along with draught and bottled beers from continental Europe. Additionally a large range of traditional ciders and perries, including a selection from East Anglia, will be on offer.

Martin Ward has organised the beer festival for a number of years, in 2011 he recounted:

'During the week of the festival we sell over 50,000 pints which is a phenomenal amount. We used to be the biggest festival in the country but other groups have expanded by using bigger and bigger marquees. We don't have that option. Our first festival was held in Blackfriars' Hall but we soon outgrew that and took over St Andrew's Hall. We now use the whole complex, including the cloisters, and have even fitted in a small marquee which allowed us to expand and include ciders and continental bottled beers. We literally can't expand any more. Even so we still rank in the top five festivals in the country. We wouldn't want to move because the venue is brilliant and makes our event unique.

'The entire event from planning to the week itself is run by volunteers and we simply couldn't afford to run it if we had to pay staff. We all give our time totally free. It takes a huge amount of planning. We start in February when we sort out the logo which will be used in marketing and be put on glasses, T-shirts etc. and just carry on from there. Many of the volunteers are CAMRA members but we have one gentleman whose been helping for 26 years who isn't a member, but he loves his ales and loves talking to people. He has a great week.

Norwich Beer Festival, Blackfriars' Hall, 2010

37

Martin Ward, 2010

Portrait of John Patteson, Blackfriars' Hall, c1803

'Although it's a beer festival it's not all about beer. We want to create a really good atmosphere which is helped along by providing entertainment. We have one section dedicated to traditional pub games such as shut-the-box and skittles, which is always popular. Also since the mid 1990s we've provided entertainment. Unfortunately because of noise restriction orders we can't offer the same variety that we used to. Nonetheless we still have an eclectic mix of performers including string quartets and brass bands. We also have a guy wandering around who makes balloons into a variety of objects from animals to flowers…in fact you name it he makes it!

'Furthermore we have a products stall which sells merchandise and also memorabilia from previous years. There's a rumour going around that in 2010 someone paid £50 for a 1986 glass . . . I hope he didn't break it on the way home!

'The ciders and continental bottled beers tend to be more popular with the younger groups so its good that we have them. It encourages younger generations to come along and hopefully gives them the opportunity to move on to sampling real ales and to discover new tastes and flavours.

'One of our members is very keen on foreign brews and the history of European brewing. He has many friends and contacts on the Continent which means that we are usually able to offer at least a couple of beers which you won't be able to buy elsewhere in England.

'When it comes to British real ales we have both the contacts and experience to ensure we have on offer a superb selection. Because we are so successful, breweries start contacting me from around February asking if we will stock their ales. If we don't know them we obviously need to try them first to ensure they are up to scratch. What is great though is that some will produce "specials" for us to showcase.

'We are really proud of the Norwich Beer Festival. The number of people who come back year after year is a testament of its success. We not only offer one of the best selections of beers that you will get anywhere in the country but do so in a medieval complex. But what is really great is that a painting of John Patteson, founder of the great brewing firm of Steward & Patteson, hangs on the wall above us. I'd like to think that he joins in the festivities . . . well in spirit at least.'

Pub Beer Festivals

Throughout the year a number of pubs hold beer festivals. The first Norwich pub festival was held at the Trafford Arms (Grove Road) as recounted by landlord Chris Higgins:

'We did our first one in February 1994, which was 12 months after we took the pub over. We saw it as a way of letting people know that the Trafford was under new ownership and that we were selling quality cask beers. We chose February as it's always a quiet month.

'Because that first festival was run around Valentine's day I linked all of the write ups on the beers to a "lonely heart" column. So for example one of our first adverts said:

Chris and Glynis Higgins at the Trafford Arms, 2011

I LOVE MY PINT
Seeking the perfect companion; look no further:
I have a great body including a wonderful nose
I have impeccable pedigree and am always
beautifully presented
A love affair that will last forever; I won't cheat on
you
I am a cask-conditioned beer; meet me at the:
TRAFFORD ARMS VALENTINE BEER FESTIVAL
If I don't suit you I am sure one of my seventy plus
friends will
We are available all week at:
TRAFFORD ARMS

'The first festival was run in the pub but for some time it has been held in a marquee. One year when we had a World Wildlife theme when we designed the entrance like a cave.

'We always stretch a point. I remember that in the first festival we had a beer from the Coach House Brewery called the "Valentine Day Massacre", which wasn't about love but a very good beer. Nearly every year we feature a beer called Sarah Hughes and one year when we had a military theme I was asked what the "link" was. Luckily I managed to convince everyone that she'd been a nurse in the Crimea!

'We aim to provide something for everyone and have now run more than 20 successful festivals – so we must be doing something right!'

The Trafford Arms' Beer Festival, 2011

Lacons' St Margaret's Brewery during the floods, 1912

Upper Goat Lane, undated

Section 2 - Norwich Pubs, Inns and Taverns

Backs' Long Bar, c1970

Origins and Evolution

King Street Gates, featuring the Cinder Ovens, by David Hodgson, undated

As early as 1577 a government survey provided the first detailed information we have on establishments selling alcohol, defined as 'inns, taverns or alehouses'. Put simply an inn serviced travellers, a tavern specialised in the sale of wine, whilst alehouses sold, and often brewed, ale. In practice there was a huge overlap between the establishments as highlighted in an 18th-century guide for magistrates: 'Every inn is not an alehouse, nor every alehouse an inn: but if an inn uses common selling of ale, it is then also an alehouse; and if an alehouse lodges and entertains travellers, it is also an inn.'

Did You Know?

In the Elizabethan era the punishment for keeping an unlicensed alehouse was one pound, and three days' imprisonment.

Over time a number of other titles have been applied, including: beerhouse, gin palace and tippling house. However, in the late 17th century the term public house started to be generally used. Its precise origin is unclear. Although it is assumed to have derived from the term 'public alehouse', it was applied indiscriminately to a range of drinking establishments.

By whichever definition we use Norwich has always been well served by drinking establishments. In 1681 the Dean of Norwich Cathedral complained to Mayor Hugh Bokenham that: '…the town swarms with alehouses every other house is almost one; and every one of them they tell is also a bawdy house.' Unfortunately for the Dean it was in the financial interest of both the tax authorities and the brewery owners, who were increasingly holding civic office, to encourage their proliferation.

Bess of Bedlam, Oak Street, 1895

By the 1880s there were over 450 pubs within the City walls. Many would have been tiny alehouses occupying little more than the downstairs room of a house where a family would live at the expense of the brewery. The landlord would usually have another job. Customers, many of whom lived in squalid conditions, resided within a few minutes' walk. After a hard day's work they returned to small overcrowded hovels. A visit to their local pub to consume cheap gin and beer with friends was their escape.

The situation could not continue and by the end of the 19th century it was widely accepted that Norwich had too many licensed premises. The 1904 Compensation Act allowed Licensing Justices to refer any houses which they felt were no longer necessary to the Compensation Authority. If the Authority agreed the licence was not renewed and compensation was paid to the brewery for loss of trade and livelihood. In Norwich around 200 premises were closed 'under compensation'.

The first house in Norwich to be closed this way was the White Horse on St Mary's Church Alley, which was referred for closure on 4th February, 1905. The licence expired in January the following year. Over the following 12 months a further 25 houses were referred for closure. Looking at various properties that were closed under the act it seems amazing that so many public houses had survived for so long. For example the Bess of Bedlam on Oak Street was closed in 1907 because 15 other licensed premises were located within 200 yards. Similarly the Globe on Botolph Street, which was closed the following year, had 17 licensed premises in the immediate vicinity. As the century progressed and Norwich City Council undertook a programme of slum clearance, many City-centre pubs were closed under compensation. In some cases their licences were transferred to new premises which were opening in the newly built estates. So, for example, in 1938 the licence was transferred from the King's Arms on Bethel Street to a new pub, also called the King's Arms, which served the newly built Mile Cross Estate.

43

Brewing memorabilia, various dates

Breweries had long recognised the advantages of controlling pubs. This was achieved by building estates of 'tied houses'. Under this system pubs were owned and controlled by specific breweries and landlords could only sell their beers. As early as 1845 a local survey indicated that over 70% of pubs were tied to one of Norwich's 'big four' breweries namely: Steward & Patteson, Morgans, Bullards or Youngs, Crawshay & Youngs. Increasingly such firms took over rivals not because they wanted to take over the brewery, which they often closed, but because of the value of the tied estate and the ready market it gave for their beers.

In 1950 over 95% of the pubs within Norwich were owned by the 'big four' Breweries. Few would have anticipated what happened over the next 20 years.

In 1958 Bullards took over Youngs, Crawshay & Youngs. They closed the brewery and kept the tied houses. Then in 1961 Bullards and Steward & Patteson bought Morgans and divided its tied estate between them, but allowed Watney Mann (Watneys) to take over Morgans' brewery and sell Watneys beers in their tied houses. At the time Watneys had started to produce a keg beer called Red Barrel which, like all keg bitter, was filtered and pasteurised to make a sterile product with a long shelf life. The carbon dioxide which was added gave the beer fizz and additional pressure which enabled it to be drawn up from the cellar. Hence keg beer did not need a traditional long-handled beer pump.

In the early days keg beer was a premium product. In principle it was a brilliant idea because it removed the perishability of the product. The beer was well packaged and sterile.

Even at this time many of Norwich's pubs were little more than alehouses, run by a couple where the landlord had another job. They often did not look after the cask beers being produced by Steward & Patteson and Bullards. By July 1962 the relative quality of Watneys' keg bitters, coupled with a strong marketing campaign, resulted in them accounting for over 50% of local bitter sales. Watneys also began to purchase shares in both Bullards and Steward & Patteson and by 1967 they had taken over both brewers. As a result this one firm came to own over 95% of all Norwich pubs.

In an effort to appease local concerns over the loss of heritage brews, Watneys produced a beer they named Norwich Bitter and a stronger brew known as Castle Bitter. Initially these brews met the tastes of the majority of local drinkers. However, over time the quality of beers declined. In particular Red Barrel, Watneys' flagship brew later reinvented as Watneys' Red, was perceived to deteriorate.

Watneys, which was taken over by Grand Metropolitan in 1972, had a near monopoly. In such an environment the number of establishments selling real ales in Norwich were few and far between. Many are still remembered fondly and indeed remain open today. Thus, for example, in the late 1960s you could get Adnams from the Maid's Head Hotel and Tolly Cobbold from the Wild Man on Bedford Street. Then in 1968 the Bystanders' Society moved to their new premises on Thorpe Road where, with help from Adnams and Greene King, they set up their Volunteer Bar and became popular for serving real ales. For a short time in the early 1970s Roger and Anthea Cawdron were landlords at Fisher's Free House on Prince of Wales Road.

Then in the mid 1970s the Ten Bells, the Plasterers' Arms and the Golden Star all opened as free houses. Peter Turner, who was the landlord at the Plasterers' Arms c1976 before taking over the lease of the Golden Star, recalls this period: 'Customers used to walk through the door of the Plasterers and see the six hand pumps, fall on their knees and bow down in front of them. It was real ale Nirvana.'

Peter Turner outside the Golden Star, c1977

1980 saw the arrival on the Norwich pub scene of Colin Keatley who now owns the Fat Cat on West End Street. He realised that despite the popularity of real ales there were only a handful of City pubs selling them, and so he bought and transformed the White Lion in Oak Street. The same decade saw Roger and Anthea Cawdron open the Ribs of Beef on Fye Bridge Street as a free house. Such free houses gave welcome support to the new microbreweries by stocking their new brews. In fact Colin had Woodforde's beers on his bar within a year of the brewery opening and has sold it ever since. He is now proud to be their longest-standing customer.

However, the pub scene in Norwich was about to change. In 1988/9 the Monopolies and Mergers Commission forced Grand Metropolitan (which had taken over Watneys) to swap 43 of its Norwich pubs with 43 Courage pubs in Bristol, where an inverse situation existed. Then in 1989 the Beer Orders restricted breweries to owning a maximum of 2,000 pubs. As a result, like many other large brewing conglomerates, Grand Metropolitan launched an umbrella property company called Inntrepreneur and its pub leases were either transferred across or, if considered unprofitable, sold. Roger Cawdron, who has been a City landlord for over 40 years says: 'Often the brewery staff moved over to the new organisation so that in practice there was not a lot of change. The Licensed Victuallers Association thought it would have been better to restrict breweries to owning a maximum of 25% of the licences in any one area. In practice this would have led to regional pub swaps between the breweries, but the end result would have been to have four or five companies owning the licences in an area rather than one holding the vast majority.'

Over the following years pub companies (Pubcos) have merged and been taken over. They have radically changed the dynamics between the pubs and their owners. Originally, tied houses were bought by the breweries to give their owners an outlet for beers. One of the many criticisms of Pubcos is that they are property companies, which are solely concerned with the value of the land. They are primed to close pubs and sell land to developers if this is the most profitable route. As a result, especially outside the City walls, we have lost many public houses including the Earl of Leicester, the Cygnet, the Little John, the Crown & Magpie and the Crawshay Arms.

But there have been many positive outcomes. The Beer Orders also gave a boost to relatively small pub-owning, non-brewing chains, such as Wetherspoons which has four outlets in Norwich. Similarly they have strengthened the foothold of smaller breweries such as Adnams, Batemans, Greene King and Woodforde's.

Bar of the Fat Cat, 2011

They also enabled many independent landlords to take over establishments. For example Colin Keatley bought the New Inn, West End Street, from Courage who assessed it as a failing, bottom-end pub. He resurrected it as the Fat Cat and has won numerous national CAMRA awards.

Another major change in both the local and national pub scene is the sale of food. Before the 1960s if you asked for food in a pub you'd get crisps or nuts and if you were really lucky a sandwich. Today in most establishments food is an important part of the business. Roger Cawdron remembers:

'I did food at my father's pub, the Edward VII, in the late 1960s which was very unusual. But we did a decent menu, which included things like steaks and scampi, which was quite novel.

'Later, at the Adam & Eve, it started with someone catching the smell of my lunch and asking if they could have the same. So I thought fair enough, prepared them a meal and charged ten bob for it. After that they started to phone an order through in advance and it sort of snowballed from there.

'We started a trend in one or two pubs and Watney Mann were keen to encourage their landlords to serve food. At the Feathers, on Prince of Wales Road, they had a steak grill behind the bar where you could actually see the food cooking, which was really novel.'

The serving of food has gone hand in hand with the increased professionalism in the trade and with the size of premises. Even as late as the 1950s many pubs were small premises run basically from a front room. Today most are a lot bigger, which has led Roger to speculate that 'although a lot of pubs have closed over the last 60 years I'd estimate that the square footage is about the same'.

So in the last 100 years the Norwich pub scene has almost changed beyond recognition. Although we have lost many of our drinking establishments we are exceptionally lucky to have retained such a rich pub heritage. The diversity is immense: from the old coaching inns to the names steeped in history, from the signs outside to the characters within. In the following pages we highlight some of the major themes common to pubs before taking a stroll around the hostelries we could have visited in the 1880s, together with those that still trade today.

Themes

A number of common threads run through the stories behind Norwich's hostelries. They cover a huge range: from how the premises acquired its name to the entertainers who performed there.

In this section we look at these features in more detail. Some of the subjects we cover are unique to Norwich but even those that are common to pubs throughout the country have a Norwich twist. They each tell us much about the huge role pubs, inns and taverns have played in the City's history.

The following themes are covered. Each has been allocated an icon which will be used to highlight relevant facts for individual pubs in the following chapters.

- Signs and Names

- Artists

- Entertainment

- Coaching Inns

- Sporting Links

- Pub Games

- Community and Clubs

- Murder and Mayhem

- Norwich Yards

- The River

Themes: Signs and Names

When the Romans conquered Britain they introduced many customs, one of which was the tavern sign. In Rome tavern keepers advertised the fact that they had new wine available by hanging a vine plant over the door. In Britain we sold ale, so when innkeepers wanted to draw attention to their new brews it became traditional to hang a branch or bush over the door. Thus the sign of 'The Bush' was born.

After the demise of the Roman Empire the tradition of hanging a bush over an alehouse seems to have survived. In the Bayeux Tapestry a building appears to have a brown pole sticking out from one corner with a lump of green on the end. This is thought by many historians to be an early depiction of a Saxon alehouse.

At the end of the 14th century authorities wanted to exert control over alehouses, which had become associated with riotous behaviour. They passed a law that all establishments selling alcohol had to hang a sign advertising the fact near the door. As it was highly unlikely that either the landlord or his customers could read, it made sense to put up a picture. At the time John of Gaunt, uncle to Richard II, was viewed by many as the most powerful man in the country. His coat of arms incorporated a Red Lion, so many landlords adopted the sign of the Red Lion to show their allegiance.

From these early times heraldry has continued to influence both pub signs and names. This trend was helped along by the fact that important families suspended their coats of arms outside their mansions which would be known by their dominant features, such as 'the house with the white lion' or 'the mansion with the blue boar'. Many of these family arms were used in later days as tavern signs by servants who retired from the service of the elite.

However, there have also been many other factors that have influenced pub names. In the words of local historian Andy Anderson: 'Much of our heritage is recollected in the names of the pubs. The pubs reflect the social and political happenings of the time. When you change the names you lose the historical connection.' Interestingly you can also lose the connection by keeping the name but changing the sign. A simple example is the name the 'Queen's Head'. Whose image does the sign painter use? A more complex example is the Stanley Arms (Magdalen Road). A plaque on the wall indicated that it originally took its name from the Earls of Derby whose family name was Stanley. Later a sign was put up of Henry Stanley meeting Doctor Livingstone. This then morphed into an image of Laurel and Hardy whilst today all we see is a stylish representation of a bowler hat, presumably as worn by Stan Laurel.

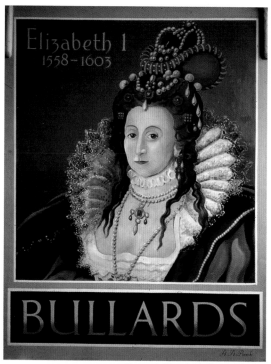

Queen's Head, Pulham Market

Lord Nelson, Reedham

Buildings and Local Landmarks

We have many examples of pubs that have been named after local buildings or landmarks, including:

- The historic Black Boys (Colegate) was rechristened the Merchants in 1980. It originally took its name from the Dominican friary that started in Colegate before eventually moving to St Andrew's and Blackfriars' Halls. The monks wore a black cloak over their white habits hence the nickname 'Black Boys'. So the pub was one of the main pointers to where the friary had once been

- In the 1790s the Cavalry Barracks were built in Pockthorpe. The soldiers here were served by a number of pubs with military connotations including the Horse Barracks, the Light Horseman and the Mounted Volunteer

- More recently the Wig & Pen (St Martin at Palace Plain) changed its name from the White Lion to reflect its proximity to the new Magistrates' Court

- The Eight Ringers (Oak Street) near St Mary's Coslany was thus called because the church had a ring of eight bells. The reasoning behind the name of the Ten Bells (St Benedict's Street) is less clear but there is a suggestion that at one time you could hear the ringing of ten church bells from outside

- In 2012 the former King's Arms (Rosary Road) was rechristened with the name Lollards' Pit, a local place of execution for heretics and other offenders

- Pubs located close to river crossings have taken their name from them. These have included the Bishop Bridge Inn (Riverside Road), Pull's Ferry Inn (Lower Close), Foundry Bridge Tavern (Rose Lane) and the Ferry Boat Inn (King Street).

Light Horseman, Barrack Street

Did You Know?

In the 1980s Ray Lince took on the Constitution (Constitution Hill). Assuming the name was connected with the American Civil War he redecorated the pub accordingly and ordered a brand new sign on the same theme. It was only afterwards that he discovered that the name referred to Anna Sewell, author of 'Black Beauty', who used to take her 'constitutionals' in the area. Ray couldn't face redecorating, so for many years it remained a tribute to 19th-century America, complete with replica guns.

The Black Boys, Colegate, 1936

Local Trades

Many pubs took the names of the local trades and guilds which met there. These took a variety of forms.

In the Middle Ages if you had an armigerous employer, that is one entitled to use a coat of arms, the alehouse that his employees frequented took on the arms of their employer. So, for example, you had the Fellmongers' Arms on Oak Street or the Plasterers' Arms on Cowgate. If you think of a community where very few could read it was an obvious way of telling people: 'Here we are.'

Some trades did stretch a point and adopted 'arms' which they were not strictly entitled to use. Hence we had the Sawyers' Arms (Fishergate) and the Wine Coopers' Arms (St Augustine's Street).

Often the tradesmen would describe themselves as 'jolly', no doubt because meeting socially in a pub somewhat cheered them. Accordingly we have the Jolly Hatters (Cowgate) and the Jolly Brewers (Magdalen Street).

Trades represented included: textiles, brewing and leather.

The textile industry, which was the main industry of late medieval Norwich, and remained so for many centuries, gave its name to a large number of pubs including: the Jolly Dyers (Fishergate), Shuttles (Botolph Street), the Yarn Factory (Cowgate), the Hot Pressers' Arms (Oak Street) and the Woolpack Inn (Golden Ball Street and Muspole Street). More obscure references come in the form of the Bishop Blaize (Fishergate), which took its name from the patron saint of woolcombers, and the Jack of Newbury (Fye Bridge Street). The latter was named after John Winchcomb of Newbury who was reputed to have been the greatest clothier in the world during the reign of Henry VIII.

Woolpack, Golden Ball Street

Not surprisingly many pub names have brewing connotations. So we have: the Jolly Brewers (Magdalen Street), the Jolly Maltsters (King Street and Cowgate), the New Brewery Inn (Barrack Street) and the Two Brewers (Magdalen Street).

The shoe and leather industries were represented by the Jolly Skinners (Oak Street), the Fellmongers' Arms (Oak Street) and the Curriers' Arms (St Giles' Street and St Stephen's Back Street).

Waterman, King Street   *Stonemasons' Arms, Aylsham*   *Shoemaker, West Earlham*

The Rose

The rose has always been a very popular tavern sign. In fact in 1884 we had 11 City-centre pubs bearing the name Rose (locations include Queen's Road and Mariners' Lane). Additionally we had three White Roses (locations include Magdalen Street and St Margaret's Church Alley), one Red Rose (Back of the Inns), one Rose & Crown (Bishopgate) and one Rose & Thistle (Heigham Street). There were a number of reasons for the popularity of the name including:

- In medieval times the rose, together with the lily, were recognised as emblems of the Virgin Mary
- During the War of the Roses innkeepers showed their allegiance either to Henry VI (House of Lancaster) or to Edward IV (House of York) by displaying a red or white rose respectively outside their establishments. Some canny landlords had both, and switched from one to another as appropriate
- After the Battle of Bosworth (1485), the York and Lancaster families united when Henry VII married Elizabeth of York. At the same time their family symbols merged to form the Tudor red and white rose. As a result innkeepers now started to display a 'Rose & Crown'
- In 1603 James VI of Scotland was crowned James I of England. He adopted a personal heraldic symbol which merged the Tudor Rose with the Scottish Thistle which gave rise to inns called the Rose & Thistle.

Astrological Features

The 'Star' together with the 'Sun' are two of the oldest inn signs. Although in medieval times the star was an emblem of the Virgin Mary, historically both signs have enjoyed some notoriety as being representative of houses frequented by harlots. We have had a number of inns in Norwich with these names, together with the occasional mention of the moon:

- References to stars include: the Golden Star (Duke Street), the Star Hotel (Haymarket) and the Morning Star (Pottergate).
- One imagines that the Man in the Moon, who gave his name to an establishment in Duke Street, was a nursery rhyme character. After all:

'The man in the moon came down too soon
and asked the way to Norwich.
He went to the south and burnt his mouth
with supping cold plum porridge.'

Sadly it is more likely to be a reference to Chapter XV of the Book of Numbers, which recounts the story of a man who gathered sticks on the Sabbath Day for which offence he was stoned to death and banished to 'lunar realms'. A modern day variation on the theme painted by sign painter Arthur Thirtle (below), shows his interpretation of the Man on the Moon.

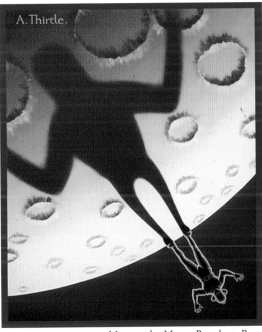

A Tudor Rose with the Crown, Frettenham

Man on the Moon, Reepham Road

Heraldry

As noted above many pub names have their origins in heraldic designs. Names and signs could be used to show where the innkeeper's allegiance lay. For example:

- The Red Lion (locations include Magdalen Street and Bishopgate) was not only the coat of arms of John of Gaunt but was also that of his son, Henry IV, who took the English throne by force from Richard II. The White Hart (locations include Ber Street and Coslany Street) in turn was the coat of arms of Richard II. It was important that innkeepers showed the appropriate sign or they could be accused of treason
- The White Lion (locations include Magdalen Street and Oak Street) was the personal emblem of Edward IV, the first Yorkist King of England
- The Spread Eagle (Sussex Street) is one of the most favoured heraldic symbols. Historically it represented strength and domination and has been linked with dynasties and countries across the world including the USA, where the bald eagle is the national bird.

People and Events

Pub names recall both local and national celebrities and events. So for example:

- The Jenny Lind (Market Place), took its name from the famous Swedish singer who was very popular in Norwich following her performances here in 1847, 1849, 1856 and 1862
- The Edith Cavell (Tombland) celebrates the life of the British nurse executed for helping Allied soldiers escape during WWI. Although many know of her courage fewer realise that she was born in Swardeston just outside Norwich
- Kett's Tavern (Kett's Hill) recalls the exploits of the Wymondham-born Robert Kett, who was executed in 1549 for committing high treason after he led a revolt against the enclosure of agricultural land
- The Waterloo (locations include the Market Place) and the Alma (Pottergate) recall famous battles
- Lord Nelson (locations include Timberhill and Bedford Street), the Duke of Marlborough (Fishergate) and the Duke of Wellington (locations include St Stephen's Street and Muspole Street) are among famous military leaders who are remembered
- Pubs also took their names from famous politicians Hence we had the Beaconsfield Arms (Pudding Lane) and the Lord Camden (Charing Cross).

Did You Know?

The white swan which hung outside the White Swan (Swan Lane) is still displayed above Dipples the jewellers shop which is located next door to what was the site of the old tavern.

Edith Cavell, Tombland, 2011

White Hart, Diss

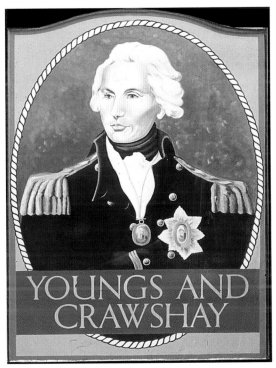

Lord Nelson, Nelson Street

Mariners' Tavern, Mariners' Lane

Kett's Tavern, Kett's Hill

Unusual names

A couple of pubs that had closed before the 1884 map was produced, deserve a mention here:

- The Five Alls stood on Bank Plain in the mid 18th century. Its name represented: the Priest, who prays for all; the Lawyer, who pleads for all; the Soldier, who fights for all; the Farmer, who grows food for all and the Labourer, who works for all. A popular addition was a sixth 'all', namely the Devil, who will carry all away

- The Nowhere Tavern was located on Westwick Street in the early 19th century. It was said to be very popular with hen-pecked husbands who could truthfully tell their dominating wives: 'I've been Nowhere.'

Finally, when the Pig & Whistle in Norwich was refurbished in 1971 a new sign was made showing a pig playing a whistle, which is the modern interpretation of the pub's original name. In fact pig comes from the Saxon word 'piggin' which means a milking pail and whistle comes from 'wassail' which means to be in good health.

 To discover more stories about pub signs and names look out for this symbol in the next chapter on 'City-centre Pubs, Inns and Taverns'.

In the days before computer graphics and fibreglass, pub signs were lovingly designed and crafted by artists including the like of John Crome and Sir Alfred Munnings. Such was the importance of signs that the breweries employed teams of artists who were responsible for their design and maintenance.

In this section we have a brief look at their lives and work.

John Crome (1768-1821)

John Crome, by John Thomas Woodhouse, 1813

Man Loaded with Mischief, John Crome

John Crome (pictured above) was the leading spirit behind the formation of the Norwich School of Artists. His long association with pubs began when he was born in the Griffin (Upper King Street) where his father was the alehouse keeper.

In August 1783 he was apprenticed to Mr Francis Whistler, a house, coach and sign painter, who had premises at 41 Bethel Street. It would have been here that Crome learnt the craft of painting. The lettering and heraldry side of the trade emphasised to him the importance of accuracy, whilst painting pictorial pub signs would have taught him how to compose pictures.

A number of pub signs, unfortunately now lost, have been ascribed to John Crome. These included his version of Hogarth's sign of the 'Man Loaded with Mischief'. Crome's sign (above right) depicts a man with a careworn face. A chain labelled 'wedlock' hangs around his neck and binds him to his wife who he carries on his back. She in turn drinks a glass of gin whilst supporting a monkey and a magpie, symbols of mischief and strife. All in all not very politically correct, but neither was his sign for the 'Labour in Vain' (Gaol Hill). This tastelessly depicted two women engaged in the fruitless task of trying to scrub a little black boy white. Other signs attributed to him include the Top Sawyer (Church Street) and the Black Boys at Aylsham.

He used to tell the story of when he was commissioned to paint 'A Shoulder of Mutton'. He duly bought the cut of meat and carefully reproduced its white and pink hues. He was dismayed when his employer angrily rejected it saying that he had ordered 'a roasted joint'. Even when his career as an artist had taken off he was still accepting commissions for this type of work. Indeed in 1803, the year the Norwich School of Artists was founded, he charged a guinea for painting a 'lame dog' and 18 shillings for writing and gilding the board of the Lamb.

His local was the Rifleman on Cross Lane. It is said that nightly this jovial and sociable artist would be found there, in the snug, enjoying a drink and a gossip in the company of his friends.

Sir Alfred James Munnings (1878-1959)

The celebrated artist Sir Alfred Munnings is renowned for his paintings of gypsies and the country life, but most especially of horses. He had a great love for Norwich and did work for many of our prestigious local firms. He was also the artist responsible for the famous Bullards' sign (below), which was later adopted and adapted by Watneys.

When Munnings was 14 his father, a Suffolk miller, was making arrangements for him to be apprenticed to Jarrolds in Norwich when, according to Munnings: 'By mere chance, my portfolio of drawings and paintings were shown to an enthusiast who declared that I must not go into the publishing world but into the lithographic.'

So instead he was apprenticed for six years to Page Brothers, the Norwich lithographers. Here he created imaginative posters, cards and advertisements, for such firms as Caley's and Colman's. In the evenings he studied at the Norwich School of Art and sold his work at exhibitions of the Norwich Art Circle.

It was in 1909 that Munnings designed the Bullards' sign. At the time, when he was apparently running short of funds. He wrote that he had received a note from: 'Bullards' brewery in Norwich asking me to do them, as usual, another yearly calendar design. Never did I sit down to do a job with such intent to finish it and get the money. The result may yet be seen on the front of all Bullards' houses around Norfolk. A Georgian landlord in a long red waistcoat, mug in hand, standing by his door, like old Willet in Barnaby Rudge. The price of £10, came by return.'

He went on to become one of Britain's best known artists and in 1944 he was knighted and elected president of the Royal Academy. Throughout his life he loved visiting and painting Norwich and in 1947 he was made a Freeman of the City. One of his favourite haunts was the Maid's Head, which he said was 'a true haven of peace and comfort'.

Bullards' sign, by Alfred Munnings, c1909

John Moray-Smith (c1889-1958)

Moray-Smith panel, Coachmakers' Arms, 2015

John Moray-Smith was thought to have been born in northern Italy. He came to England as a prisoner during WWI. Whilst studying at the Slade School of Art in London he met his future wife Katin and took her name when they married. Unfortunately John's own surname is unknown. Whilst working for Morgans' brewery he created a series of outstanding bas-reliefs (i.e. large-scale relief murals modelled or cast in plaster) which are remarkable for their detail and beauty.

The only interior panels still on show in a Norwich pub can be seen at the Woolpack (Golden Ball Street). It was in 1938 that Morgans commissioned a series of six panels, in celebration of Norwich's wool trade, when they rebuilt the premises. Originally positioned in a side room they were put behind the bar in 1982. At this time one was surplus to requirements and was returned to the brewery Unfortunately it is now lost. The remaining panels include delightful scenes of: wool sales and dying, sheep farming and shearing.

Of the three exterior panels on display in the City-centre two are based on a series of engravings made by Henry Ninham of the City gates c1792. Accordingly outside the Berstrete Gates (Ber Street) we see a depiction of the gates from which the establishment took its name. Meanwhile mounted on the wall of the Coachmakers' Arms (St Stephen's Road) is a view of St Stephen's Gate, which was beautifully renovated and repainted in 2013. Another stunning piece of Moray-Smith's work, measuring 12 feet by 9, can be viewed on the gable wall of the Prince of Denmark (Sprowston Road). Local artist and sign painter, Cass Hooton, describes the Prince as being 'elegantly bedecked as a beau of the late 17th century, astride a prancing white charger, reminiscent of the carousel horse in its bright colours and ornamentation'. It is said that Mrs Moray-Smith stood behind her husband when he was painting the Prince and advised him on colours. Described by the Norwich Society as being 'the most startling single public structure in Norwich', it was beautifully restored in 2007 by Antony Murray.

Apart from his work for the brewery Moray-Smith is known to have been an expert in decorative plasterwork and worked in private houses and churches across the county. Today the Gressenhall Museum store a selection of his pieces whilst the Cromer museum are in possession of a beach scene and a portrait of the famed lifeboat man, Henry Blogg.

Restoring the Prince of Denmark

The Prince of Denmark, by John Moray-Smith, commissioned 1939. Restored by Antony Murray in 2007

In 2007 Antony Murray, a decorative painter who had attended the Norwich School of Art, was commissioned by landlord Martin Woods to repaint the Prince. He recalls that it was an interesting assignment:

'I'd never tackled anything on this scale before but decided to approach the project as though it was a huge model soldier. I also applied theatrical techniques, particularly on the metal work, as I wanted to give the image a three-dimensional aspect which I felt would really bring it to life.

'I spent a lot of time rubbing it down and as I did I found lots of different layers of paint underneath. I got down almost to the original but I needed to research costume dress and military books so that I could restore the image accurately. That said, at times I did apply some artistic licence, for example, red heels were probably somewhat unfashionable. Also I painted the flowers and other details at the foot of the horse in the colours which I thought would be the most artistically pleasing. Because I was working on scaffolding covered with green mesh I couldn't stand back to check what I had done. As the scaffolding came down I touched up my work.

'It took me four weeks to complete and was finished on 14th July, 2007. I'm delighted with the feedback I've had. In particular the Norwich Society said that I had repainted it "with the delicate shading so typical of Moray-Smith's work". I would really love the opportunity to work on the other Moray-Smith's in the City . . . you never know, one day I may be asked.'

Antony Murray, 2007

Sign Departments at the Norwich Breweries

Sign artists at Steward & Patteson, 1960s

This section wouldn't be complete without reference to the sign artists who worked for the breweries. Until the late 20th century they were responsible for meticulously researching and hand painting each sign.

The process began when the sign artists drew a scene or design. The sketches would often be retained for over 20 years. They were not only referred to when a sign needed renovating but were also sometimes used to reproduce a sign for another pub with the same name in a different location. On average each sign needed work doing on it at least every five years. If they were in a bad condition the previous painting would be burnt off and the artist would have to start again from scratch. The average time taken to paint a sign would be about ten days, from the priming to the final coat of varnish. In the early 1980s they cost around £500 to make, including the posts and iron work.

Old signs would be kept for a while, but then would have been recycled, which was an easy thing to do as signs were of a standard size. Trainees would have started by doing lettering jobs and it could be many years before they progressed to doing a picture.

In 1983 Ted Newson was the chief sign artist at the Norwich Brewery, where he headed a team of five. He believed that to be a good sign artist '. . . you have to be dramatic. I tell the lads anything that looks good on the easel doesn't necessarily look good from a distance.'

The sign department was involved in a lot of research, particularly when it came to heraldic signs. They always ensured a sign contained salient features but would simplify it to ensure the sign had impact.

Arthur Pank, Peter Burrows and Dave Devlin all worked in brewery sign departments:

Arthur Pank

On 3rd October 1949, Arthur Pank received a letter from Cecil Golding (Architect at Youngs, Crawshay & Youngs) asking him to 'commence work here as a signwriter at a fixed salary of £9 per week'. This marked the start of Arthur's 33 year career in the industry during which he also worked for Bullards and the Norwich Brewery.

Arthur's diaries show that the first sign he worked on was for the Bell at Barnham Broom, the last was the Cross Keys at Wymondham. In between he painted and restored over 1,000 signs around East Anglia including the Yeoman (Salhouse Road) and the Crocodile (Heigham Street).

Arthur took great pride in his work. This was particularly evident when in 1953 he was asked to paint a sign for the Fellmongers' Arms on Oak Street. At the time fellmongering (dealing in hides or skins which could also involve preparing skins for tanning) was a vanishing trade. However, Arthur was so determined to paint an accurate picture that he went to great efforts to locate a retired fellmonger who was persuaded to bring out his old tools and go through the motions of removing the fat from a sheepskin. It was reported in

'Over the Tea Table', a popular section in the Eastern Evening News, that the resulting sign presented 'a charming picture . . . which commemorates this old trade'. It was also observed that 'the sign will be a memorial to an old trade and in years to come no doubt will be one of historic interest'. Sadly the pub was demolished c1967 and the sign is believed to have been destroyed. Luckily Arthur photographed it and looking at the image (below left) I think all would still agree with the observation made by the journalist who wrote about it over 50 years ago.

In 1972, when the Rose Tavern on St Augustine's Street) was given a face lift and a change of name to 'Old Crome' (after the famous Norwich artist), Arthur competed a more unusual commission. He reproduced one of John Crome's paintings, which hung in the bar for many years.

After he retired, in 1982, Arthur continued to paint his favourite subjects of sailing ships and the East Anglian countryside and became well recognised for his evocative scenes of Norfolk, including the Broads and the north Norfolk coast.

Fellmongers' Arms sign, by Arthur Pank

Arthur Pank, 1957

Peter Burrows

Peter joined Morgans as an apprentice in the signwriting department in 1954. As part of his training he attended Norwich Art School. Early in his career Peter worked with Moray-Smith, who gave him one of his palettes. In 1961, when Morgans was taken over, Peter transferred across to Bullards and then to Watney Mann. At the end of 1968 he started the marketing department at the Norwich Brewery where he stayed until 1983.

Peter particularly enjoyed painting heraldic signs These often involved a lot of gilding, which was one of his specialities. It was through his interest and skill in heraldry that in 1996 he was elected to become a Craft Member of the Society of Heraldic Arts.

After he left the brewery to become self-employed he painted many more pub signs before his death in 2002. Peter's work is still displayed at various pubs in Norwich including the Sir Garnet Wolseley (Market Place), the Prince of Denmark (Sprowston Road) and Kett's Tavern (Kett's Hill).

Dave Devlin

In the early 1980s Dave Devlin worked in the sign department at the Norwich Brewery and still does restoration work with his wife, Cass Hooton:

'Signwriting was an art form in itself. The amount of preparation it took to paint a sign was incredible. You'd start with lead primers and layer up from there. The artists had two or three signs going at any one time because they'd always be waiting for paints and varnishes to dry. Typically a new sign would take around 30 hours to complete from scratch but that would be undertaken over a two-week period.

'I was more involved in lettering and heraldic signs unlike the master craftsmen who worked there. They all took great pride in their work. One of which was Arthur Thirtle who first joined Bullards as a full-time artist in 1947. During WWII he'd put his skills to good use when he painted mock-up targets for use by bomber crews. He moved on to work with the Norwich Brewery when Watneys took over. When he retired more than 30 years later it was estimated that he had painted over 1,200 signs across East Anglia. He was a really nice unassuming man. He could paint anything. Although an ex-RAF man one of his specialities was ships. He was also very good at signs that pictured trains. He was known to take his time and if anyone tried to rush him he had a habit of slowing down.

'Today signwriting is a dying art. The majority of pub signs images are now computer generated and scanned or stuck onto something like fibreglass. When the signs were hand-painted great care was taken to make each sign individual. It was great because you could recognise who had painted a sign just by looking at an image.'

Peter Burrows, June 1999

Southwell Arms, Hall Road, Arthur Thirtle

60

Cass Hooton

'After I left art school in the early 1980s I drank at the White Lion (Oak Street) and knew the landlord Colin Keatley had signs that he wanted restoring but I didn't know what was involved. By chance I read an article in the newspaper about Ted Newson retiring from the Norwich Brewery, so I rang him up and he kindly invited me to visit the brewery sign workshop. That's how I started painting and restoring pub signs.

'Over the years I've completed a lot of work for Colin, including the design and execution of the signs for the Pottergate Tavern (Pottergate), the Brewery Tap (Lawson Road) and the Fat Cat (West End Street). Looking at the Fat Cat sign you can tell from the herring bones hanging out of the dustbin that I was an avid Beano reader. As regards the Pottergate Tavern, there were always books in the Art School library which could be used for reference for artwork. So after much browsing I chose a black-and-white photo of a man in a bowler. He looked like a bit of a toff and I wanted to have a bowler hat in the picture to continue the "Brown Darby" sort of feel. I added the pint of beer and did my own thing with the clothing and colours. Another sign on display at the Fat Cat is one I painted of Queen Victoria. For that my inspiration was an old cigarette card that I found in an antique shop.

'Colin has a wide selection of old signs on display at both the Fat Cat and the Brewery Tap. I've restored many of them. Others I've painted from scratch. I'm particularly proud of the sign I painted of the Green Man which was used for an exhibition on superstition at the Sainsbury Centre. You can recognise my original work as it's signed Cass H.'

Cass Hooton and Dave Devlin, 2011

A Final Observation

In April 1948 the Brewing Trade Review praised Morgans' brewery for introducing six exquisite panels designed by Moray-Smith into the Jolly Farmers at King's Lynn. The article expressed the view that the appreciation of art should extend to licensed premises. They conveyed the strong opinion that '...each house calls for separate thought and treatment and the one thing to be avoided like the plague is anything approaching standardisation'.

Sadly, with the loss of hand painted signs some of this individualism has been lost. Although many landlords do not find it cost-effective to maintain hand painted signs it is great when they are still on show. Fine collections of restored signs and other memorabilia are on display at both the Fat Cat (West End Street) and the Fat Cat Brewery Tap (Lawson Road).

Pottergate Tavern, Cass Hooton

To find more links between artists and individual public houses look out for this symbol in the chapter on 'City-centre Pubs, Inns and Taverns'.

Strolling Players Rehearsing in a Barn, by William Hogarth (1697-1764), undated

In the late 17th century a wide variety of amusements was being offered by Norwich's various hostelries. These ranged from boxing to musical soirees and wild beast shows to performances of 'Shakespeare's finest plays'.

The mind boggles at the animals which visited Norwich's inns and taverns. For instance, in 1685 a pair of elephants visited the Angel (later the Royal Hotel on Gentleman's Walk), whilst in 1801 'lovers of natural curiosities' were invited to visit the Church Stile (later the Beaconsfield Arms on Pudding Lane) to 'view the largest rattlesnake ever seen in England'. At such shows the feeding of reptiles with a live 'quadruped' was a big attraction especially as it was customary to admit persons free of charge who produced live cats and rabbits at the pay box!

For those who required a little more culture a visit to the White Swan (St Peter's Street) was in order. Before it was superseded by the Theatre Royal (c1758) this coaching inn doubled up as a playhouse. Sometimes called the 'Metropolis of the East', it was also the HQ of the Norwich Company of Comedians from c1730 until 1758.

Another inn famed for offering outstanding entertainments, including prize fights, plays and natural curiosities was the King's Head (Market Place). Thus it was here in 1729 that the Norwich Company of Comedians presented 'Macbeth with all the witches songs and dances', whilst in 1797 the major attraction was the 'greatest' man in the world who stood 8 feet four inches tall. The Rampant Horse Hotel (Rampant Horse Street) also offered a variety of amusements which in 1785 included the 'learned pig' which was able to spell words and numbers from letters and figures put in front of it.

In September 1854 the first music hall in Norwich was opened at the Boar's Head (Surrey Street). An advertisement for the venue in the Norfolk Chronicle announced: 'There is to be a vocal and instrumental concert by London professionals, who are almost weekly changed.' A room capable of holding 200 was set aside for the performances and called 'The Shades'. Unfortunately the venture was not successful which, in retrospect, is not surprising as the old-fashioned music hall kind of entertainment never took off in Norwich.

The Swinging Sixties and Beyond

The Continentals, l to r: Danny Zagni, Andy Field, Denny Royal, Harvey Platt, 1966

Such events make 20th century pub entertainment seem rather tame; nevertheless by today's standards it was impressive. In particular the period from 1960 to 1980 saw an incredible array of artists appearing at two Norwich venues: the Orford Cellar and the Jacquard Club.

The 1960s was a golden era at the Orford Cellar (Orford Arms, Red Lion Street). Andy Field, a member of the popular 1960s group The Continentals, who performed there remembers it well: 'It held about 300 people in those pre "Health and Safety" days. The only way in and out was one little staircase, which was so narrow people couldn't pass on it. It was hot, it was black, it had condensation dripping off the walls. It really was Norwich's "Cavern".' Acts that performed there included: Rod Stewart, Eric Clapton, Georgie Fame, the Graham Bond Organisation and Ronnie Scott. It was also the place to see popular local groups such as Gary Freeman and the Contours or Lucas and the Emperors.

Around the same time brothers Albert and Tony Cooper founded what was originally the Jacquard Folk Club. The club ran at its first venue at the Mischief (Fye Bridge Street) from 1964 until 1968. Albert Cooper recalls: 'You could fit in 80 people at a squeeze. Mind you it was then so packed you couldn't move. Performers included Judy Collins and Paul Simon. They didn't want much, I suppose we paid them about £15. I performed as "Albert and the Jacquards" backed by Gerry Parish and Dave Keeley.' In 1971 Albert and Tony bought and renovated the old White

Lion pub at 135 Magdalen Street and the Jacquard Club was re-formed. Over the next seven years acts included: George Melly, Stephane Grappelli, Eddie 'Guitar' Burns, The Strawbs, Elkie Brooks and Mike Carr's Quintet.

Albert Cooper, c2000

63

Anna and the Jolly Butchers, various dates

One cannot move on from this era without recalling the Jolly Butchers (Ber Street), together with its indomitable landlady Antoinette Hannent, known today as Black Anna. Sophie Tucker was Anna's idol and she too sang jazz and blues in a deep, husky voice. Anna was very popular with US airmen during WWII largely because of her ability to sing American music with spirit and gusto. After the War, until Anna's death in 1976, the Jolly Butchers with Anna at the helm became a Norwich institution. Anna was renowned for singing songs with double entendres such as 'Lovely Water Melon'. She also performed many calypsos. Other performers at the Jolly Butchers included Beryl Bryden, the Dolly Sisters and Albert Cooper.

Anna accompanied by Albert Cooper on guitar, c1960

Orford Arms, 1957

Today pubs still provide a range of amusements. Sadly at some point singing along to the pub piano gave way to karaoke and wild animal shows made way for Sky Television. However, many pubs still provide live entertainment including: the Rumsey Wells (St Andrew's Street), the Blueberry (Cowgate) and the Birdcage (Pottergate).

 To find more links between entertainment and individual public houses look out for this symbol in the chapter on 'City-centre Pubs, Inns and Taverns'.

Anna (2nd from right) with American forces, c1950

Gary Freeman and the Contours, c1967

A stagecoach leaving the King's Head, Robert Dighton, 1799

Stagecoaches began to run in England around 1657. Although details of early coach travel from Norwich are sketchy, we do know that a coach was running between Norwich and the Four Swans in Bishopsgate, London as early as 1696. In subsequent years a number of coaches left the City. As early as December 1745 adverts appeared in the Norwich Mercury informing the public that 'Christmas Coaches carrying fowles and presents to London' would be leaving from such premises as the Castle Inn, the Maid's Head and the Duke's Palace. These vehicles remained popular until the end of the Coaching Age i.e. 1846.

In 1762 the Norwich Machine provided the first regular coach service linking Norwich and London. It ran between the Maid's Head on Tombland and the Green Dragon in Bishopsgate and took two days. By 1769 the Flying Machine was advertised as doing the journey in one day.

But 1800 to c1840 was the golden age of coaching. In this period thousands of people travelled on coaches to and from every corner of England.

In 1802 the Norwich Mail Coach Office was established at the King's Head on the Market Place (pictured above). It ran two coaches a day to London via both Ipswich and Newmarket. At least half a dozen other coaches were travelling the routes between London and Norwich. One of the quickest left the Bull in Bishopsgate at 5.30am and arrived in Norwich at the White Swan on St Peter's Street just 12½ hours later.

A number of other coaches provided local services. For example the Day post-coach took two-and-a half hours to travel between the Angel (Market Place) and the King's Head in Yarmouth, whilst passengers could connect with coaches to the Midlands and the north by taking the Wellington coach to Stamford.

Did You Know?

On 30th December 1809 it was estimated that in the previous ten days 6,000 turkeys had been transported from Norwich to London on the 'Christmas Coaches'.

Norwich mail coach, undated

The coaches not only transported people and goods they also brought information. Accordingly in 1812 the mail coach brought news of Wellington's victory near Salamanca to Norwich whilst on 23rd June 1815 the Expedition coach brought tidings of the victorious Battle of Waterloo.

In the early 1840s seven coaches were leaving daily from Norwich to London. As more coaches took to the road proprietors became much more competitive. This brought many benefits. For example, vehicles became more comfortable, whilst stages were shortened and horses were changed more often resulting in quicker journeys.

Despite such improvements the death knell sounded for coach travel on 1st May 1844 when the Yarmouth to Norwich rail route was opened. On 30th July the following year the first through train left Trowse station on its way to London. The end was swift and on 17th January 1846, the Norfolk Chronicle announced that all coaches between Norwich and London had ceased to run . . . the coaching era had ended.

Did You Know?

In the early 19th century many coachmen considered it to be a matter of honour not to be passed by a rival and they drove accordingly.

Did You Know?

Between 14th July 1822 and 3rd November 1825, a Mr Thorogood drove the Times coach daily between Norwich and London. Over this period it is estimated that he travelled some 182,352 miles.

Star Inn, Haymarket, artist unknown, undated

The coaching inns not only acted as termini for vehicles, they also provided food, shelter and lodgings for travellers, coaches and horses alike. Norwich's principal inns included the Angel (later the Royal Hotel), the Bell, the Norfolk Hotel, the King's Head and the Maid's Head. These were supplemented by lesser establishments such as the Lamb.

One of the areas best served with inns was the area around the market. At least four opened onto the Walk and were all of similar construction. Narrow gateways opened onto long yards which were overlooked by guest rooms on the first and second floors. Public rooms were grouped around the ground floor which incorporated warehouses used by itinerant dealers for the storage and sale of their stock.

In many cases the inns would have provided quality accommodation and as befits such establishments they also provided entertainment for their guests. Take for example the King's Head, which was located on the Market Place until c1813. The establishment was much favoured by Parson Woodforde (1740-1803),

Rector of Weston Longville. Here residents were treated to an eclectic variety of entertainments ranging from shows of natural curiosities to a performance of Macbeth.

A number of inns survived the end of the coaching era and continued to operate as hotels and hostelries, although their fortunes varied considerably. Even today many of the buildings still survive and indeed some are still trading. In particular the Maid's Head is now a hotel whilst both the Bell and the Lamb are popular pubs. The Angel was renovated and reopened as the Royal in 1840 before being reinvented in 1899 as the beautiful Royal Arcade.

 To discover more stories about coaching inns look out for this symbol in the next chapter on 'City-centre Pubs, Inns and Taverns'.

There has always been a close relationship between sport and pubs. This has taken numerous forms and covered many disciplines.

Cockfighting

Many pubs in the City had cockpits, the most notable of which were at the White Swan (St Peter's Street), the Maid's Head (Wensum Street) and the Lobster (Lobster Lane). The sport was taken very seriously, with trainers and breeders of fighting cocks enjoying high esteem. Champion birds would even represent the City or county in matches.

In the early 19th century there was increasing concern for the welfare of animals and in 1824 the Society for the Prevention of Cruelty to Animals was formed. In Norwich the last reported cockfight took place in the City in 1823, although the sport probably continued 'underground'. At around the same time there was a growth in boxing, in the form of prizefighting.

Cockfighting, by William Hogarth, undated

> ### Did You Know?
> Jem Mace prepared his fists for fighting by 'pickling' them in a concoction made of copper, gunpowder, whisky and horseradish.

> ### Did You Know?
> In the 20th century the boxers Ginger Sadd and Chucky Robinson trained at the Bishop Bridge Inn.

Boxing

Prizefighting was especially popular in Norwich during the 19th century and much of it was linked to pubs. The Green Dragon (Little London Street) and the Sun & Anchor (Lobster Lane) were especially renowned for their pugilistic encounters, but many other establishments also staged fights. For example, in 1807 the King's Head (Market Place) held an exhibition of sparring between Tom Cribb and John Gully, two noted boxers, which is said to have attracted 200 spectators.

Many boxers were also pub landlords. For instance if you had visited the White Swan on Swan Lane around 1859 there was a very good chance that you would have been served by the famed pugilist Jem Mace. Two years later you'd have been able to tell your family that you'd been served by the middleweight champion of England.

Jem Mace, undated

Other local pugilists included:

- John 'Licker' Pratt, one time Norwich champion boxer, was the landlord of a number of Norwich pubs, including the Jolly Skinners (Oak Street) and the Hampshire Hog (St Swithin's Alley). 'Licker' received his nickname after a fight in Drayton in 1850 when he beat Jem Mace in a 69-round bout. Subsequently Mace defeated Pratt in ten rounds

- Ned Painter, a renowned Norfolk boxer, kept the Sun and Anchor on Lobster Lane. An advert he placed in the Norfolk Chronicle on 1st January 1820, not only extolled the qualities of his ale and of spirits, but also informed amateurs of the 'noble art' that he intended to give private lessons in sparring: 'in the most scientific style, at all hours of the day'.

Surprisingly boxing is not widely remembered in the name of pubs. One exception is the Champion on Chapelfield, but even this does not celebrate local talent. Instead it was named after the London-born champion Daniel Mendoza. Mendoza, who was acclaimed as 'the first scientific boxer', toured the country's theatres after retirement and obviously made an excellent impression when he visited Norwich in 1790.

Football

On the 23rd July 1902, the first meeting of the Norwich City Football Club (NCFC) took place and straightaway links between City pubs and its new football team were established. At the meeting Arthur Turner, who was also the manager of the Boar's Head on Surrey Street, was appointed as City's secretary and effectively their first manager. Subsequently from 1908 to 1916 the Boar's Head became the headquarters of City's first Supporters' Club. In the coming years many professionals from the club took over pubs. For example:

- In 1928 Albert Gosnell, manager 1920-1926, became the licensee of the Raven Stores (St Giles' Street)

- Fred Hall, City's goalkeeper in the 1930s and through WWII, became landlord at the Old Barge (King Street)

- Bob Young, manager during WWII, became licensee at the Kingsway (King Street) from 1945 until his death in 1960.

Our football heritage is not widely reflected in the names of pubs. NCFC tried to rectify this in 1980 when for a short time it opened a public house in the rear of the new River End Stand which was called the Nest in memory of the team's previous ground, it was later rechristened 'Strikers'.

Boar's Head, Surrey Street, 1934

Cricket

It was in 1827 that the Norfolk County Cricket Team first played at their Lakenham ground. In the same year Lord Suffield presided at their annual dinner at the Rampant Horse Hotel (Rampant Horse Street). Lakenham remained their home for over 170 years until August 2000 when they moved their headquarters to Horsford Cricket Club.

There were two pubs in the vicinity which took their names from the sport. The Cricketers' Rest was located on Queen's Road and the Cricketers' Arms on Lindley Street. The latter had a lovely sign of a bearded cricketer being bowled out. It recorded the occasion in 1902 when W. G. Grace, the celebrated cricketer, came to play at the Lakenham ground and was dismissed early in his innings.

The Cricketers' Arms is now the premises of Allcock Family Funeral Services which is owned by Terry Allcock's family. In a final sporting twist many will remember Terry's long and illustrious career at NCFC. He joined City in March 1958 and played his last game in April 1969 over which time he made almost 400 appearances, scored 127 goals (placing him second on City's all-time goal scoring list) and after scoring 37 times in the 1962-63 season, he still holds the club record for scoring the most goals in one season.

 To find more links between sport and individual public houses look out for this symbol in the next chapter on 'City-centre Pubs, Inns and Taverns'.

Mike Spivey (left) gives encouragement during the Norwich Beer Festival, 2010

Historically, pubs have offered their customers the opportunity to play a range of games. Sadly many of these have died out. For example if you had visited the Hampshire Hog (St Swithin's Alley) in the 18th century you would probably have played logats, which was similar to skittles but the logats (applewood pins about 22 inches long) were thrown at the jack.

Other traditional games include the 'Norfolk Twister'. This unusual pastime required a room with a low ceiling as players were required to spin a pointer on a board which was attached to it. Ten of the segments on the board were numbered and the rest marked with symbols including a glass of wine and a pint of beer. The player would spin a pointer. If this landed on a number you scored points but if it pointed to a drink symbol you had to down the pictured tipple before your next go. A board dating back to the 1830s can still be seen at the Horse Shoes Inn at Alby.

Another old game, 'ringing the bull', involved swinging a bull's nose-ring attached to a string in an arc. The aim was to hook it onto a bull's horn attached to the wall. It can still be played at the Duke of Wellington (Waterloo Road).

Although both the Queen Adelaide and its skittle alley (Pitt Street) have long since gone and few pubs retain their shove ha'penny boards, you can still play billiards at a handful of City pubs including the White Lion (Oak Street) and the King's Head (Magdalen Street).

Finally, enthusiasts should visit the annual CAMRA beer festival where the 'traditional pub game section' is always extremely popular.

 To find more links between pub games and individual public houses look out for this symbol in the next chapter on 'City-centre Pubs, Inns and Taverns'.

Woodcock, c1980

Pubs have long been at the heart of communities. More so in the days before motorised transport. Accordingly in the City Council's slum clearance programmes of the early 1900s, which involved moving whole communities to new estates on the outskirts of the City, public houses were considered integral to the new developments. Often City-centre licences were transferred to estate pubs. For example, in 1935 the licence of the King's Head on Barrack Street was transferred to the newly built Woodcock pub on the Catton Grove estate. Mike Holmes remembers the importance of the pub to his family in the 1950s:

'The Woodcock was our nearest pub and hence our local. I remember my grandparents would always go there on a Friday night for a pint or two of mild and a sherry. My parents would occasionally go as well but in the early days with three kids to look after it was not so easy. Sometimes we would tag along and be given our perfunctory glass of orange squash. We didn't go inside but could play in the sunken garden. It was great when we were included in such activities as the coach trip to the seaside. I distinctly remember the day we went to Skegness, which in those days was unbelievably exotic, as the yearly Sunday school trip to Gorleston was the furthest we normally went.

'When we became teenagers, and for many years after, Friday was the night that we'd catch up with our parents and grandparents at the Woodcock. In later years it was modernised and was given both inside loos and a carpeted comfy lounge. After this we became very posh and frequented the lounge even though beer was 1d a pint more expensive than in the bar.'

Thorn Tavern, coach outing, c1950

Trafford Arms, Grove Road, 2011

Over the years the contribution made by pubs to their local communities has taken many forms, one of which has been to provide a meeting place for clubs and societies. For instance, fishing was one of the most popular pastimes in Edwardian Norwich, probably because it appealed to all ages and needed very little outlay to begin with. Shortly before WWI it is estimated that Norwich had at least 100 fishing clubs, most of which were affiliated to pubs. Chris Baker remembers such activities at the Golden Can (Middle Street) in the 1930s: 'The landlord, like many of the others, used to organise fishing outings for the men. They often arranged a coach, but sometimes we cycled to places like Ludham and Wroxham.'

Around the same time canary breeding was very popular, in fact in the early 20th century there were 13 such clubs in the City. The pastime is thought to have originated with Norwich's Flemish weavers. One club met at the Spread Eagle (Sussex Street) whose landlord, William Drake, is reputed to be the first man to breed a crested canary!

Examining the history of pubs some really stand out as being 'community' pubs'. One such was the Golden Star in the late 1970s and early 1980s when it was owned by Peter and Carol Turner. Carol recalls:

'It was a lovely pub, we ran it like a social club. We provided a meeting place for a range of groups ranging from Compassion in World Farming to the Norwich branch of the Norse Film and Pageant Society.'

Today pubs continue to contribute much to their local communities. The Trafford Arms (Grove Road), where Chris and Glynis Higgins have worked with their customers to raise thousands of pounds for local charities, epitomises this approach. Chris has no doubt as to the importance of pubs in society: 'We are a pub at the hub of the community, which is what we think all pubs should be.'

St Faith's Tavern, Mountergate Street, c1930

A Community Pub: The Little John

Pub outing, c1920

The Little John, on the corner of Northumberland and Armes streets was destroyed in April 1942 during the Norwich blitz. Undeterred, the pub reopened a few months later in a wooden hut which it occupied until a new pub was rebuilt in 1957. Janet Hope's family ran the pub from 1943 until 1979. Here she shares her memories of a local which really was at the heart of the community:

'My grandparents, Walter and Gertrude Whitmore, took over in October 1943, but it wasn't until 1957 that the pub transferred from the hut back into a brand new building. It had a snug, a bar which was always open and where everything went on and also a lounge which we opened at the weekends and for special occasions.

'I spent a lot of time there. I loved helping. I can even remember serving behind the bar on a Saturday night in the early 1960s when I was only ten.

'It was a great local pub with lots of characters. We provided our own entertainment. My grandad loved getting dressed up and sitting with the customers who often amused themselves by playing the piano and starting a sing-a-long. We had lots of outings, particularly with the darts teams and the fishing club. Everyone knew each other. People didn't travel far because cars weren't really about so they were all neighbours and friends to each other and to us.

Little John in the 1950s, from left: ladies dart team; Walter and Gertrude Whitmore; dressing in style

The Fishing Club outside the 'Hut', c1955

'Down the road was Clarks' shoe factory so the employees often came in. Particularly at Christmas and the New Year we were chock-a-block because everyone used us for their parties.

'It was very different to pubs today. Apart from sandwiches, for darts games and sometimes in the evenings, the only food we served then was crisps and nuts. Obviously customers smoked so decorating was always a problem because the nicotine turned everything yellow. Although we closed at around 10.30pm in accordance with licensing laws, that didn't mean to say customers left. On Saturday nights especially we always had a "lock in" when most didn't leave until after midnight. Luckily one of our customers worked for Thomson's Fish & Chip Shop, which was just up the road, so he brought us all a late night snack. We didn't have underage drinkers . . . well only me. I used to enjoy a "pink lady", which was a pink Babycham.

'My grandmother died in 1969 and my mother, Phyllis Barnes, moved in to help my grandfather. In the early 1970s the atmosphere started to change. More people had cars and they started travelling further afield for their evening entertainment. My family finally left the pub in 1980, I still miss it.'

The Little John was closed in May 2002 and demolished in 2005.

Little John, 2002

To find more links with the community and clubs look out for this symbol in the chapter on 'City-centre Pubs, Inns and Taverns'.

The Gardeners' Arms (Timber Hill) is better known by its nickname of 'The Murderers'. At least two gruesome stories are linked to the premises. The first tells of a prostitute who quarrelled with a client who stabbed and killed her in 1895. More recently landlord, Philip Cutter, has unearthed the murder of the landlady's daughter Milly by her estranged husband Frank. Visitors to the pub are always reminded of its sinister past when they look up at the sign which shows the Gardeners' Arms on one side and The Murderers (above) on the other.

We would like to say that this tale of infamy relating to a Norwich pub was unusual, but that would be far

from the truth. A quick look through the history books turns up numerous horrific stories, whilst a handful of ghosts, bearing testimony to tragic ends, still haunt various premises today. These include:

- The ghost of a 13th-century Rabbi who has been sighted in the cellars of the old Curat House on Gentleman's Walk (now part of Fat Face)

- John Aggas, landlord of the Lamb (Old Haymarket) in the 18th century, who was murdered by his brother-in-law

- William Sheward, a 19th-century landlord of the Key & Castle on Oak Street, who murdered his wife and distributed her remains around the City.

Did You Know?

Bodysnatching became very popular in the 19th century. At this time trunks containing cadavers would be left at coaching inns for collection and delivery to London hospitals. The Coach & Horses (Redwell Street), the Duke's Palace Inn (Duke Street), the Rampant Horse Inn (which gave its name to the street) were particularly noted for their involvement in this grisly trade.

 To find out more about these and other macabre stories look out out for this symbol in the chapter on 'City-centre Pubs, Inns and Taverns'.

A Brief History

In the Middle Ages Norwich was a rich trading centre. Its citizens were protected by a wall. Within its perimeter were the larger houses of the gentry, as well as those occupied by their less prosperous neighbours.

As time progressed and the population increased, rather than build in open spaces within the walls large houses were subdivided and speculative builders put up inadequate building in the courtyards and land behind the properties that lined the main streets. Thus the quintessential old courts and yards made their appearance. They were already characterised as being shoddy, rough dwellings.

This pattern of infilling behind older properties lining the street continued through to the late 19th century.

Pope's Head Yard, c1920

View from St Peter Mancroft Church tower, c1932

By 1900 more than 650 yards were located within the City. This type of housing, which was notorious for containing the City's worst accommodation, proliferated into the early 20th century for a number of reasons. In particular, from the end of the 18th century Norwich lost its major industry, the textile trade, and went into decline. Although new trades were established, including the production of shoes, most were characterised by low wages and seasonal employment.

At the same time, there was a depression in agriculture which resulted in many farm labourers moving into the City, which in turn contributed to a massive expansion in population. Over the 19th century Norwich's population grew from 39,000 to 112,000 generating a huge increase in demand for cheap housing. In response, speculative builders squeezed dwellings into every available space which often included the stable yards of public houses and alehouses.

In Norwich a typical old yard or court (the terms are interchangeable) was located behind an ancient building which fronted the street. It was entered through a narrow opening, often tunnel-like which led to a cul-de-sac. Around its perimeter were shoddy dwellings, which shared inadequate water supplies, toilets and waste-disposal facilities. The only water available to families was often by means of a single pump in the yard. Privies would generally have been shared by a number of households. Until the 20th

century these were not flush toilets and often consisted of a 'bin' covered with a toilet seat. Occupants living in yards suffered from both a lack of ventilation and dismal light. Living conditions in the yards were squalid. Landlords were reluctant to take on their responsibility of cleaning the yards. Yet despite all of this, although inhabitants may have had few material possessions, the interior of the houses would often be exceptionally clean and neat. People lived in yards because they could not afford to live anywhere else.

WWI generated a mood for change. People rebelled against poor housing and increased living costs, all of which put the City Council under pressure to make major improvements. However, it was only in the 1930s that legislation changed and new council estates were built specifically to rehouse residents living in slum properties, many of which were located in the old yards. As tenants were moved to new housing estates, such as Lakenham, the old yards were demolished. Many that survived these clearances were bombed in WWII or demolished as a result of post-war road-improvement schemes.

Today as you wander along Norwich's streets you will still see narrow entrances and alleyways accompanied by signs proclaiming the existence of a court or yard. These may lead to a pretty square containing attractive properties, but more often than not they lead …nowhere. There are now many modern yards and a handful of renovated old yards in the City centre,

Swan Yard, King Street, 2015

but in a single generation, their use and appearance have changed almost beyond recognition. Often they contain desirable properties ranging from bijou residential developments to the setting for attractive eateries. Most poignantly some of the old names live on in social housing schemes that have replaced the deprivation of the past. New communities no longer occupy insanitary accommodation, but live in well-constructed dwellings which provide them with comfort and security beyond the dreams of previous residents.

Pubs and Yards

If we transported ourselves back to the 1880s and took a 400-yard stroll down St Benedict's Street between the White Lion and Plough public houses we would see the very clear relationship which existed between the pubs and yards. In this short space we could have visited:

- The White Lion public house and the adjacent Great White Lion Yard
- The Beehive with the Beehive Yard behind
- The Cardinal's Cap with its Cardinal's Cap Yard
- The Queen of Hungary adjacent to the Queen of Hungary Yard

- The Plough which lies between Plough Yard and Little Plough Yard.

A similar situation existed on all of the major thoroughfares. This was because the stable yards adjacent to pubs were perfect spaces for speculative builders to infill with inadequate housing. Subsequently the pubs gave their names to the new developments. This gave rise to the fact that paradoxically some slum dwellings had rather exotic addresses, such as Arabian Horse Yard (Oak Street) or Moon & Stars Yard (Colegate).

Today only a handful of City pubs still lie adjacent to yards. These include the Plough on St Benedict's and the King's Head on Magdalen Street. However, yards have often survived the demise of pubs which gave them their name. For example today we can still visit:

- The Labour in Vain Yard on Guildhall Hill
- Jolly Butchers' Yard on Ber Street
- Old Barge Yard on King Street.

 To find out more links between the yards and individual pubs look out for this symbol in the next chapter on 'City-centre Pubs, Inns and Taverns'.

The River Wensum has played a large part in the development of pubs within Norwich. In turn they have much to tell about the River itself.

Wherries

The River Wensum links Norwich to Yarmouth. In the early 16th century, depending on the wind, sailing boats would have taken from eight hours to more than two days to make the journey. Despite this it was preferable to risking a trip by foot, or on horseback, across the treacherous swamps which divided Norwich from the sea. The journey by river was hard and travellers relied on innkeepers to provide them with sustenance and warmth in their breaks from travelling.

Vessels of the period had square sails which was fine if the wind was astern and the tide worked in your favour. However, on a twisty river this never happened consistently through the journey. In 1570 evacuees from religious persecutors in the Low Countries sailed to Yarmouth and tied their vessels up on Yarmouth Quay. Local keel men saw that the immigrants vessels had fore-and-aft-rigging which enabled them to sail against the wind as well as with it. They realised that this was an ideal set-up for river sailing and successfully adapted it to fit their own smaller passenger-carrying vessels which they called wherries. The word 'wherry' was new to East Anglia and it evolved into a generic term for many kinds of passenger-carrying craft. For many years the wherry remained small and speedy, whilst keel boats were big and cumbersome and carried a square sail.

The wherry was much better suited for river travel and soon larger craft were given new rigging and used to carry cargo between Norwich and Yarmouth. By the early years of the 19th century their superiority over the keel boats was recognised and the wherrymen enjoyed a golden era as they became the accepted carriers of all goods on the waterways. At their peak over 300 traditional Norfolk wherries sailed the county's rivers. However, like coach travel the wind was literally taken out of their sails with the arrival of the railway. By the turn of the 20th century the wherry fleets had been decimated and the subsequent growth of road travel led to their virtual demise.

The wherries influenced pub names and played their part in local folklore. Thus until 1964 the Keel & Wherry pub was located on King Street, whilst Elizabeth Howes, a 19th-century landlady at the Adam & Eve, owned a wherry of the same name which she is reputed to have used for smuggling contraband liquor. Around the same time Richard Buttle, landlord of the New Star on Quayside, owned a wherry named 'Amphion', which he presumably used for more legitimate purposes than Mrs Howes, as he was also a coal merchant. Finally, drinkers of Woodforde's beers remember our sailing heritage every time they order a glass of Wherry Bitter.

Did You Know?

Steward & Patteson owned their own steam wherry, Annie, which transported goods between Norwich and Yarmouth. Although this photograph is not very clear 'Annie' seems to be loaded with cases of bottled beer and some casks of presumably S&P bitter.

Did You Know?

In 1985, to mark the opening of the Ribs of Beef, Woodforde's hired a Norfolk wherry to sail there from the Hotel Nelson. Woodforde's founder, Ray Ashworth (far left), was spotted on board by his 5 year old daughter. Seeing him standing near the town crier, who was resplendent in his red coat and tricorn hat, she asked: 'What's that pirate doing with my daddy?'

Mutford Bridge, c1800

Norwich Harbour

Around 1820 a grandiose scheme was devised for connecting the sea at Lowestoft with the Waveney at Oulton (via Mutford lock) which would then be linked to the River Yare at Reedham. It was devised to allow sea-going vessels to travel from Lowestoft to Norwich. With great optimism the Lowestoft to Norwich Navigation Act of 1827 was passed, and the lock at Lowestoft and the 'new cut' linking Haddiscoe and Reedham were made. It was also decreed that a huge harbour was to be built on the land now occupied by Thorpe railway station and named after the Duke of Clarence, subsequently William IV. Unfortunately it never happened. In 1833 there was much rejoicing when the 'Squire' and the 'City of Norwich' sailed into Norwich on the new navigation, but sadly the celebrations were short lived. Steam began to replace sail and the tonnage of the average seagoing ship increased beyond anything which could travel on the newly devised waterway.

Clarence Harbour, Carrow Road, undated

As would be expected, various pubs adopted names that reflected these developments, including two short-lived hostelries called Norwich A Port located on Carrow Road and Bridewell Alley. Additionally the Clarence Harbour pub was built c1837 with the intention of providing accommodation for workers on the new harbour. It traded for over 150 years on Carrow Road before being demolished in 2004 to make way for a residential development.

Did You Know?

In Elizabethan times a rule was introduced forbidding skippers who transported passengers from Yarmouth and Norwich from carrying 'any suspect person, or common, rogue, or harlot or suchlike'.

Ferries

In the absence of bridges ferries have long been used to transport passengers across river crossings. Running a ferry service could provide a lucrative second income to landlords.

An arched gateway, now known as 'Pull's Ferry', was built in the 15th century to guard the river approach to Norwich Priory and Cathedral. It spanned the narrow waterway that connected the River Wensum to the Priory. In the late 16th century, after the Reformation forced the closure of the Priory, a ferryman's house was built beside the gate. Innkeeping became an additional source of income for the ferryman John Pull (or Poole) who operated the service from 1796 until 1841 during which time he was also landlord at the Pull's Ferry Inn.

A group of musicians who practised at the inn held concerts on the 'Apollo', a river barge which was moored at the bottom of the ferryman's garden. The barge's owner lived in the Cathedral Close and became known as the 'Admiral of the Flotilla'. Although its later history is unclear it would appear that by 1868 the inn had been renamed the Ferry House and had been delicensed by 1884.

Many will still remember the Ferry Boat Inn on Lower King Street, which closed as recently as 2006. Its name derives from the activity of a former landlord, William Thompson, who (like John Pull) set up a ferry service across the Wensum.

Pull's Ferry, 2011

 To find more links between the river and individual public houses look out out for this symbol in the next chapter on 'City-centre Pubs, Inns and Taverns'.

Thompson's Ferry, c1890

City-centre Pubs, Inns and Taverns

In 1884-5 an OS map of Norwich City-centre was produced giving the name and location of over 450 hostelries. In this section we have divided the map into eight areas and highlighted all that were open then. To give some idea of where we are today we have added a number of pubs which did not exist then but are now trading.

The diagram on the right shows how the City has been divided. Each map covers the following areas:

- Map 1 = North-West Norwich
- Map 2 = North-East Norwich
- Map 3 = Coslany and St Benedict's Street
- Map 4 = Cathedral and Historic Heart
- Map 5 = Market Place and Surrounding Area
- Map 6 = South-East Central Norwich
- Map 7 = South-West Norwich
- Map 8 = South-East Norwich

Each section contains a pub index, map, historical overview, additional information on a selection of hostelries and a picture gallery.

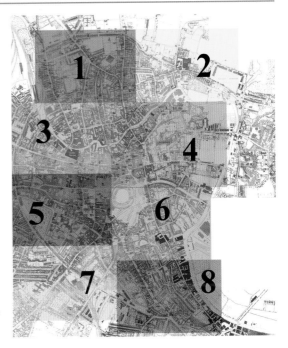

We have inserted the following 'icons' to highlight topics of particular interest. More information is given on these in the previous chapter on 'Themes'.

 Signs & Names

 Artists

 Entertainment

 Coaching Inns

 Sporting Links

 Pub Games

 Community and Clubs

 Murder & Mayhem

 Norwich Yards

 The River

Please note the following:

- If a pub was open in 1884/5 the name on the map and index is the name it had in 1884/5. If it is still open, but its name has changed, the new name is given in brackets in the index.
- If a pub is open today but was NOT open in 1884/5 the name on the map and index is the name it has today.
- If a pub is recorded at more than one address, or the street name has changed, the address quoted in the index is the one we consider to be the most appropriate.

Key for Map:

 Open in 1884/5

 Open in 2015 (may also have been open in 1884/5)

 Brewery or malthouse

 Religious buildings

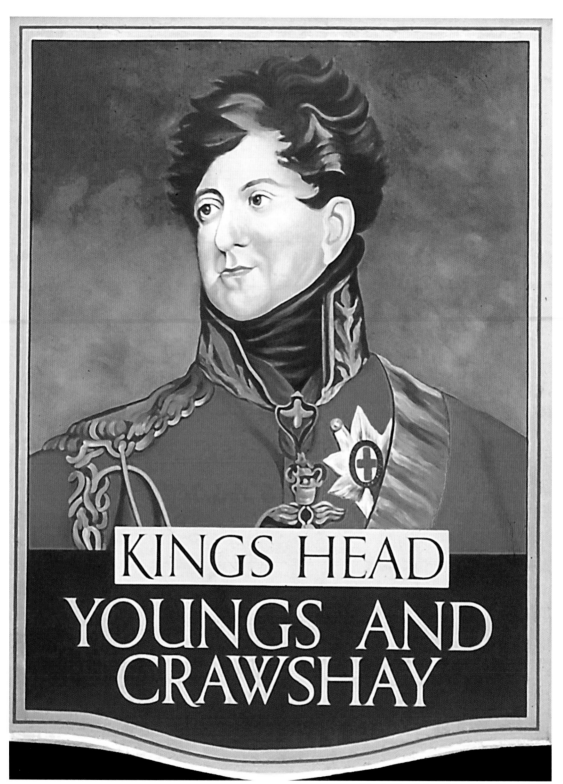

King's Head sign, Magdalen Street, 1957

Below is a list of the pubs, inns and taverns located in this area of Norwich. Those with a page reference have an entry or illustration. For further details see page 83.

Page	Pub Name	Location
99	Anchor of Hope	114 Oak Street
99	Angel	154 Oak Street
89	Arabian Horse	70 Oak Street
89	Artichoke	1 Magdalen Road
90	Bess of Bedlam	20 Oak Street
	Boatswain's Call	57 Botolph Street
99	Britannia Tavern	73 Botolph Street
	Buck	139 Oak Street
	Bushel	27 St Augustine's Street
90	Cat & Fiddle	105 Magdalen Street
91	Catherine Wheel	61 St Augustine's Street
	Cherry Tree	43 Pitt Street
91	Cross Keys	106 Magdalen Street
	Crown & Anchor	105 St George's Middle St
99	Duke of Sussex	42 Botolph Street
99	Duncan Arms	49 Magdalen Street
99	Dun Cow	167 Oak Street
	Edinburgh Castle	8 Botolph Street
	Elephant	60 Magdalen Street
	Fanciers' Arms	140 Oak Street
99	Flower in Hand	20 Pitt Street
99	Flower Pot	129 Oak Street
	Fortune of War	48 Calvert Street
	Free Trade Tavern	11 St Augustine's Street
91	Globe Tavern	37 Botolph Street
92	Golden Dog	34 Magdalen Street
	Hope Brewery	19 St Saviour's Lane
99	Hope Tavern	64 Calvert Street
	Jolly Brewers	134 Magdalen Street
	Jolly Skinners	91 Oak Street
92	Key & Castle	105 Oak Street
99	King's Arms	38 Botolph Street

Page	Pub Name	Location
	King's Arms	26 Oak Street
93	King's Head	42 Magdalen Street
99	King's Head	49 St George's Middle St
100	Light Horseman	4 Botolph Street
94	Magpie	34 Magpie Road
94	Mischief Tavern	44 Peacock Street
	Pelican	33 Pitt Street
100	Pineapple	47 St Martin's Lane
	Prince of Wales	39 St Augustine's Street
	Queen Adelaide	57 Pitt Street
	Queen Caroline	61 Oak Street
100	Queen Victoria	51 Magdalen Street
95	Queen's Arms (Cactus)	102 Magdalen Street
100	Railway Arms	90 Oak Street
100	Red Lion	157 Magdalen Street
95	Rose Tavern	5 - 7 St Augustine's Street
100	Royal Oak	132 Oak Street
96	Royal Oak	64 St Augustine's Street
96	St Paul's Tavern (Blueberry)	20 Cowgate
100	Shuttles	62 Botolph Street
97	Spread Eagle	35 Sussex Street
	Staff of Life	72 St Augustine's Street
100	Suffolk Arms	199 Oak Street
	Sussex Arms	40 - 42 St Augustine's St
	Two Brewers	151 Magdalen Street
100	White Horse	84 Magdalen Street
98	White Lion	135 Magdalen Street
97	White Lion	73 Oak Street
98	White Rose	77 Magdalen Street
100	White Swan	154 Magdalen Street
	William IV	108 St George's Middle St
	Wine Coopers' Arms	30 St Augustine's Street

Kings Arms

Staff of Life

Cathe.
Wh

Royal Oak

Dun Cow

Spread Eagle

Buck

Flower Pot

Angel

Suffolk Arms

Fanciers Arms

Royal Oak

Key & Castle

Anchor of Hope

Baptist Chapel

Malthouse

Jolly Skinners

Railway Arms

Bess of Bedlam

Pineapple

White Lion

Arabian Horse

Saint Martin Church

Queen Caroline

Smith & Carman Brewery

Artichoke

Magpie

White Swan

Red Lion

Two Brewers

Jolly Brewers

White Lion

Sussex Arms

Prince of Wales

Bushel

Winecoopers Arms

Free Trade Tavern

Rose Tavern

Cross Keys

Britannia Tavern

Queens Arms

Cat & Fiddle

Saint Augustine Church

Boatswains Call

Shuttles

Phoenix Brewery

Duke of Sussex

Globe Tavern

White Horse

St Paul's Tavern

William IV

Kings Arms

White Rose

Crown & Anchor

Queen Adelaide

Edinburgh Castle

Light Horseman

Cherry Tree

Elephant

Queen Victoria

Mischief Tavern

Baptist Chapel

Hope Tavern

Methodist Chapel

Duncan Arms

Hope Brewery

Pelican

Saint Saviour Church

Flower in Hand

Fortune of War

Kings Head

Gospel Hall

Golden Dog

Kings Head

North-West Norwich: Historical Background

Magdalen Street: cranes loom as the bank (centre right) awaits destruction to make way for the flyover, c1970

Norwich was the largest walled city in England. The walls, which were completed by the mid 14th century, gave its citizens security. To outsiders they were a tangible symbol of power. As one would expect the gates allowed entry and exit, but their use went beyond that. For example, when used for civic functions they would be decorated with coats of arms, whilst after executions they proved a handy place to display the heads and quarters of miscreants! Both the walls and gates also had a commercial purpose, as they could be used to control and tax goods as they passed in and out of the City. Most of the gates were demolished around 1793, although the Magdalen Gate was not removed until 1808. The gateways would have been shut at night hence travellers who were prevented from finishing their journeys needed refreshment and lodgings. This enabled inns and taverns, located in the nearby vicinity, such as the Artichoke, to thrive.

This area encompasses the three gates which controlled the traffic of goods and people to the north of the city namely: Magdalen Gate, St Augustine's Gate and St Martin's Gate. Even in 1885, long after they were removed, you would have had no difficulty finding a tavern to suit your needs as there were over 60 to choose from. Today just a handful remain. Many of the premises were deemed superfluous and were closed 'under compensation'. Looking at the facts it is easy to understand why so many met their demise under this system. For example the Light Horseman (Botolph Street) was closed in June 1911 after it was reported that there were '14 other licensed houses within 200 yards, including the Edinburgh Castle which was six yards away'. Although many are now lost their names are still remembered in the names of the yards and streets that lay adjacent to them.

Subsequently many pubs were demolished c1970 to make way for the controversial Magdalen Street flyover including: the Flower in Hand (Pitt Street), Fortune of War (Calvert Street) and the Elephant (Magdalen Street). Regretfully, many of the hostelries which survived this event have also met untimely ends. Luckily others continue to flourish.

Arabian Horse

The licence of the Arabian Horse (Oak Street) can be traced back to the 18th century. The horse has given its name to many of our public houses. However, it is rarely mentioned without a preceding adjective. Here the name is taken from the stallion known as the Godolphin Arabian that was imported into Britain in 1729 by Edward Coke. The stallion sired many champion racehorses before its death in 1753.

Walter Wicks tells the story of Dick Nichols, landlord from 1872 to 1886, whom he recalls as a 'guardian of the peace' at Conservative Party meetings and demonstrations: 'Dick was generally in charge of a band of trusty stewards engaged to render assistance in the tactful duty of ejecting turbulent interrupters; and judging from external appearances these gentlemen had in the days of the prize ring suffered heavy battery, and apparently, were equally capable of administering it.' Today they would be called bouncers!

It was closed under compensation in 1911.

Did You Know?

The term 'plonk' is believed to have originated during WWI. When soldiers serving in trenches visited French bars and mispronounced 'vin blanc'.

Artichoke

The current building was erected on Magdalen Road in the 1930s. This is, however, somewhat misleading as the Artichoke has traded on this site since at least the 18th century. It used to be housed in a 15th-century building which had previously, and somewhat incongruously, been used as a leper house, an almshouse and a workhouse, before becoming an alehouse.

In its early days the inn would have been located just outside the City gates when it would have provided lodgings for travellers who were unable to enter when these were locked. However, once restrictions were lifted its popularity waned. Interestingly, when it was redesigned in the 20th century, the pub's design was supposed to be reminiscent of the towers that used to flank the City's gates.

From the Middle Ages, a Rush Fair (so called because domestic items made of rush were sold there) was held in the yard at the rear of the Artichoke. The fair raised funds for the St Magdalen leper hospital that was housed nearby on Sprowston Road. Walter Wicks noted in 1925 that the custom continued and even his contemporaries could remember country people selling similar items at the pub's popular Saturday markets.

Today the Artichoke is a lively venue offering a wide range of entertainment.

Artichoke, 2011

Bess of Bedlam

Bess of Bedlam, c1890

Cat & Fiddle

Cat & Fiddle, 1997

 It is unclear whether the Bess of Bedlam (Oak Street) was also known as Tom of Bedlam or if the two houses were adjacent. The names remind us of the times when the mentally ill were uncared for. The name 'Tom of Bedlam' is taken from the character of poor Tom in Shakespeare's King Lear.

In 1906 the licensing inspector said that this was an old house and was structurally deficient for the requirements of the licensed trade. Furthermore that the tenant, Robert Arthurton, who had taken over the lease in 1884 was engaged as a job master and did not give the pub proper supervision. No doubt further influenced by the fact that there were 15 other licensed premises within 200 yards, the authorities refused the renewal of the licence. The premises were closed under compensation in 1907.

Did You Know?

 The Queen Adelaide (Pitt Street) housed a skittle alley which was utilised as the pub after the main building was damaged during enemy action in April 1942. Until the pub's closure in 1965 it still displayed some of the large flattened stones, known as cheeses, which were thrown at the skittles.

By the 18th century the Cat & Fiddle was trading on Magdalen Street. There are many Cat & Fiddle public houses in Britain, indeed records show that historically there have been four located in and around Norwich. But what is the origin of the somewhat unusual name?

 Some suggest that it could derive from 'chat fidele' which is French for 'faithful cat'. Another possibility is that it derives from 'Catherine la Fidele', Catherine the Faithful, a nickname for Catherine of Aragon who was Henry VIII's first wife. However, one should perhaps just look at the sign, apply common sense and assume it is taken from the old nursery rhyme: 'Hey diddle diddle, The cat and the fiddle.' But herein lies another tale. Some suggest that 'Hey diddle diddle' offers a cryptic commentary on Richard III's path to the English throne. Following the death of his brother Edward IV, Richard took over the position of regent on behalf of his young nephew, Edward V. He than placed the young king together with his younger brother in the Tower of London whence they mysteriously disappeared. The finger of suspicion pointed at Richard III but his subjects were too frightened to voice their worries openly, hence they used nonsense verse. Here 'cat' refers to Richard's aide Sir William Catesby who, it was whispered, had thought up the 'fiddle' that put Richard on the throne.

The pub closed c2011.

Catherine Wheel

St Catherine was one of the most popular saints in the Middle Ages. She lived in the 4th century and was daughter of the King of Cyprus. A number of legends are recorded as to why she was martyred at the hands of the Roman Emperor Maxentius, including both her refusal to marry him and to sacrifice to his gods. However, all agree that she was tortured and killed by being attached to a gigantic spiked wheel. Thus we have the birth of that most iconic of fireworks, the catherine wheel. The catherine wheel was also adopted as the arms of the Knights of St Catherine of Mount Sinai, an ancient order created for the protection of Mount Sinai. It is presumed that the Catherine Wheel (St Augustine's Street), along with many pubs of the same name, adopted the name because of the symbolic protection the knights offered to wayfarers.

The pub can trace its origins back to the 18th century. In 1790 it was in the news when it was reported that: 'Dame Fortune has thrown £500 of the present lottery into the laps of 30 industrious individuals, who assemble as a club at the Catherine Wheel, St Augustine's.'

Today the pub advertises itself as 'a safe, fun friendly and fabulous venue for the LGBT members of the Norwich community... and anyone else who would like to join us'. Here you can attend a variety of theme evenings including: quizzes, karaoke and cabaret. You can still view their 16th-century well, a quirky fireplace (which following a revamp is now curiously located behind the bar), whilst from upstairs you can view parts of the old City Wall.

Catherine Wheel, 2011

Cross Keys

Cross Keys, by Edward Pococke, c1890

The Cross Keys (Magdalen Street) can trace its licence back to 1760. It is likely that at one time it had strong religious connections as the keys in question were the symbol of St Peter, the guardian of the gate of heaven.

The Chief Constable objected to the licence renewal at the February 1906 Sessions. This was an old house, in bad repair. The bar and taproom were inconveniently small and supervision from the living room was not possible. The sanitary accommodation was bad. The house was very unsuitable as licensed premises, with 12 other houses within 200 yards.

It was closed under compensation in February 1907.

Globe Tavern

A tragic event enables us to trace the history of the Globe Tavern (Botolph Street), back to the turn of the 18th century.

In 1701 Robert Watts, a weaver, murdered his wife. Watts, who often frequented the Globe, was well known for his jealous disposition. One evening, whilst visiting the tavern, a mischievous person made a bet with the weaver that he would be able to secure Mrs Watts' wedding ring. He then went straight to their house and asked to borrow the ring with the excuse that her husband had made a wager about its weight. When the man returned triumphantly to Watts, who was still in the Globe, he was furious. Believing his wife to be unfaithful Watts rushed home and murdered her. It is said that the unfortunate wife haunted Watts' house for many years afterwards and it was only when the building was pulled down in 1875 that the spirit took flight.

The Globe (later called the Old Globe) was closed under compensation in 1908. With 17 other licensed premises within 200 yards this 'small and inconvenient house' was basically considered to be superfluous to requirements.

Golden Dog

Key & Castle

Former site of the Golden Dog, 1938

In the 17th century it is understood that Golden Dog Lane led to an old inn of the same name. In 1850, James Hubbard, an established brewer, set up a small brewery down the lane together with a new tavern on the corner at 34 Magdalen Street. Both establishments took the name of the Golden Dog. The tavern was considered to be a fairly rough establishment (even for those times) and in 1886 was fined what was then the huge sum of £5 for not allowing the police to enter the pub.

In 1894, the brewery and pub were bought by Morgans. The pub continued to trade until 1933 when it was closed under compensation.

Did You Know?

At the turn of the 20th century the upstairs rooms of the Jolly Brewers (Magdalen Street) were the home of an illegal gambling club. Late one night the gamesters heard a fire engine draw up outside. However, they were so engrossed in their game they failed to see a number of policemen disembark from the phoney fire engine and enter the pub. Following their subsequent arrest the illicit gamblers were taken away in two black marias which had trailed the fire engine at a discreet distance.

Key & Castle, 1938

 This is an unusual name for a Norwich pub as the 'key and castle' was the badge of the 12th Suffolk Regiment, leading to some speculation that at one time it had links with a veteran of the corps. Interestingly the Suffolk Arms is located nearby, also on Oak Street.

 In 1869 the pub became notorious when its landlord, William Sheward, confessed to having murdered his wife back in 1851 when they had lived in Tabernacle Street, which was later renamed Bishopgate. At the time the crime was committed portions of an adult female body had been discovered in various parts of Norwich, including Thorpe, Lakenham and Mile Cross. It was eventually decided that medical students were playing a gruesome practical joke designed to terrify local citizens. At his trial Sheward retracted the confession saying that he was drunk when he made the statement. Nevertheless he was found guilty, convicted and sentenced to death. He was executed at Norwich City Gaol by the notorious hangman Calcraft who was known for his 'short drops', which resulted in the majority of his clients been 'strangled to death' rather than having their necks broken.

The tavern ceased trading in 1958.

King's Head

The licence of this pub, located at 42 Magdalen Street, can be traced back to 1760 and remarkably, 300 years later, it is still trading. Despite an extensive renovation in 2004/5, the entrance to the adjacent court still depicts the emblem of the Crown Brewery, dating back to when it was tied to Youngs, Crawshay & Youngs. Similarly the carvings between the windows, of a 'king's head', have been retained.

The building was restored in 2005 but still retains a traditional feel. As would be expected from an establishment which has been given the award 'CAMRA Pub of the Year', it boasts an impressive selection of real ales which are served in a welcoming friendly atmosphere.

 On top of all this the King's Head is one of the few pubs in the City with its own bar billiards table and hosts the Norwich bar billiard league.

King's Head, 1935 (above), 2011 (below)

93

Magpie

Magpie, c1900

The origins of the Magpie Tavern can be traced back to 1806.

At one time an antiquated weighing machine was attached to the front of the house which had a large beam from which huge chains hung down. It was used to weigh wagons and their merchandise before they entered the City through Magdalen Gates. Locals nicknamed the Magpie the 'Weighing Chains'.

 There used to be four 'Magpies' in Norwich. It is believed that the name could be a corruption of Magotty Pie recalled in the nursery rhyme:

'Round about, round about, Maggoty Pie
My father loves good ale, and so do I.'

In 1910 a survey of the City wall found evidence of its 'foundation cropping out of the ground against the east wall of the house'. They went on to surmise that 'this was possibly also the site of the second tower east of St Augustine's Gate'. Outside there is now no sign of the surviving wall although it is understood that part of the wall is visible in the cellar.

In 1975 John Riddington Young described the Magpie as 'a very warm hearted little beer parlour with its cosy carpeted public bar and brightly painted Britannia tables . . . [and a] fine Edwardian dresser'. Although it survived into the 21st century it is now closed.

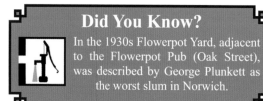

Did You Know?

In the 1930s Flowerpot Yard, adjacent to the Flowerpot Pub (Oak Street), was described by George Plunkett as the worst slum in Norwich.

Mischief Tavern

The Mischief sign attributed to John Crome, undated

The original pub of this name was located on Peacock Street. Over the years it has been given a number of names including 'Man Loaded With Mischief' and the 'Bundle of Mischief'.

The original sign of 'The Man Loaded with Mischief' was attributed to the 18th-century artist Hogarth and hung in Oxford Street, London. Crome is said to have painted the Norwich version (pictured above). It depicted a careworn man labouring under the weight of his wife who is sitting happily on his back with a glass of gin in her hand. The mischief and strife he suffered were illustrated by a monkey and a magpie, perched upon his wife's shoulders. Around his neck he had a padlocked chain engraved 'wedlock'.

The pub was owned by St Saviour's Church, leading some to assume that their clerics' consciences got the better of them when it closed. However, along with so many other houses in the area its licence was refused in February 1914 and it was closed under compensation at the end of that year. The Norfolk Chronicle of 11th February, 1905 gives an interesting explanation of why it was deemed superfluous to requirements: '[The Mischief]…is an 8ft by 14ft room, leased by Youngs, Crawshay & Youngs. Two other houses are within 100 yards, six are housed within 150 yards and a total of 11 (licensed) houses are within 200 yards.'

Queen's Arms (Cactus)

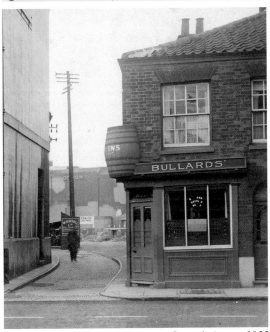

Queen's Arms, c1955

A pub has been trading on the same site on Magdalen Street since the 1830s. Around 1950 it became the property of Messrs Backs, when it was one of their famed free houses. During this time a huge barrel was hung outside as a sign that Backs kept their cellars fully stocked. This led to the house being known locally as the 'Tub'. Other public houses in the Backs' empire included the Curat House (Haymarket) and the Griffin (Prince of Wales Road).

Today it trades as the Cactus Café Bar.

Red Lion

In Victorian times the Red Lion (Magdalen Street) was a house of ill repute where a young girl called Sara was murdered whilst 'entertaining' one of her customers. Over the years, even after the pub was closed, there were many reports that the building was haunted by her friendly ghost. Unexplained activities included typewriters working on their own and paper flying through the air. Eventually staff working in the building held a Ouija board session and claimed that the messages they received were from Sara, who didn't know she was dead and just wanted people to talk to her.

Despite being exorcised it is said that you can still feel Sara's presence in the building. Indeed not only do many visitors claim to have smelt lavender and heard footsteps when standing in the back room, but they also report that they have seen the ghostly face of a young girl staring down at them from a window . . .

Rose Tavern

Rose Tavern, 1938

An inn was first located on this site (St Augustine's Street) in the 14th century when it would have provided sustenance to knights and revellers after they had completed their jousting tournaments, and other exertions, at the nearby Gildencroft.

 The Gildencroft was a large, grassed, open area which is believed to have covered around ten acres. It once filled the whole space between the City wall and St Martin at Oak, and between St Augustine's Street and Pitt Street on the east, and Oak Street on the west. Parts would have been an early recreation ground where youths probably played an East Anglian type of street football with few rules known as camping. Others would have indulged in the ancient arts of jousting and archery. For those less interested in taking part in such sports there was a little shelter on the field called 'Tabor's Folly'. This is thought to have held the musicians, a tabor being a drum, who played as maidens and youths danced.

In 1714 the area was very different to today. At this time the Rose had yards, gardens, stables, an orchard and even pasture. In the early 19th century it was here that the Primitive Methodists held their first Norwich meeting.

In 1972 the Rose Tavern was given both a £10,000 face lift and a name change when it was rechristened 'Old Crome'. The latter was decided by a competition in the Evening News and was given in memory of the famous artist John Crome (1768-1821) who is accredited with painting a number of Norwich pub signs, including the Two Brewers and the Labour in Vain. He was known as Old Crome to distinguish him from his son, also called John, who was also a well-known artist. To mark the occasion three of John Crome's more famous pictures were reproduced by sign artists Arthur Thirtle, Ted Newson and Arthur Pank. These hung in the bar together with a picture of the artist himself.

Writing in 1975 John Riddington Young reports that by then the exterior of the pub had been painted red by the owners Watney Mann to promote their well know 'Red Barrel'. He also extolled the virtues 'of the fine old yard where one can still enjoy a drink on a quaint old settle (type of bench) when weather permits'. Alas no more. In the early 1980s, after around 500 years of trading, it was closed and delicensed.

Royal Oak

Royal Oak, 1936

The licence of the Royal Oak (St Augustine's Street) can be traced back to 1806. The name commemorates the escape of Charles II, who visited Norwich in 1671. It refers to the time that he secreted himself in the oak tree at Boscobel in Staffordshire to avoid capture. Unsurprisingly the title was a favourite in Restoration days with both tradesmen and publicans, being an ideal way of publicly showing your allegiance to the monarchy. After the Restoration, the King's birthday (29th May) was designated Oak Apple Day to commemorate the event. For about 200 years it was customary for people to wear a sprig of oak leaves on their coat on this particular day.

Royal Oak (cont.)

Public houses also ran 'Royal Oak Lotteries', believed to honour the same event. Walter Wicks refers to one such lottery being permitted at the White Horse (Haymarket) in 1669 and 1670. He speculates that often the proceeds were 'for the benefit of loyal and indigent officers . . . who probably served King and country in the troubled days of Charles I'.

The Royal Oak stood opposite the Catherine Wheel and was the larger of the two establishments. The archway adjoining it led to a smithy where visiting horses could be shod. It closed around 1965.

St Paul's Tavern (Blueberry)

Blueberry, 2009

The licence of St Paul's Tavern (Cowgate) can be traced back to 1836, since which time it has undergone a number of transformations. In 1996 it became the Blueberry and is currently known as the Blueberry Music House. As you would suspect the emphasis is now on entertainment, which includes jazz nights and acoustic sessions.

Did You Know?

In the 1st century AD ale used to be drunk in large tankards which would be passed from one person to the next. In AD 975 King Edgar tried to curb consumption by sticking pegs onto the tankard to mark one-pint measures. Theoretically each person was only allowed to drink one measure. Needless to say the system totally failed as everyone drank well beyond their allotted pint. It is thought this is the origin of the saying 'take a person down a peg or two'.

Spread Eagle

William Drake with his canaries, c1900

The licence of the Spread Eagle (Sussex Street) can be traced back to 1830. Writing in 1975 John Riddington Young was highly appreciative of the fact that, at that time, the front door of the pub was decorated by a beautiful hand-painted eagle.

 The Spread Eagle is much favoured as a pub name. In heraldry the eagle is the king of the skies. Throughout history it has represented strength and domination. Thus to identify themselves to the enemy, Roman legions would display the legionary eagle, whilst an image of an eagle with outstretched wings and talons has been connected with dynasties and countries across the world including the USA, where the bald eagle is the national bird. Nevertheless, there is also some speculation that the name could be referring to a Royal Navy punishment whereby a sailor was tied to a mast or over a cannon, with his arms and legs outstretched in a position known as the spread eagle, after which he would be subjected to a whipping.

 In the early 20th century the Spread Eagle played host to another bird, strongly associated with Norwich, namely the canary. I have to admit that when I found out it was the meeting place of the Norwich Canary Club, I assumed the club in question was linked to Norwich City Football Club. But here the canaries in question were of the small, yellow and feathered variety. In the photo above we see William Drake, publican and shoe factory worker, who is reputed to be the first man to breed a crested canary. This photograph was taken in the Spread Eagle, during the time Drake ran the pub from around 1888 to 1912. In 1975 pictures of canaries still decorated the walls of the smoke room to the left of the main door.

It was closed and sold as a private dwelling in 2010.

White Lion (Oak Street)

White Lion Oak Street, 1986

In 1884 there were 16 pubs trading on Oak Street, the White Lion is the sole survivor.

Amazingly parts of the building date back to the late 16th century. The premises themselves were licensed in the late 18th century, although it was probably trading before this date. For a short period, from 1830 to the early 1840s the landlord, James Butcher, also operated the White Lion Brewery from the premises.

In the early 1930s the pub was better known as Dancocks after a long-serving landlord, George Frederick Dancock, who held sway from 1907 through to 1935. In April 1942, the building narrowly escaped destruction during the so-called Baedeker Air Raids. The adjoining property was not so lucky; it was wrecked and later rebuilt as a single-storey building, which has since been incorporated into the pub.

From 1982 to 1989, under the ownership of Colin Keatley (who now presides over the Fat Cat), the pub prospered, being one of only a handful in the City selling real ales. In the years that followed it went into decline, and was eventually closed and boarded up in April 2005.

For some time it looked as though this historic pub would not survive, but on 29 September 2008 it was reopened under the ownership of the Milton Brewery (based in Cambridge). It has since flourished winning the accolade of CAMRA East Anglian Cider Pub of the Year in 2012.

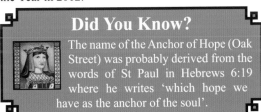

Did You Know?

The name of the Anchor of Hope (Oak Street) was probably derived from the words of St Paul in Hebrews 6:19 where he writes 'which hope we have as the anchor of the soul'.

White Lion (Magdalen Street)

White Lion, 1938

Fitzgerald, who was touring the country, but she was charging around £3,000 a night and we just couldn't afford her.

'In 1974 we opened the City's first dedicated wine bar, the Wine Cooper, in our upstairs room. Imported wine had become the trend in London so I added my own touch to the idea. In London prices were astronomical, I just added a pound to every bottle. It became one of the club's major attractions.

'We eventually sold up in 1978. It went for a fraction of what it was worth. We got around £30,000 for the lot. I don't regret selling as it was time to move on, but I wish we'd taken the name with us. The British jazz legend Ronnie Scott, who performed at the Jacquard in October '72, said of us "the club was exceptional", now that was a real compliment.'

 The licence of the White Lion (Magdalen Street) can be traced back to the 18th century and it traded as a pub until c1962. However, for many it will be best remembered as the second home of the Jacquard Club (also see the Mischief Tavern, Map 4). Albert Cooper continues the story:

'In 1971 my brother Tony and I bought the old White Lion for around £10,000. I worked hard with friends converting and renovating it. At the time Watneys were knocking down pubs and I wanted to buy old stuff such as tables, mirrors, stained glass and the like. I approached the brewery and was taken to a huge warehouse like an Aladdin's cave filled with old pub fittings. We paid a few quid and could literally have what we wanted. We also got permission to take the 'Long Bar' from Backs (the Curat House) that had closed on Gentleman's Walk. We cut it into two. One piece became the ground floor bar, the other formed another bar in the front upstairs room. Needless to say the golden cherubs that we had rescued from the old Hippodrome and originally installed in the Mischief also came with us!

'We relaunched the club on 14th October 1971 when I played the opening set. In fact I always did the warm up. Sometimes I played with the Jacquards or alternatively the larger collective that we called 'Albert's Banned'. Early acts included Eddie 'Guitar' Burns, the Strawbs and Elkie Brooks. As we became more established we attracted big names such as George Melly, Stephan Grappelli and Mike Carr's quintet. It was a real privilege to hear these performers in a club that only held 200 people. We were offered Ella

White Rose

Rose, 1936

In 1866 this Bullards' house (Magdalen Street) was known as St Paul's Rose, by 1884 it was the White Rose and by 1911, when Michael Holmes' grandparents were licensees, it was known simply as the Rose. Michael recalls:

'My grandfather, Bertie Holmes, had the licence from 1911. When he was called up in 1916 to go to the North-West Frontier of Afghanistan my grandmother Beatrice took over until Bertie's return in 1919. Unfortunately Bertie was caught selling after hours more often than the brewery would tolerate and they had to leave in 1927. My Uncle Arthur remembers the pub with its big spare room where he played and the back yard where he kept his tortoise between the many beer barrels. He also recalls the fierce chickens which would always attack him.'

Watneys eventually closed the pub in 1971 and a year later it was destroyed in a major fire.

Anchor of Hope, 1937
114 Oak Street
George Plunkett

Angel, 1936
154 Oak Street
George Plunkett

Britannia Tavern, 1938
73 Botolph Street
George Plunkett

Duke of Sussex, 1938
42 Botolph Street
George Plunkett

Duncan Arms, 1938
49 Magdalen Street
George Plunkett

Dun Cow, undated
167 Oak Street
Derek McDonald's collection

Flower in Hand, 1965
20 Pitt Street
Derek McDonald's collection

Flowerpot, 1938
129 Oak Street
George Plunkett

Hope Tavern, 1961
64 Calvert Street
George Swain

King's Arms, 1936
38 Botolph Street
George Plunkett

King's Head, 1938
49 St George's Middle St
George Plunkett

Light Horseman, c1890
4 Botolph Street
unknown photographer

Pineapple, 1936
47 St Martin's Lane
George Plunkett

Queen Victoria, 1938
51 Magdalen Street
George Plunkett

Railway Arms, 1936
90 Oak Street
George Plunkett

Red Lion, 1936
157 Magdalen Street
George Plunkett

Royal Oak, 1938
132 Oak Street
George Plunkett

Suffolk Arms, 1938
199 Oak Street
George Plunkett

Shuttles, 1967
62 Botolph Street
George Plunkett

White Horse, 1936
84 Magdalen Street
George Plunkett

White Swan, 1964
154 Magdalen Street
George Plunkett

North-East Norwich

Below is a list of the pubs, inns and taverns located in this area of Norwich. Those with a page reference have an entry or illustration. For further details see page 83.

Page	Pub Name	Location
	Anchor	1 Silver Road
110	Bird in Hand	53 Barrack Street
	Black Chequers	133 Cowgate
	Bricklayers' Arms	38 Bull Close
	Bull Inn	18 St Paul's Plain
	Bull	40 Bull Close
106	Cellar House	72 Barrack Street
106	Cottage	5 Silver Road
	Dove	43 Barrack Street
	Dun Cow	118 Barrack Street
	General Windham	122 Cowgate
110	Griffin	93 Barrack Street
107	Horse Barracks	173 Barrack Street
	Jolly Gardeners	20 Mousehold Street
	Jolly Hatters	123 Cowgate
	Jolly Maltsters	47 Cowgate
	King's Head	24 Barrack Street
107	Leopard	98 - 100 Bull Close

Page	Pub Name	Location
	Light Horseman	130 Barrack Street
108	Marquis of Granby	177 Barrack Street
	Mounted Volunteer	12 Silver Road
	New Brewery	Barrack Street
109	Plasterers' Arms	43 Cowgate
	Prince of Wales	96 Cowgate
	Robin Hood	Barrack Street
	Rose Tavern	109 Cowgate
	Seven Stars	112 Barrack Street
110	Ship Tavern	106 Cowgate
110	Sportsman	108 Barrack Street
	Staff of Life	51 Fishergate
	Swan	79 Cowgate
110	Tiger	47 Fishergate
110	Windsor Castle	47 Barrack Street
	Wrestlers	58 Barrack Street
110	Yarn Factory	152 Cowgate

101

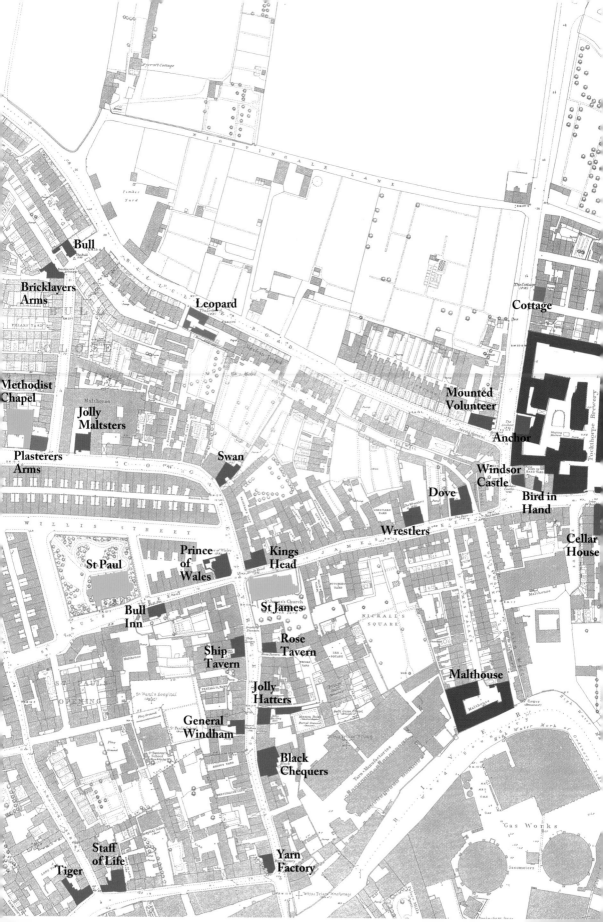

Bull

Bricklayers
Arms

Leopard

Cottage

Methodist
Chapel

Jolly
Maltsters

Mounted
Volunteer

Anchor

Plasterers
Arms

Swan

Windsor
Castle

Dove

Bird in
Hand

Wrestlers

Cellar
House

St Paul

Prince
of
Wales

Kings
Head

Bull
Inn

St James

Ship
Tavern

Rose
Tavern

Jolly
Hatters

Malthouse

General
Windham

Black
Chequers

Staff
of Life

Tiger

Yarn
Factory

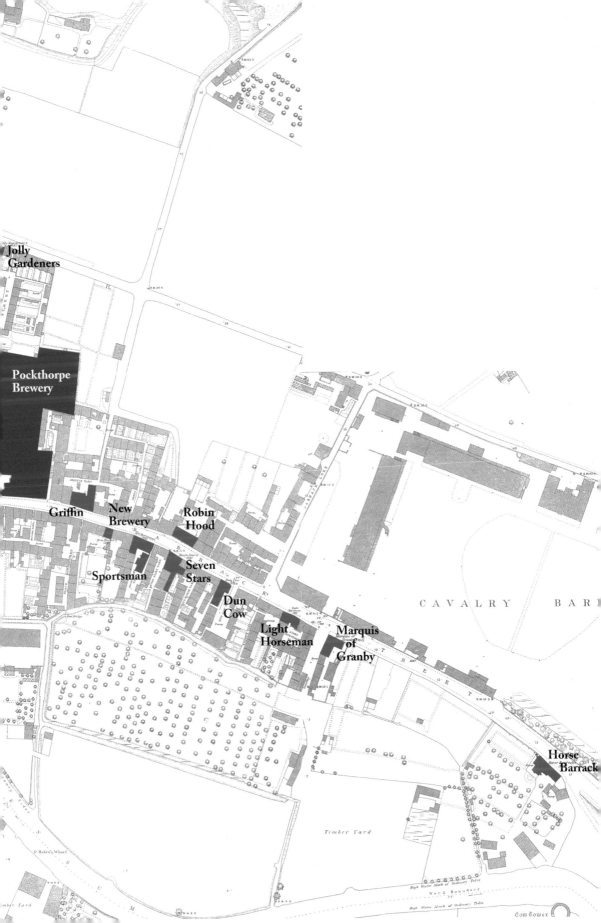

Jolly
Gardeners

Pockthorpe
Brewery

Griffin

New
Brewery

Robin
Hood

Sportsman

Seven
Stars

Dun
Cow

Light
Horseman

Marquis
of
Granby

C A V A L R Y   B A R

Horse
Barrack

Timber Yard

North-East Norwich: Historical Background

Pockthorpe Brewery, c1960

This section encompasses the area around Pockthorpe, which historically was the poorest in the City. It was an area of slum dwellings. In 1884 walking along St James' Street (now Barrack Street) between the King's Head and the Wrestlers, a distance of some 100 yards, you would have passed the entrances to no less than nine yards, including Butchers' Yard and Wrestlers' Yard, and this was not unusual. The area was also notorious for being rough. In fact it was rumoured that policemen always went around in pairs.

Despite the poor conditions residents had a strong sense of pride and local identity. In 1772 the 'Pockthorpe Corporation', also called the 'Pockthorpe Guild', was set up. Although its early history is sketchy, by the early 19th century it was known to be flourishing.

A pageant was held annually on the day following the Guild Day of the 'adjacent City of Norwich'. Resplendent robes and insignia of office were provided for the 'Mayor' of Pockthorpe, the 'Sheriffs' and 'Officers'. There was also a knight in armour and a 'Snapdragon', a reminder of the medieval Guild of St George. A grand procession took place along flag bedecked streets for a banquet at the Dun Cow Hotel, which doubled up as the 'Guildhall'. Afterwards 'convivial proceedings and sports' were held in the Cellar House gardens.

A number of factories were located in the area, including yarn factories and timber yards. However, the largest industrial site was occupied by Steward & Patteson's Pockthorpe Brewery. Originally Charles Greeves' brewery, in 1793 it was bought by John Patteson with a view to finding an occupation for his son. By 1961 it was one of the largest non-metropolitan breweries in the country. On 27th January 1970, only nine years later, the last brew in Pockthorpe was made. Today all that remains are the brewery offices on Barrack Street.

Did You Know?

A window bill from the early 19th century announced:

'Pockthorpe! Sublime great venerated name,
As years roll on, so will thy well earned fame;
The Patriot's home, his hope our Senate's guide
At once thy country's Bulwark and its Pride!'

St Paul's, September 1948

St James, looking along Cowgate from the west, 1932

The two medieval churches of St Paul's and St James' Pockthorpe were located in the area. Of these only the latter survives and now it is better known as the Puppet Theatre.

The Cavalry Barracks were erected between 1791 and 1793. Built of red brick they provided accommodation for 500 men and 340 horses.

Many pubs sprung up around the barracks to cater for the soldiery including the Light Horseman, the Horse Barracks and the Mounted Volunteer.

In 1923 the Cavalry Barracks was renamed the Nelson Barracks. Its buildings, together with most of the adjoining properties, were finally demolished in the mid 1960s to make way for a large housing estate. Today all that remains is a wall at the corner of Gurney Road and Barrack Street. Sadly, like the Barracks, many of the pubs that served the soldiers are also long since gone.

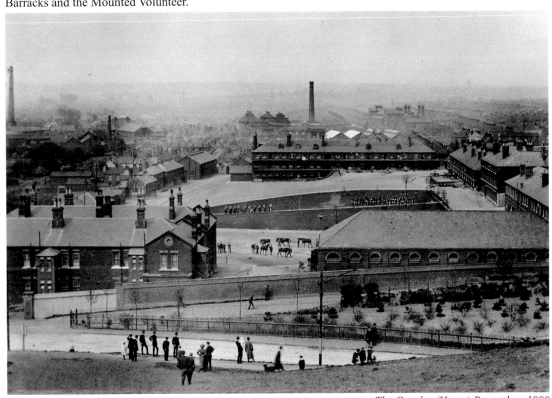

The Cavalry (Horse) Barracks, c1900

Cellar House

The Cellar House, which was located opposite the entrance to Steward & Patteson's brewery, played an important role in the Pockthorpe Guild Day. It was to the Cellar House gardens that revellers came at the end of the festivities to take part in 'convivial proceedings' and sports. In 1823, when John Patteson was elected Mayor of Norwich, the Pockthorpe Guild made a special effort to outdo themselves. After all he did preside over the Pockthorpe Brewery. Conscious of the importance of the day Mr Patteson is reputed to have contributed a most welcome sheep (presumably dead) to the promoters, which would appear to have added much to the day's enjoyment. However, it was the sports at the Cellar House which the majority looked forward to. On this occasion games included such Olympiad activities as:

- A contest to determine which lady could drink the hottest gunpowder tea
- Wheelbarrow races for blindfolded septuagenarians, to the tune of 'Now speed ye well my brave old boys'
- Climbing a greasy pole some 80 feet high, 'which commanded a view of Norwich and the Brandon railway', to win a leg of mutton.

Throughout there were concerts by banjo players and minstrels which John Patteson kindly conducted whilst playing a mouth organ...those were the days!

In the 1930s large areas of Pockthorpe were demolished as part of the City's programme of slum clearance. Residents were given accommodation in the newly built council estates where new pubs had been built. In 1938, as part of the programme, the licence of the Cellar House was transferred to the Grove on Cadge Road which formed part of the new Larkman estate. The Grove closed July 2009

Cellar House, 1937

Cottage

Cottage, 2011

The Cottage on Silver Road is one of the few pubs in the area still trading.

Its licence can be traced back to 1830. Within ten years of opening it was the subject of some concern when

it hosted meetings of a radical Chartist club inspired by John Love, Norwich's first Chartist leader. Other public houses where gatherings took place included the Angel (Oak Street) and the Shuttles (Botolph Street). Unsurprisingly all were located in the poorest areas of Norwich.

In 2015 the pub was taken over and renovated by the Grain Brewery.

Did You Know?

In April 1831 Richard Nockolds was executed after being found guilty of setting fire to straw stacks at Wood Dalling. His poverty-stricken widow displayed Richard's body outside the Barrack Gates in Pockthorpe charging a penny for a view. Apparently she raised a 'considerable sum' before burying him at St James' Pockthorpe Church.

Horse Barracks

Horse Barracks, June 1937

 Located on Barrack Street the licence of this pub can be traced back to 1822. The name reflects its proximity to the Cavalry Barracks. An old sign, long since destroyed, pictured a seal issued to the troops to buy food early in the 19th century.

It is reported that a sergeant who returned from the Boer War brought a baboon home from Africa with him. When he became landlord of the inn, hoping to attract customers, he kept it up a tree in front of the premises. Unfortunately his scheme misfired when the animal went mad and a cavalry officer had to be sent across from the barracks to shoot it!

The original house was demolished in the 1930s as part of a road-widening scheme and rebuilt c1938, but was partly destroyed during an air raid on 29th April 1942. Undeterred it reopened in January the following year in a temporary building.

 In the 1960s Les Eyre, an inside left for NCFC from 1946 to 1951, was the landlord. Around the same time it was the 'home' of local pop group Malcolm and the Toffs. It continued to trade as the Horse Barracks until 1975 when it was renamed the John W. Stokes. It was subsequently closed in 1989.

John W Stokes, c1980

Leopard

Leopard's old sign, 2002

 The Leopard, on Bull Close Road, can trace its licence back to the early 19th century. Normally when an animal appears on a pub sign it is of heraldic origin and design, which is why we have so many White Horses and Red Lions. It is rare that a non-heraldic, aggressive animal gives its name to a pub, yet in this area we have both the Leopard and the Tiger. No one is quite sure why, although it isn't beyond the realms of possibility that the signs were once very badly painted lions. Alternatively it could be explained by the cavalry telling of their exploits whilst defending the Empire.

 Unfortunately a new sign now replaces the rather splendid image of a reclining leopard which graced the outside wall for so long and which is pictured above.

From c2007 the premises was owned by Batemans who sold it in 2013. The following year, following an extensive refurbishment, the pub reopened as a free house.

Leopard, May 2008

Marquis of Granby

Marquis of Granby, July 1938

Marquis of Granby, sign by Arthur Thirtle, c1960

Located on Barrack Street, the licence of the pub can be traced back to c1763 immediately after the end of the Seven-Years War. It was during this campaign that John Manners (1721-1770), the Marquess of Granby (the traditional title of the eldest son of the Duke of Rutland), distinguished himself.

Until then his career had been somewhat chequered. In fact it is rumoured that he was described by George II as both a drunkard and a bully. However, subsequent events showed that though he enjoyed a drink and may have been a tyrant he was not a coward. During the war, as a Colonel of the Horse Guards, he took part in a number of successful engagements including the Battle at Minden. Then on 31st July, 1760 he led the cavalry on a daring charge against the French at the Battle of Warburg, capturing nearly 2,000 enemy soldiers and many guns. Although Granby had been bald since his early twenties, regardless of prevailing fashions he never wore a wig. During the charge he lost his hat but kept advancing, giving rise to the expression 'going at it bald headed'. Joshua Reynolds was commissioned to paint his portrait and it was a replica of this image showing a wigless Marquess which hung outside the tavern (above).

This is one of many pubs across the country celebrating the Marquess. Here, as in many others, his title was spelt as Marquis in the European way. Although it does not seem to be the case in Norwich, he often helped members of his old regiment establish themselves as innkeepers. Accordingly many honoured their former leader by calling their hostelries after him.

In 1869 the pub was at the centre of a controversy following allegations of corruption after the 1868 election. Investigations by the Bribery Commission led them to Pockthorpe, St James' Street, St Paul's Plain and St Paul's Opening, which were described as areas where the lowest (and poorest) class of voters in the City lived. They went so far as to describe Pockthorpe as the most corrupt ward in the City. Concern was raised about the Marquis of Granby, whose landlord John Mackley was a Liberal supporter, and where they thought that Liberal votes had been bought. This may have been a little unfair as it was the Conservative Sir Henry Stracey who was found to have offered bribes and not the Liberal Sir William Russell.

Nevertheless the pub survived the scandal for another 100 years before finally closing its doors in 1969.

Plasterers' Arms

Plasterers' Arms, 2011

PLASTERERS ARMS

The Plasterers' Arms (Cowgate) is one of the many taverns in the City which bore the name of some trade or occupation. Typically the name would be given to an establishment where workers met either socially or to discuss the business of their guild. Often, as happened here, the tavern would take on the name of their 'arms' which would then be depicted on the pub sign. Interestingly the Bricklayers' Arms and Plasterers' Arms, both representing the building trade, were located within 200 yards of each other. The pub sign (above right) depicts the actual Arms of the Plasterers with its motto of: 'Let brotherly love continue.' The central shield contains images of a trowel between two plasterers' hammers whilst below the chevron we see a plasterer's bush.

The licence of the pub, which still trades, can be traced back to the early 19th century. In the mid 1970s it became a real ale hot spot when in 1976 it was bought for £12,600 by Derek Howard, who also owned the Ten Bells on St Benedict's Street. Pete Turner, who later took over the Golden Star, was installed as landlord and recalls: 'At the time it was virtually impossible to get draft beers in Norwich. We sold Tolly Cobbold, Adnams, Greene King, IPA and Abbott. Customers used to walk through the door of the Plasterers and see the six hand pumps, fall on their knees and bow down in front of them. It was real ale Nirvana. The crowd at the bar was regularly six deep, it was a real scrum.'

Bram Lowe, first chairman of the local branch of CAMRA, remembers visiting the Plasterers on New Year's Eve 1976: 'I went in early and saw that Pete had a massive punch bowl. First he selected a bottle of gin which all went in, then a bottle of vodka which was also emptied in and so on across the entire spirit range. "Are you going to serve it like that?" I asked. To which I received the response: "I am". So I had to ask what he was going to call it: "Sudden death", he replied. There were many very merry people at the Plasterers that night.'

Did You Know?

The Cavalry Barracks were built on the site of Hassett's Hall, the home of the Blennerhasset family. It was rumoured that many years after his death 'Old Hassett' was seen riding his coach and four over Bishop's Bridge. Moreover soldiers working in the Cavalry Barracks' hospital often complained that they saw strange ghostly manifestations . . .

Did You Know?

The Ship Tavern traded from 106 Cowgate between 1830 and 1907. The premises is believed to date from the 15th century when it was the home of Sir John Fastolf (1378 - 1459). 100 years after his death Shakespeare based the character of Falstaff on Sir John.

Bird in Hand, 1929
53 Barrack Street
NCC Library & Info Service

Griffin, 1936
93 Barrack Street
George Plunkett

Ship Tavern, 1936
106 Cowgate
George Swain

Sportsman, 2003
108 Barrack Street
Derek McDonald's collection

Tiger, 1934
47 Fishergate
George Plunkett

Windsor Castle, 1929
47 Barrack Street
NCC Library & Info Service

Yarn Factory, 1938
152 Cowgate
Philip Armes Collection

Coslany and St Benedict's Street

Below is a list of the pubs, inns and taverns located in this area of Norwich. Those with a page reference have an entry or illustration. For further details see page 83.

	Pub Name	Location
	Alexandra	4 St Benedict's Street
115	Alma Tavern (Micawber's Tavern)	92 Pottergate
	Anchor	4 Ten Bell Lane
125	Anchor Brewery Stores	Coslany Street
	Bakers' Arms	45 Lower Westwick Street
	Balloon Tavern	62 Lower Westwick Street
125	Barn Tavern	1 Dereham Road
	Beehive	67 St Benedict's Street
125	Black Boys	30 Colegate
	Blackfriars' Tavern	37 Bridge Street
125	Builders' Arms	51 Pottergate
125	Bull & Butcher	131 Pottergate
125	Cardinal's Cap	86 St Benedict's Street
	Colchester Arms	79 Lower Westwick Street
	Cork Cutters' Arms	51 Bridge Street
	Corn Exchange Tavern	61 Bridge Street
	Crocodile	27 Heigham Street
	Crooked Billet	12 Heigham Street
	Crown	48 Bridge Street
	Crown	71 St Benedict's Street
	Dolphin	56 Coslany Street
	Dove Tavern	Muspole Street
	Drum	63 Lower Westwick Street
	Duke's Head	Duke Street
115	Duke's Palace Inn	7 Duke Street
	Eagle Tavern	110 Lower Westwick Street
126	Eight Ringers	14 Oak Street
116	Festival House (St Andrews Brewhouse)	2 - 6 St George's Street
	Fleece	8 Bridewell Alley
126	Fountain Inn	89 St Benedict's Street
	Garibaldi	68 Duke Street
	Golden Can	15 - 17 St Andrew's Broad St
120	Golden Can	26 Middle Street
	Golden Lion	15 St John's Street
117	Golden Star	57 Colegate
	Grapes Tavern	72 Colegate
	Greenland Fishery	30 Oak Street
120	Hampshire Hog	St Swithin's Alley
	Hen & Chickens	28 St. Mary's Plain
	Hot Pressers' Arms	17 Oak Street
126	Lord Camden	15 Charing Cross
121	Mash Tun	16 Charing Cross

	Pub Name	Location
	Moon & Stars	23 Duke Street
121	Morning Star (Birdcage)	23 Pottergate
126	New Brewery Inn	90 Lower Westwick Street
126	Nightingale Tavern	26 Colegate
126	Omnibus Tavern	91 St Benedict's Street
126	Pheasant Cock	3 Oak Street
122	Plough	58 St Benedict's Street
	Post Office Tavern	29 - 31 Exchange Street
	Prince of Wales	48 St Benedict's Street
127	Queen Anne	57 Colegate
	Queen of Hungary	85 St Benedict's Street
	Railway Stores	2 Heigham Street
	Red Cow	14 Cow Hill
122	Red Lion (Dog House)	18 St George's Street
127	Red Lion	26 Coslany Street
123	Rifleman	5 Cross Lane
	Rose Tavern	53 Oak Street
	Rose Tavern	24 St Mary's Plain
	Rose & Thistle	1 Heigham Street
	Rosemary Tavern	1 Rosemary Lane
123	Rumsey Wells	4 St Andrew's Street
	St Andrew's Hall Stores	26 Bridge Street
127	St Margaret's Stores	46 - 48 Lower Westwick St
	Shakespeare Tavern	42 Colegate
123	Shrub House	2 Charing Cross
	Staff of Life	31 - 33 Oak street
127	Stag	65 St Benedict's Street
124	Ten Bells	96 St Benedict's Street
	Three Kings	46 St Benedict's Street
127	Three Pigeons	St Benedict's Street
	Two Quarts	70 Bridge Street
127	Unicorn	39 Oak Street
	Vine	2 St Benedict's Street
	Waggon & Horses	23 Coslany Street
	Wellington	16 Wellington Lane
124	Wellington Tavern	18 Muspole Street
127	Whip & Nag	3 Pitt Street
	White Hart	28 Coslany Street
	White Horse	10 St Mary's Church Alley
	White Horse	10 St Andrew's Broad Street
127	White Lion	106 St Benedict's Street
	White Rose	6 St Margaret's Church Alley
124	Woolpack (Woolpack Yard)	2 Muspole Street

111

Crocodile

Crooked Billet

Railway Stores

Rose & Thistle

Eagle Tavern

Rose Tavern

Dolphin

Unicorn

Staff of Life

New Brewery Inn

Drum

Balloon Tavern

Miss Room

St Margaret Brewery

Barn Tavern

Colchester Arms

Fountain Inn

Hampshire Hog

White Rose

Omnibus Tavern

Beehive

Crown

St Margarets Stores

White Lion

Stag

St Swithin

Queen of Hungary

Bakers Arms

Cardinals Cap

St Margaret

Ten Bells

St Benedict

Plough

St Law

Anchor

Three Kings

Prince of Wales

Bull & Butcher

Baptist Chapel

Alma Tavern

Builders Arms

Wellington

Red Cow

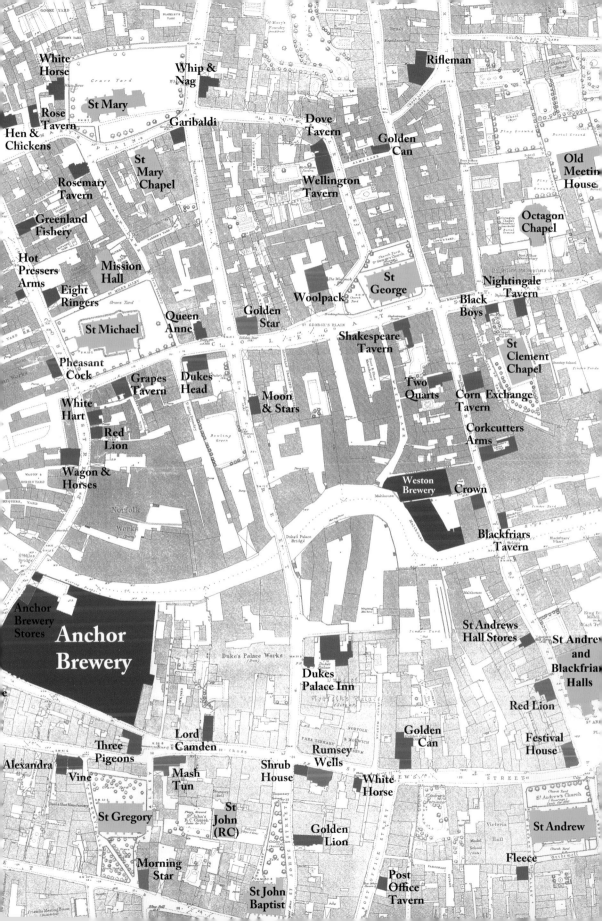

White Horse

Whip & Nag

Rifleman

Rose Tavern

St Mary

Garibaldi

Dove Tavern

Golden Can

Hen & Chickens

Old Meeting House

Rosemary Tavern

St Mary Chapel

Wellington Tavern

Octagon Chapel

Greenland Fishery

Hot Pressers Arms

Mission Hall

Woolpack

St George

Nightingale Tavern

Eight Ringers

Black Boys

St Clement Chapel

Queen Anne

Golden Star

Shakespeare Tavern

St Michael

Pheasant Cock

Grapes Tavern

Dukes Head

Moon & Stars

Two Quarts

Corn Exchange Tavern

Corkcutters Arms

White Hart

Red Lion

Weston Brewery

Crown

Wagon & Horses

Blackfriars Tavern

St Andrews Hall Stores

St Andrew and Blackfriars Halls

Anchor Brewery Stores

Anchor Brewery

Dukes Palace Inn

Red Lion

Golden Can

Festival House

Lord Camden

Rumsey Wells

Golden Can

Three Pigeons

Shrub House

White Horse

Alexandra

Vine

Mash Tun

St Gregory

St John (RC)

Golden Lion

St Andrew

Morning Star

Fleece

St John Baptist

Post Office Tavern

Coslany and St Benedict's Street: Historical Background

St Benedict's Street looking west, c1920

It is often quoted that Norwich had a pub for every day of the year and a church for every Sunday. Consequently it is not particularly surprising that in 1884 there were over 80 pubs and 17 churches in this relatively small, but highly populated, area of the City.

Additionally Bullards' Anchor Brewery, the Weston Brewery and St Margaret's Brewery were all located in the area. Furthermore in the 1980s the Star (later the Tap) micro brewery was briefly located next door to the Golden Star on Duke Street.

Of the ten medieval churches on the map nine are still intact. Sadly all that remains of St Benedict's, following the Baedeker Raids of late April 1942, is a tower. The same raid severely damaged the nearby Crown, Stag and Cardinal's Cap. Despite only St George Colegate and St Andrew's continuing to be parish churches, the other church buildings continue to play an important role in the City's life, but not as places of worship. Now in the care of either the Churches Conservation Trust (a national charity that protects churches at risk) or the Norwich Historic Churches Trust (responsible for seeking new and suitable uses for the churches in its care) the churches have a multitude of uses. For example, St Swithin is home to the Norwich Arts' Centre and St Margaret de Westwick is used as an exhibition space.

Not only does this area boast an impressive selection of medieval churches but according to Simon Jenkins, Chairman of the National Trust, it also has two of the 'most impressive Dissenter chapels' in England within 100 yards of each other along Colegate.

The Old Meeting House has been a meeting place for Congregationalists since it was built in 1693 on the site of the Blackfriars' garden. Its exterior indicates the influence and association with kindred worshippers in Holland. The neighbouring Octagon Chapel is more accessible and welcoming in design. It was erected in 1756 for the Presbyterians, but handed to the Unitarians in 1820. Charles Wesley, the 18th-century English leader of the Methodist movement, described it as 'the most elegant Meeting House in Europe…furnished in the highest taste and as clean as any gentleman's saloon'.

On the eastern periphery of the map are located Saint Andrew's and Blackfriars' Halls which are the most complete medieval friary complex to survive in England. They were built more than 600 years ago as the home of the Dominicans. After the Dissolution of the Monasteries in the 1530s, Augustine Steward (three times mayor of Norwich) bought the Halls for the people of Norwich. Since then they have had many uses: from playing host to ceremonial banquets to being a workhouse. Nonetheless for many they will be best known for being the location of CAMRA's annual beer festival.

Did You Know?

Norwich has 31 medieval churches, which is more than any other city north of the Alps.

Alma Tavern (Micawber's Tavern)

Micawber's Tavern, 2011

 The Alma Tavern on Pottergate was built in 1772. It was originally called the Duke of York but was renamed the Alma c1856 to commemorate Lord Raglan's victory over the Russians in 1854, in what was the first key battle of the Crimean War.

John Curson's aunt, Mariah Land, was landlady from 1926 to 1952 and he remembers visiting the pub around 1930: 'When I was a little lad I recall sitting outside on the step with my bottle of pop and, if I was lucky, a packet of crisps. My uncle wasn't about during the day because he was a drayman for Steward & Patteson. It was very small then, I think they've extended it now by knocking out part of the living quarters. There was a bar and a snug that held two or three people, which was used by ladies who enjoyed a drink but didn't want people to notice. When Mariah died the brewery allowed my cousin Jessie to take over. It wasn't often that licences were passed across to children but the brewery made an exception because Mariah had been there for so long.'

John Riddington Young recalls the autumn of 1971 when a party was held to mark the closure of the pub. The dartboard and ashtrays were given away and festivities extended well beyond closing time. The following morning the Brewery paid a visit to the licensees, Jessie and Billy, to tell them there had been a mistake and it wasn't to close at all. So the dartboard was returned and another party was held to celebrate the reopening!

It eventually closed c1975. Two years later it was reopened as Micawber's Tavern a name which, despite a brief period as Seamus O'Rourke's, it still has today.

Duke's Palace Inn

This little inn has a fascinating history. Located on Duke Street it was originally part of the home of the Dukes of Norfolk who first settled here during the reign of Henry VIII. In 1602 the original house was pulled down and work was started on a magnificent new palace.

In its heyday it must have been glorious. Sir Thomas Browne describes the Christmas festivities that took place in 1664: 'They had dancing every night and gave entertainments to all that would come. He [Henry Howard] built up a room on purpose to dance in, very large and hung with the bravest hangings I ever saw…A banquet was given every night after dancing and three coaches were employed to fetch ladies every afternoon.' Even Charles II was entertained there when he visited the City in 1671.

However, all the jollifications came to an end in 1708. At the time it was customary for companies of strolling players to enjoy the support of a nobleman which allowed the troupe to call themselves, for example, the 'Servants of His Grace the Duke of Norfolk'. This meant that they were properly constituted and unlikely to be taken up as common vagrants. The Duke of Norfolk's Company of Comedians seemed to have enjoyed privileges which extended to the right to play trumpets and fly banners whenever they entered the City. In 1708 Mayor Thomas Havers took exception to this behaviour and withdrew the entitlement. This led to a heated altercation between the two men and resulted in the Duke taking the rather extreme action of pulling down part of the palace and quitting the City.

The Duke set up a workhouse in part of the remaining building, the inmates living in somewhat different conditions from its previous inhabitants. Additionally the Duke's Palace Inn was established there.

 It is unclear when the inn started trading, but on 14th December 1745 the Norwich Mercury announced the departure of the 'Christmas Coach' for London from here. It was obviously a well-endowed establishment able to furnish gentlefolk with 'a landau, a handsome glass coach, chaise and chariot, mourning coach and horse…to any part of England'.

 In 1803 the inn played host to Mr Polito's Wild Beast Show. The exhibition included: a royal lion, a striped Bengal tiger, a beautiful leopard, a laughing hyena and a ravenous wolf. All were displayed in four 'commodious and safe' caravans in the yard.

Duke's Palace Inn (cont.)

Duke's Palace Inn, 1967

During 1815 strange and macabre events took place here. All started innocently enough with the landlord hiring out a spare stable and loft to an apple merchant. Ben, the ostler, objected to sharing the stables and took to spying on the merchant who he suspected of being a crook. Late one November night Ben, who strongly believed in ghosts, heard the sound of wheels passing over the cobblestones outside. In some trepidation he lit his lantern and crossed the yard only to find the apple merchant, unloading his cart, rather than the eerie spirit that he had been expecting. Ben bid the merchant good night and returned inside. But he was unable to rest and could not resist returning to investigate the sacks that he had seen being unloaded. It was now that a grisly sight met his eyes for these were not sacks of fruit but three dead bodies. Mr Robert Paraman, the head constable and governor of Norwich gaol, was called in to investigate. However, it did not take him long to solve the crime as next morning he was visited by the Rector of Hainford, who came to report that his parishioners had witnessed strange happenings in his churchyard the night before. Mr Paraman is said to have commented to the somewhat astonished vicar: 'Ah, those apples.' He then took the Rector across to the inn and reintroduced him to three parishioner he had recently buried! The apple merchant had in fact been a 'resurrection man' who sold dead bodies to the medical profession for dissection.

In 1855 the inn was host to happier events when a grand dinner was held here to celebrate the abolition of tolls on the nearby Duke's Palace Bridge.

When the 1884 map was produced neighbours on the old Palace site included Norwich's earliest museum and the City's Public Library, the first in England. The inn continued to trade well into the 20th century. Sadly all this history was lost in the 1960s when the it was demolished and St Andrew's car park built.

Festival House (St Andrews Brew House)

St Andrews Brewhouse, 2015

On 1st August 1898 a fire broke out at Chamberlin's department store which occupied a block fronting Guildhall Hill stretching back along the length of Dove Street. The Edinburgh, which stood next door to the store, appeared unaffected. Then four days later, just after the end of lunchtime trading, the building collapsed. It was decided to transfer the licence to premises on St George's Street, which at the time was a grocer's shop, and open the Festival House.

The Festival House took its name from the Norfolk and Norwich Triennial Music Festival which was first held at the nearby St Andrew's Hall in 1824. In its time the Festival played host to such great musicians as Edward Elgar and Vaughan Williams.

Until 1980 the corner bar was a Victorian gem complete with carved wood and mirrors. Unfortunately around this time it was 'modernised' and the bar was removed. Subsequently from 1992 to 2000 it was renamed several times, at one point being called the Grocer's Ghost, recalling the building's earlier use. From 2001 to January 2015 it operated as an Irish theme pub called Delaneys. Since when it has been taken over by City Pub Company (East). The premises, which has been refurbished and renamed St Andrews Brewhouse, now incorporates a micro brewery and even a smoke house.

Did You Know?

The Railway Stores, which was located on Heigham Street before being bombed in 1942, used to be called the Cow & Hare. This unusual name referred to an old superstition that witches could turn into hares and in this form would rob cows of their milk.

Golden Star

Golden Star, 2011

The licence of the Golden Star on Duke Street can be traced back to the 1860s. In 1970 it was closed by Watney Mann and it seemed that the building was likely to be demolished. Then in 1975 Peter Turner negotiated the lease from the City Council and he, together with his wife Carol, got to work. This is their story:

'At the time the "Northern traffic loop" proposals included the widening of Duke Street and the pub, along with other buildings along Duke Street, was threatened with demolition. Luckily we obtained a protection order, as did other buildings in the street, and they were unable to go ahead.

'When we moved in during 1976 it was derelict and inside was positively grim. We had to do a lot of work before we opened, which included knocking down walls and a total refurbishment. We didn't have carpets but wanted to create a traditional drinkers' pub with bare floorboards, wooden panelling and wooden seats. We even had a mulling iron, which stood by the open fire in the back bar, for those wanting to drink mulled ale.

'In March 1977 we made national headlines when we created a house bitter brewed by Paine's Brewery at St Neots which we called "Wife Beater Bitter". On the day of the launch we arrived at the pub to be met by a crowd of protesters from the Women's Lib movement and the UEA carrying banners with such slogans as: "Broken jaws, black eyes. What's so amusing about wife beating?" Demonstrators asked me not to serve anyone who asked for a pint of "wife beater". I never meant to cause offence so I changed the name to Golden Star XXX but all that happened was that regulars started asking for "Golden Star Unmentionable" or "a pint of Unspeakable".

 'It was a lovely pub. We ran it like a social club. We had music nearly every night, groups came in but some evenings we just had customers playing the piano. On Saturdays the Jubilee Rag Time Jazz band pulled in huge audiences playing their versions of such classics as "You Are My Sunshine" and "Tell Me Your Dreams".

 'The Norwich branch of the Norse Film and Pageant Society met in the pub. On one occasion we catered for their Viking banquet and served such delicacies as suckling pig and mead to 70 guests who wore full battle dress, including horned helmets, fur boots and axes!

'We also ran a Golden Star Summer Chess League. We were really proud when one of our members, "Supertim" Love, became County Champion whilst part of the Norwich Anonymous Golden Star Team.

'When our son Max was born in 1979 parents came in with their babies during the day and we turned the back bar into a crèche. We provided a meeting place for a range of groups from Compassion in World Farming to the Norwich Twenty Group.

'The Golden Star Morris team started at the pub around 1979/80 they were quite unusual because they were a "mixed side" and welcomed female members. They're still going strong. Also the Lost Garden Ceilidh Band (an anagram of Golden Star) met there.

'We really enjoyed being at the hub of the community.'

In 1984 when Carol and Peter sold the Golden Star to Greene King the Evening News reported: 'There was genuine sadness at the demise of the pub which had been a last bastion of resistance to juke boxes, video games and fruit machines…It was the end of an era.' On their final night at the pub a wake was held which spilled onto the streets outside. Performers who had been regulars at the pub, including the Golden Star Morris, entertained the crowds.

200 customers, who feared that Greene King would alter the Star's interior and ruin its unique character, signed a petition. The new owners listened, retained the old Golden Star spirit and opened to ecstatic reviews. It continues to trade today.

Peter Turner (right), c1978

Carol and Peter Turner (front) with friends, c1981

Carol Turner (left), 1981

The Star Brewery

During his tenure as landlord Peter created history when he opened the Star micro brewery. In his words:

'In August 1979 I was given approval from the City planners to turn three empty houses next door to the Golden Star into a brewery. I set it up with Sam Spall and employed Ted Willems, who previously worked for Watneys, as head brewer. We bought much of the brewing equipment second hand from different parts of the country.

'We launched Turner's Star Brewery in April 1981. It was thought to be the first new independent brewery to open in Norwich that century. It cost around £35,000 to convert the terrace houses. Our first batch of beer was a bit of an experiment. We'd wanted to give it away and ask customers to make a contribution to charity. However, legally we couldn't, so instead we sold it as a trial brew for 30p a pint. Luckily it went down well, with Terry Storer from CAMRA describing it as 'very palatable'. Learning from our experience in the pub we chose less controversial names for the beers such as Royal Flush. We even had a horse and dray (pictured above) to make local deliveries.

'Unfortunately in May 1982 we ceased trading. We just weren't making any money and the quality of the beer wasn't consistently good enough. In January 1983 we sold it to Hashmat Jalil. During the time it was closed the "S" and foot of the "R" had fallen off the "STAR Brewery" sign, so it seemed logical to open it as the Tap Brewery. It only lasted another 13 months and closed for good in March 1984.'

Did You Know?

Heigham Street Gate, between the Railway Stores and the Eagle Tavern, was also known by the rather macabre name of 'Porta Ubfern' or 'Hell Gate'. There are a number of explanations for this unusual soubriquet. It could be because it was both the most low lying of the Norwich gates and near a swampy, unapproachable river bank. Alternatively it was on Lower Westwick Street which was possibly one of the City's 'bad streets'. Finally 'hell' could be a corruption of 'holl' or 'hole', the Norfolk dialect for a ditch.

Golden Can

Golden Can, Middle Street, 1937

The Golden Can took its name from an old nursery rhyme which began: 'Little Brown Betty lived at the Golden Can, where she brewed good ale for gentlemen.'

Ruby Baker remembers back to the 1930s: 'I used to live in Stonemasons' Square. My dad worked in the shoe factories during the day and in the evenings used to make and mend shoes at home. At ten o'clock every night, if he had sixpence in his pocket, he stopped work and went for a pint at the Golden Can on Middle Street. By then he'd earned it.

'The Golden Can had a proper bar, a little lounge and a snug. There was always a fire in the corner of the bar commandeered by two old boys who smoked pipes. In winter you could get a special brew called "old". So you'd get half a pint of "old" which you'd put in a metal cone with a handle, like a pan, which you'd then rest in the coals for a couple of minutes to warm the beer. Once it was warm you'd pour it back into your glass to drink. It happened in a lot of the little pubs.'

When Ruby met her future husband Chris, he also got to know the pub: 'The landlord, like many of the others, used to arrange fishing outings for the men. They often organised a coach, but sometimes we cycled to places like Ludham and Wroxham. I used to go with Ruby's father. I went so often that Ruby used to say to me: "I don't know if you're courting me or my father." We've now been married 70 years so she must know by now.'

The Golden Can was destroyed during enemy action in 1942.

Hampshire Hog

The licence of the Hampshire Hog, can be traced back to the 1820s, however, there is some suggestion that it was trading long before this time. When Peter Seaman, Sheriff 1699 and Mayor in 1707, died in 1715 he left a public house in St Swithin's Alley to be sold for the benefit of apprenticing boys and it is assumed that this was the pub in question.

The Hampshire Hog is an unusual name for a pub and is assumed to derive from a poem by Drayton with the somewhat unusual line: 'Hampshire long hath had the term of hogs.'

In the late 19th century its landlord was the boxer John 'Licker' Pratt (1825 - 1903). John had a long association with pubs. He was born at the Jolly Gardeners (Angel Road) and subsequently went on to be landlord at the Jolly Skinners (Oak Street), the Rose Inn (St Augustine's Street), the Prince of Denmark (Sprowston Road) and the Brickmakers' Arms (Sprowston Road). He subsequently took over the Hampshire Hog c1880 where he remained until just before his death. In 1850 he beat the celebrated boxer Jem Mace, who later became the middleweight champion of England, in a memorable fight that lasted over two hours. Although records indicate that Pratt was the better man on the day, pub historian Walter Wicks who knew him reports: 'Pratt always said the fight was won because he could stand punishment better than Mace, not because he outclassed him as a boxer. Up to the last he declared that Mace "had the science".'

The Hampshire Hog's other claim to fame is that it was the last house in Norwich, and possibly East Anglia, where logats was played. Logats were 22 inches long and were similar to Indian clubs. Each competitor had three logats and the aim of the game was to toss them as close as possible to a jack that had been placed at the other end of the ground. It was similar to the game of 'Aunt Sally'. It would seem that such games were very popular in Norwich, as an entry from 1723 in the Mayoralty Court Books reports: 'Great disorders are committed and inconveniency arise by persons playing nine pins, ten pins and logats at public houses in the City.'

Did You Know?

The Cardinal's Cap (St Benedict's) was named in honour of Cardinal Wolsey, who visited Norwich in 1517 and again in 1520, when the Cardinal was accompanied by Queen Catherine of Aragon.

Mash Tun

Mash Tun, 2015

In 1891 the Three Pigeons, which was located on the corner of St Benedict and Westwick streets, was destroyed to allow the road to be improved. The licence was transferred across to 16 Charing Cross where a pub continues to trade. In 1977 it was rechristened as the Hog in Armour a term which dates from the 18th century and seems to be a variation on the phrase that 'you can't make a silk purse out of a sow's ear'.

The sign (below), by Peter Burrows, reflects the view of the Baptist preacher Charles Spurgeon (1834-92) who said: 'A hog in a silk waistcoat is still a hog.'

In 2014 following a substantial renovation, which included the opening of a 'decadent gin palace', the premises was renamed as the Mash Tun.

Morning Star (Birdcage)

Morning Star, 1938

In 1937 the traditional building occupied by the Morning Star on Pottergate was demolished and replaced by the contemporary building we see today. It did not meet universal approval and in 1945 was described in the City of Norwich Plan as being 'incongruous in design and out of place in an ancient street'.

In the late 1980s it was briefly operated by Colin Keatley, now very well known for his success at the Fat Cat. As you would expect from Colin, during his tenure it sold a range of real ales. When he took it on it was known as the Brown Derby, but he renamed it the Pottergate Tavern and engaged Cass Hooton to make a new sign. Her design depicted a man in a bowler hat, which she felt carried on the 'Brown Darby' sort of feel. She deliberately drew him to look like a toff obviously enjoying his pint of beer.

Today it is the home of the Birdcage, where one can enjoy 'wines, wifi, work and play, coffee, cup cakes, cocktails, board games, bloody marys and a bit of Bohemia'.

The Birdcage incorporates a gallery space where it hosts a variety of events, including DJ slots, poetry readings, art events and cabaret.

Did You Know?

Naming a pub that stands on Oak Street the Greenland Fishery seems a little strange. The title dates back to at least the 18th century when both Yarmouth and King's Lynn were involved with the Greenland, or whale, fishery. Understandably these towns both had hostelries with this name and doubtless it was copied by an enterprising, if slightly misguided, Norwich publican.

121

Plough

The Plough (St Benedict's Street) is located in a 17th-century merchant's house. The pub gave its name to both Plough Yard and Little Plough Yard, which it stands between.

A plasterwork plough in a distinct 'Wedgwood' style is highlighted on the front wall. The sign was popular in agricultural areas and Norwich's other Plough, which stood near to the Cattle Market on Farmers' Avenue, had this connection. The plough was also the main heraldic device on the Crawshay family's coat of arms.

In 2009 the Plough was closed and subsequently bought by the Grain Brewery, a small venture located at Alburgh in the Waveney Valley. Following an extensive renovation it was reopened in April 2010 to rapturous reviews.

Particularly popular is the beautiful beer garden, a rare commodity in Norwich.

Did You Know?

Not only did Lord Camden give his name to the hostelry on Charing Cross but he is also remembered in the name of Camden Town, the settlement he started in London.

Red Lion (Dog House)

The building occupied by the Red Lion on St George's Street is around 300 years old. An Elizabethan report of a previous establishment states that the innkeeper was accused of harbouring 'ill disposed persons and playing unlawful games with them day and night to the displeasure of Almighty God and to the evil example of others'.

In the 1950s and 1960s the Red Lion was part of the music scene and was one of the first Norwich pubs to feature a skiffle group, namely the Alley Cats.

In 1973 the premises was subject to a £27,000 conversion during which an impressive inglenook fireplace was uncovered.

For many years the Red Lion was the nearest pub to the Norwich School of Art, now transformed into the Norwich University of the Arts, and was a favoured meeting place for staff and students, both past and present.

The Red Lion closed c2005 and following a further conversion it reopened as the Dog House Bar.

Plough, 2010

Dog House, 2010

Rifleman

Rifleman, 1936

Built in 1626, the Rifleman was well known for being John Crome's local. It is said that the artist would be found nightly in the snug.

In 1826 the rather unusually named Dirty Shirt Club was founded at the Rifleman. It originated when a local master weaver paid his men here and they stayed on to gossip and drink. The name originated from the fact that they still wore their working clothes. Each member had his own churchwarden pipe with his initials inscribed upon the bowl which would be given to him when he entered. New members had the honour of smoking from a silver pipe.

Rumsey Wells and Shrub House

Shrub House, 1989

The licence to the Shrub House, originally located on 2 St Andrew's Street, can be traced back to 1842. Initially it was the premises of Ward & Seaman who traded in wines and spirits. In 1974 the premises was extended to incorporate 4 St Andrew's Street which had been Wells & Son hat shop.

Rumsey Wells, c1935

In 1979 the Shrub House closed and the original corner bar (2 St Andrew's Street) became a newsagents. Around 1984 the remaining property was reopened as Blueberries. It has since traded as both the St Andrew's Tavern and the Rumsey Wells. Today it retains the latter name and prides itself on providing premium booze, a good selection of real ales and foreign beer, pub grub that 'resembles good British home cooking' and regular live music.

But who was Rumsey Wells? The story starts in 1815 when the Wells family established themselves as regimental and school outfitters in a shop on Cockey Lane (now London Street). By 1879, under the leadership of Thomas Wells, they were manufacturing hats and caps in a three-storey building on St Andrew's Hill. Thomas' son Herbert Rumsey Wells was born in 1877. He became a partner in the family business in 1904, by which time the firm had moved to 4 St Andrew's Street. Rumsey was known as being quite a character who sported elegant whiskers, fine hats and a cloak. With Rumsey at the helm the firm were renowned for the quality of their products, sense of humour and service. One middle-aged man returning to Norwich after many years and wanting a new hat was amazed to find that the shop still had the measurements for his school cap. By 1935 his firm was advertising their caps as being the most expensive in the world. Rumsey died in 1937 but the business continued until 1974 during which time the shop sported a sign depicting three wells and the rising sun, a rebus for Wells & Son. One suspects that Rumsey Wells would be quite chuffed to know that his name still appears outside the premises where he presided so long ago.

Ten Bells

Ten Bells, 2011

 There has been much speculation as to the origin of the Ten Bells' name. It has been trading here on St Benedict's Street since at least the 18th century and is thought to allude to the fact that at one time you could stand on this stretch of street and clearly hear the bells from ten different churches. In the mid 1970s it was a free house and one of the few places in Norwich that you could buy real ale. It now serves a wide variety of spirits, craft cocktails and real ales.

Woolpack (Woolpack Yard)

Woolpack, 1936

 The licence of the Woolpack (Muspole Street) can be traced back to the 18th century, though it may have been trading before then. Its name very much reflects that it is set in the midst of an area once occupied by the textile trade. The building it occupies was built in the 15th century and it is said that there was once a tunnel connecting it to the nearby St George's Colegate Church.

After a short period as 'Woolies', it has been rechristened the Woolpack Yard. Inside, the building boasts beautiful wooden beams whilst the outside patio overlooks the medieval St George's Church.

Wellington Tavern

 The Wellington traded on Muspole Street from the mid 1840s through to 1962. In 1952 Walter Freeman became landlord. His son Gary, known to many for his performances with well-known local group the Contours, recalls his early career:

'I started singing in pubs when I was a young lad. My dad used to take me to his local, lift me up onto the bar and I would perform such songs as "Sons of the Sea". I thought it was great because people gave me pennies.

'My dad had a bakery on Adelaide Street but had always wanted a pub. Then in 1952 when I was 14, he had the chance to take over the Wellington in Muspole Street. He worked hard to build it up.

'We had a good pianist and customers often joined in a singalong. When I was 16 I started performing there. At the time I was a real fan of Frankie Laine so I always tried to sing in his style. On Saturday nights you couldn't get in. I like to think that they came to hear me sing!'

Wellington Tavern, c1952

Anchor Brewery Stores, 1984
Coslany Street
George Plunkett

Barn Tavern, c1940
1 Dereham Road
Derek McDonald's collection

Black Boys, 1932
30 Colegate
George Plunkett

Builders' Arms, undated
51 Pottergate
George Swain

Bull & Butcher (Paul Pry in background), 1964
131 Pottergate
George Swain

Cardinal's Cap, 1936
86 St Benedict's Street
George Plunkett

Eight Ringers, 1938
14 Oak Street
George Plunkett

Fountain Inn, 1936
89 St Benedict's Street
George Plunkett

Lord Camden, 1938
15 Charing Cross
George Plunkett

New Brewery Inn, 1939
90 Lower Westwick Street
George Plunkett

Nightingale Tavern, c1900
26 Colegate
NCC Library & Info Service

Omnibus Tavern, c1920
91 St Benedict's Street
Philip Standley's collection

Pheasant Cock, 1938
3 Oak Street
George Plunkett

Coslany and St Benedict's Street: Photo Gallery

Queen Anne, c1900
57 Colegate
NCC Library and Information Service

Red Lion, 1939
26 Coslany Street
George Plunkett

Stag, 1938
65 St Benedict's Street
George Plunkett

St Margaret's Stores, 1936
48 Lower Westwick Street
George Plunkett

Three Pigeons, c1900
St Benedict's Street,
NCC Library & Info Service

Unicorn, 1938
39 Oak Street
George Plunkett

Whip & Nag, 1936
3 Pitt Street
George Plunkett

White Lion, 1936
106 St Benedict's Street
George Plunkett

Britons Arms, Elm Hill, Henry Ninham, undated

Below is a list of the pubs, inns and taverns located in this area of Norwich. Those with a page reference have an entry or illustration. For further details see page 83.

Page	Pub Name	Location
135	Adam & Eve	17 Bishopgate
134	All Bar One	1 Upper King Street
	Bakers' Arms	St. Martin at Palace Plain
	Bank Stores	1 Prince of Wales Road
	Bank Tavern	10 Bank Street
148	Beehive	St Martin at Palace Plain
137	Bishop Bridge Inn	Riverside Road
148	Black Bull	5 - 7 Magdalen Street
	Black Horse Tavern	10 Wensum Street
	Bolingbroke Stores	66 London Street
137	Britons Arms	9 Elm Hill
	Cabinetmakers' Arms	6 Redwell Street
148	City Arms	2 Princes Street
	Compasses	4 Upper King Street
	Coopers	1 Queen Street
	Coopers' Arms	24 Princes Street
	County Arms	11 Castle Meadow
148	Crown	29 Elm Hill
148	Cupid & Bow	St Martin at Palace Plain
148	Duke of Connaught	72 Prince of Wales Road
148	Duke of Marlborough	29 Fishergate
	Duke of York	21 Bishop Bridge Road
149	Evening Gun	7 Rosary Road
	Flint House Tavern	13 St Andrew's Hill
137	Glass House	11 - 13 Wensum Street
138	Grapes (Lawyer)	14 Wensum Street
	Griffin	64 - 66 Prince of Wales Rd
	Horse Shoes	21 Palace Street

Page	Pub Name	Location
149	Jack of Newbury	19 Fye Bridge Street
149	Jolly Dyers	16 Fishergate
138	King's Arms (Lollards' Pit)	1 Rosary Road
	London Tavern	1 St Andrew's Hill
149	Lord Raglan	30 Bishop Bridge Road
139	Maid's Head Hotel	1 - 7 Wensum Street
	Marquis of Granby	23 Bishopgate
149	Masonic Tavern	24 Elm Hill
134	Mr Postles' Apothecary	2 Upper King Street
149	New Star	8 Quay Side
	Norwich Tap House	8 Redwell Street
140	Prince of Wales	8 - 10 Prince of Wales Rd
	Queen	25 Castle Meadow
	Rampant Horse	31 Fishergate
	Red Lion	19 Magdalen Street
140	Red Lion	79 Bishopgate
	Red Lion	63 London Street
134	Revolucion de Cuba	7 - 9 Queen Street
134	Revolution	6 Queen Street
141	Ribs of Beef	24 Fye Bridge Street
	Rose & Crown	35 Bishopgate
144	Tombland Stores (Edith Cavell)	7 Tombland
145	Turkey Cock	40 Elm Hill
145	Waggon & Horses (Take 5)	17 Tombland
149	White Friars	13 Whitefriars' Street
146	White Lion (Wig & Pen)	6 St Martin at Palace Plain
146	Wild Man	29 Bedford Street
147	Wine Vaults (Mischief)	8 Fye Bridge Street
	World's End	6 World's End Lane

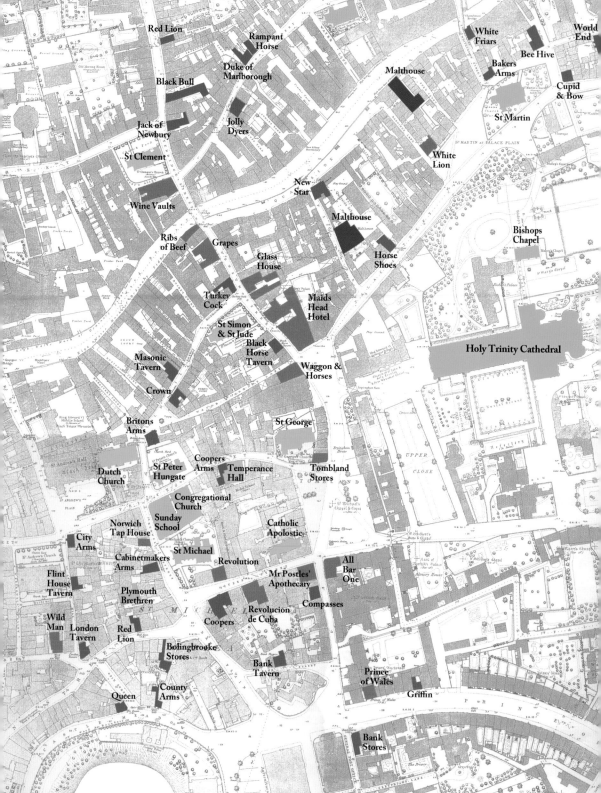

St Edmund

Red Lion

Rampant Horse

Duke of Marlborough

Black Bull

White Friars

Bee Hive

World End

Bakers Arms

Malthouse

Cupid & Bow

St Martin

Jack of Newbury

Jolly Dyers

St Clement

White Lion

New Star

Wine Vaults

Malthouse

Bishops Chapel

Ribs of Beef

Grapes

Glass House

Horse Shoes

Turkey Cock

Maids Head Hotel

St Simon & St Jude

Masonic Tavern

Black Horse Tavern

Holy Trinity Cathedral

Crown

Waggon & Horses

Britons Arms

St George

Coopers Arms

Dutch Church

St Peter Hungate

Temperance Hall

Tombland Stores

Congregational Church

Sunday School

Norwich Tap House

Catholic Apolostic

City Arms

St Michael

All Bar One

Cabinetmakers Arms

Revolution

Flint House Tavern

Mr Postles' Apothecary

Plymouth Brethren

Compasses

Wild Man

London Tavern

Red Lion

Coopers

Revolucion de Cuba

Bolingbrooke Stores

Bank Tavern

Prince of Wales

Griffin

Queen

County Arms

Bank Stores

The Tabernacle

Adam & Eve

Lord Raglan

Duke of York

St Helen

Marquis of Granby

Rose & Crown

Red Lion

Bishop Bridge Inn

Kings Arms

Evening Gun

Cricket Ground

St Matthew

Duke of Connaught

Distillery & Vinegar Works

Cathedral and Historic Heart: Historical Background

Norwich Cathedral, 2007

For many people this area of Norwich is its most picturesque. It features a treasure trove of medieval buildings set in a beautiful landscape.

This section of the City is of course dominated by the Cathedral with its majestic spire and beautiful Close leading down to the river. It was in 1096 that Bishop Herbert de Losinga laid the foundation stone for the Cathedral and by 1145 it was the largest building in East Anglia. The Cathedral has survived many disasters including devastating gales, fires, riots and wars. Today this iconic Norman structure is the most recognisable building in the City.

Behind the Cathedral on Bishopgate is another medieval complex of great beauty and interest, the Great Hospital. Originally known as St Giles' Hospital, it was founded by Bishop Walter Suffield in 1249. It would not have provided medical treatment as we understand it today but would have offered residents shelter and food. St Helen's Church was the lynchpin of the hospital complex. It was rebuilt in the 14th and 15th centuries when the refectory and cloister were added. The City acquired the Hospital in 1547, post Reformation, after which it offered medical as well as spiritual and physical care to residents.

Elm Hill, 2005

Over the years its appearance and use has changed. Although the central part of the church is retained for worship, the chancel was converted into accommodation which includes the Eagle Ward, thus named because it was painted with more than 250 eagles in honour of Anne of Bohemia, who visited Norwich in 1383 with her husband King Richard II. Today the Great Hospital gives sheltered accommodation to its residents although parts of the complex are used for dinners, conferences and meetings.

Elm Hill is the City's most famous Tudor street. It acquired its name from the elm trees that were first planted there in the early 16th century by St Peter Hungate's church warden. In 1507 many properties were destroyed by a fire which swept through the area. These were subsequently rebuilt by the prosperous merchants, craftsmen and civic dignitaries who lived there. Most of these properties still survive. By the 1920s Elm Hill was dilapidated and run down. Its many courts and yards contained slum dwellings and it was eventually saved from demolition by a majority decision of one vote by Norwich City Council. Today the cobbled street is a photographer's dream.

If the above weren't enough, this area is still home to an additional five medieval churches including St George Tombland and St Michael at Plea. Moreover Bishop Bridge, built between 1337 and 1341, is one of the oldest surviving water crossings in England.

Many of the inns, pubs and taverns located in the area also have impressive pedigrees. These include the Maid's Head Hotel, which is reputed to be one of the oldest inns in England, and the Adam & Eve, housed in a building dating back to the 13th century. Although many of the pubs dating from 1884/5 no longer exist, unlike many other areas of the City, here some parts have as many hostelries now as they did then. For example in the 100 yards separating the Mischief Tavern and the Maid's Head there are five establishments. All different in character, they offer their clientele a choice of ambience, food and beers.

In the following pages we describe hostelries of particular interest but before we do so we consider the question of the difference between a pub and a bar.

Did You Know?

Norwich Cathedral spire which rises to 315ft is the second-highest spire in England.

A man walked into a bar – or was it a pub?

Revolucion de Cuba, 2015

Revolution, 2015

One of the challenges in completing this book has been defining 'What is a pub?' We have many licensed premises in the City which are obviously not pubs, but other cases are not so clear cut. There are many examples in this section of the City, including the run from Revolution on Queen Street down past the Revolucion de Cuba and Mr Postles' Apothecary finishing at All Bar One on Upper King Street. All of the establishments contain bars and serve food. None openly describe themselves as pubs.

The area is popular because it is both in the heart of Norwich's tourist area and also adjacent to its most popular nightclubs leading down Prince of Wales Road. They all sell their clients a 'concept'. For example, Revolution describes itself as 'one of Norwich's best-loved bars' and boasts that it has an 'infamous clubroom'. Meanwhile Revolucion de Cuba guarantees a 'slice of the Cuban good life' whilst All Bar One describes itself as a 'stylish city bar' offering a 'sophisticated space to indulge in an excellent selection of food and drink. At Mr Postles'

Apothecary customers are invited to partake of the 'magical potions and eccentric elixirs on sale at the counter' whilst enjoying a laid back 1820s atmosphere.

In truth all could describe themselves as pubs using the Oxford English Dictionary's definition: 'An establishment for the sale of beer and other drinks, and sometimes also food, to be consumed on the premises.' All prefer to describe themselves as 'bars', technically an 'establishment where alcohol and sometimes other refreshments are served'. The main difference is the emphasis on serving beer. A concept clearly followed by CAMRA who annually list the best pubs in the country in their Good Beer Guide. Here they unequivocally state: 'Beer quality, above all, determines the choice of (good) pubs'. Although they fully acknowledge that history, architecture, food and ambience all contribute to the enjoyments of a visit to a pub 'the aroma and flavour of the beer in the glass is our prime consideration', a view shared by many pub landlords and their clients.

All Bar One, 2011

Mr Postles' Apothecary, 2015

Adam & Eve

Adam & Eve, 2011

 Many inns were called the Adam & Eve in the Middle Ages when the sign was the arms of the Fruiterers' Company. It was common at this time for Eve to be depicted tempting Adam with an apple accompanied by a serpent coiled around the trunk of the 'tree of knowledge'. In 1972 a new rather risqué sign was produced for this inn that excited so many complaints that the landlord had to return it to the brewery, where the sign painters added two large and strategically placed fig leaves!

The Adam & Eve (Bishopgate) is believed to be the oldest public house in the City still serving ales. Earliest references date back to 1249 when it was owned by the monks at the Great Hospital who used it as a brew house. At this time records indicate that it was frequented by labourers working on the Cathedral who were paid with 'bread and ale'. The original building was extended over the 14th and 15th centuries when living accommodation and Flemish gable ends were added.

 It will come as no surprise that the Adam & Eve is supposedly haunted. The resident ghost is said to be Lord Sheffield who was killed in the vicinity during Kett's Rebellion of 1549. However, in no way does he have exclusivity as it is also rumoured that sundry other ghosts often waft across from the nearby monks' cemetery. If this weren't enough the notorious 19th-century murderer James Rush was a regular at the Adam & Eve and is reputed to have plotted the murders of Isaac Jeremy, Recorder of Norwich, and his son at the inn. Rush was captured and spent his last night in the dungeons of Norwich Castle before being hung in 1849.

 Around the same time landlady Elizabeth Howes had an interesting sideline. She owned a wherry also called the Adam & Eve, which she used to transport sand from Yarmouth which she subsequently sold to local pubs for their floors and spittoons. On the face of it all was very respectable, but hidden in the sand was contraband liquor which she successfully smuggled into Norwich for years!

Both John Riddington Young and Leonard Thompson write fondly of the Adam & Eve which is still very popular today. Roger and Anthea Cawdron presided here for 12 years from 1971. They have many memories:

'It was derelict when we took it over but the brewery did a good conversion and we had many successful years there. We installed a bar, the previous tenant would have taken orders at customers' tables more like a restaurant style of service. We also excavated the cellar and in the process found the remains of a body, which caused a certain amount of alarm. We called the police in to make sure no one had been murdered but after examination the coroner declared it to be the remains of a medieval monk. He was taken away for reburial and we could continue. At the time we were trying to lower the floor by 4 inches as until then the ceiling height was only 5 foot 4 inches.

'Because it was a Watneys' house we were tied to selling Norwich Bitter and Mild. Despite this many of our customers followed us across from Fisher's (Prince of Wales Road), which was a free house, and of course we were next door to the Close so we were joined by many solicitors and accountants who just wandered over from their offices during their lunch break.

'Also we had the Great Hospital on our boundary. Many of the residents who were still mobile used to come in at lunchtimes but didn't want to carry extra supplies back because of the dangers of dropping their bottles. So every Thursday I used to take Guinness and Mackeson over to them and to those that were disabled and unable to get across. I was a bit like their weekly milkman. Sometimes if the old boys had a bowling competition I just took over a couple of jugs. It was great to be able to see their magnificent Eagle Ward and cloisters.

'We've always worked closely with the local police. On one occasion I took a call from the local sergeant who said: "You've Reggie Kray coming in. Can you just give him a beer and keep an eye on him."

'What that was supposed to mean I really never knew. But sure enough he came in, had his beer, read the newspaper and luckily just walked out.

'On another occasion a huge man squeezed through the door and asked for a drink just on closing time. I served him of course. It was Joe Bugner the British contender for the World Heavyweight title!

 'For entertainment we had the Jerry Pot Banjo band complete with washboard and tea chests and at the other end of the scale Mick and John who played guitars and performed hits by such groups as the Eagles.'

The Great Hospital, recreational area, c1920

Bishop Bridge Inn

Bishop Bridge Inn, 1960

 The Bishop Bridge Inn took its name from the nearby river crossing. The licence can be traced back to the early 19th century but it was demolished for road improvements in the early 1960s. Pub historian Derek McDonald has happy memories of the pub:

'My grandparents, Billy and May Goodson, kept the Bishop Bridge Tavern from 1942 to 1956. It stood on the corner of Bishop Bridge and backed down to the River Wensum. My father worked there on Saturday mornings when I also used to help nan with a bit of shopping.

'It was a big old place. On the corner was the main bar and there was also a smoke room where they kept the dartboard. You went through into the kitchen that looked out over the car park. Their living quarters had a big veranda with steps that took you into a wood yard that led down to the river.

 'We had a big hall known as a sports room where Ginger Sadd and Chucky Robinson boxed, I think it was just to train. It was also useful for social events. I particularly recall the kiddies' parties. I remember it as a lovely pub.'

Billy and May Goodson, Bishop Bridge Inn, c1950

Britons Arms

Britons Arms, 1934

The picturesque Britons Arms on Elm Hill dates from the reign of Edward III. It is one of the few thatched buildings in the City. It has had an eclectic range of uses. These have included being a beguinage (similar to a convent) and the HQ of the ARP firewatches during WWII. However, for about 200 years it was a pub. Originally called the King's Arms, in the spirit of nationalism it was rechristened the Britons Arms around the time of the French Revolution. Today it houses a restaurant

Glass House

 In 2001 the Glass House (Wensum Street) was the third J.D. Wetherspoon pub to open in the centre of the City. As its name suggests it is partly housed in the premises of a former glass merchant. The premises is light and airy and with an attractive outside seating area.

The chain was founded in 1979 when the 24 year old law graduate Tim Martin opened his first pub in Colney Hatch Lane, London. Wetherspoon's is a strong champion of cask ale and are proud to regularly have more pubs than any other pub company in CAMRA's 'Good Beer Guide'.

Glass House, 2011

Grapes (Lawyer)

King's Arms (Lollards' Pit)

Lollards' Pit, 2015

Lawyer, 2011

In the late 18th century a Joseph Geldart occupied this building on Wensum Street where he traded as a wholesale and retail dealer in 'wine, brandy, rum and other spirits'. In the early 19th century the premises were licensed as the Grapes. Between 1911 and 1972 it was part of the local chain established by P. G. Back. Subsequently it underwent many name changes.

Around 2004 it was attractively refurbished and renamed as the Lawyer. It is described as a 'London-style bar' offering 'real ales, premium lagers, and a huge wine selection'.

The King's Arms was in existence by 1749. It was located on the site of the infamous Lollards' Pit which in the 16th century was a place of execution for heretics and other offenders. It has been rumoured that at one time the building was a prison where heretics were held prior to suffering a horrific execution. Writing in 1975 John Riddington Young noted that: 'Many of the older regulars went down to the cellars to see the chains hanging from the walls before the dungeons were bricked up a few years ago.' It is even claimed that the drinkers in the pub have seen ghostly manifestations, but of course this may have been after a pint or two!

It is therefore very appropriate that after a short time being called the Bridge House (from 1975) in 2012 the revamped pub was reopened as the Lollards' Pit. It even has a grisly sign portraying a group of Protestant martyrs going up in flames. Despite its somewhat gruesome past you can be assured of a friendly welcome and a choice of real ales.

Maid's Head Hotel

The Maid's Head Hotel can trace its origins back to 1287, and is believed to be the sixth-oldest inn in England. It stands on the site of a bishop's palace built by Herbert de Losinga, who was responsible for the foundation of the Cathedral. Over time the palace became a hospice and was let to Hugh Bigod, a lay brother, who called it the 'Molde Fishe' or 'Murtle Fishe' Tavern. There is no clear explanation why the name altered to the Maid's Head. Suggestions that it was changed to honour Queen Elizabeth I, who visited Norwich in 1578, sound plausible. Unfortunately they are somewhat wide of the mark as over 100 years earlier, in 1472, nobleman John Paston referred to the 'Mayd's Hedde' in letters to his wife Margaret. Two other theories remain. The first suggests that the murtle fish may have been akin to a skate, for which Norfolk fishermen's colloquialism has long been a maid's head. A second explanation is that an early widowed tenant of the inn called Mathilde put up the sign of Mathilde Hedde, which eventually became shortened to 'Maid's Head'.

Many important historical events have been linked with the Maid's Head. In 1359 it is reputed to have been visited by the Black Prince, who came to Norwich to attend the jousting at Gildencroft. Subsequently in 1520 guests are said to have included Cardinal Wolsey and Queen Catherine. Then in 1549 the King's commanders breakfasted here on the morning of the last battle of Kett's Rebellion.

In the early 17th century the Maid's Head was often at the centre of local celebrations but it was in the early 19th century during the 'Golden Age' of coach travel that the inn had its real heyday. During this period coaches ran regularly from the Maid's Head to London.

Whilst other hostelries offered visitors to Norwich wild beast and freak shows, the Maid's Head put on musical evenings and banquets. However, not all entertainments were above reproach. Such diversions included a visit by the charlatan Dr Graham, the Director of the Temple of Health in Pall Mall, who gave sex lectures. His assistant was the 'Goddess of Health', a scantily clad Emma Hart, who later became Lady Hamilton, better known as Lord Nelson's paramour.

In this period it was also a very attractive place for gamesters and sportsmen to meet having no less than five cockpits. It is said that there was more cockfighting here than at any other hostelry in Norwich.

Many clubs and societies met at the Maid's Head, including a drinking organisation called 'The Everlasting Club'. The initiation ceremony consisted of plying new members with alcohol until they could not sit astride the wall of the nearby church of St Simon and St Jude. It was also here that the Masonic Craft had their first lodge in the City.

In the 19th century, with the coming of the railway, many of its rivals, including the Royal (Market Place) and the Norfolk Hotel (St Giles' Street), failed. However, the Maid's Head was still thriving at the end of the century when the Norfolk Chronicle wrote that there was 'an air of comfort and antique dignity about the inn and its elaborate apartments'.

In the 1970s the Maid's Head became very popular with real ale drinkers, being one of the few outlets in the City were you could buy cask ales.

Today it continues to meld the old with the new. You can still visit the old coach yard which is now a restaurant. It also has picturesque rooms and seating areas. Like so many of its illustrious visitors over the years, guests are ideally placed to wander around the historic heart of Norwich and some of its famed local hostelries.

Coloured postcards such as these were popular in the early 20th century.

The view looking down Wensum Street

The dining room

Prince of Wales

Prince of Wales, 2004

The Prince of Wales (Prince of Wales Road) has operated from here since the late 19th century, despite being damaged during air raids in April 1942. It is now adjacent to some of Norwich's most popular nightclub venues.

Red Lion

The Red Lion along with the Adam & Eve (both located on Bishopgate) were once owned by the monks who resided at the nearby Great Hospital. Parts of the building it still trades from today can be traced right back to the 16th century. In the 1970s it was renowned for its musical evenings and it is said to have been the venue where the Mutton Chop Banjo Band was launched!

It continues to be a very attractive pub in a beautiful location.

Did You Know?

Norwich Cathedral has the largest surviving monastic cloisters in England and the Great Hospital has the smallest.

The Red Lion overlooking Bishop Bridge, 2011

140

Ribs of Beef

The Ribs of Beef is one of Norwich's most popular City-centre pubs. As early as 1743 it was operating as a licensed premises. In 1898 the front half of the building was demolished as part of a road-widening scheme to allow electric tramway tracks to be laid. Nevertheless the remaining building was rescued and the pub reopened in 1904. In 1929 it was renamed the Fye Bridge Tavern in anticipation of the new twin span bridge that was built to prevent the River Wensum flooding the City as it had in 1912. In 1958 the pub was delicensed.

Over the following years the building housed an antique shop, an electrical shop and a ladies fashion boutique before Roger and Anthea Cawdron relicensed it in 1985 as the Ribs of Beef. Most real ale pubs at the time had floorboards and benches but the new thick carpet and leather seats appealed to the locals and professional clientele who required more comfort. Serving a range of cask ales from all over the UK and excellent food and wines, it quickly established itself as 'the City's favourite local'.

Roger Cawdron has been in the pub trade for over 40 years. During this time he has served as both Chairman and President of the Norwich and Norfolk Licensed Victuallers' Association and the Anglia Region Chairman of the British Institute of Innkeeping. Roger, and his wife Anthea, have run a number of hostelries including: the Mischief Tavern (Fye Bridge Street), the Black Horse (Earlham Road) and the George & Dragon (Hay Hill). Roger was already well versed in running pubs before becoming a landlord:

'Many members of my family were involved in the pub trade. My father Ted took on the King Edward VII in Aylsham Road around 1966. It was one of the biggest barrelage houses in Norwich. In those days there was no cellar refrigeration and I can remember going with my father to Valori's, the fish merchants, in our van and returning with it full of big blocks of ice. We used to lay sacks over the 36-gallon wooden barrels and lay the ice in between. It took about three days for the ice to melt and was a good way to keep the beer relatively cool.

'Fruit machines were unheard of then but Ted kept a mini sega machine which took sixpence in old money (2½p) and paid out £20, a huge amount in those days. Later on we had one of the first "Chieftain one-armed bandits" imported from America, along with a Wurlitzer juke box which played 45s (records which revolved at 45 revolutions per minute).

'As a lad I used to visit my Uncle Albert's pub, the Norfolk & Norwich Arms on Sprowston Road. I still remember sitting outside with my bottle of lemonade and packet of Smiths crisps listening to the noise and watching the smoke rise from the bar. My Uncle Freddie also kept both the Magpie in Magpie Road and the King's Arms in Botolph Street. I pulled my first pint of "twos" at the King's Arms. It cost 10½ old pennies, which would be 4p today .

'In 1970 I was working at the Edward VII one night when I was approached by a gentleman called Geoffrey Fisher. He'd just bought a couple of bars,

Ribs of Beef, by Edward Pococke, c1890

Ribs of Beef, 2011

one of which was on Prince of Wales Road, and he asked if I wanted to manage it. I said yes, and largely because there were so few free houses in the City, Fisher's Free House was an overnight success. We sold an enormous selection of beers compared to local pubs, most of which were tied to Watneys. We served keg beers such as Trumans, William Youngers and Newcastle Exhibition, also Tuborg Lager. Later on we sold a couple of cask beers such as Sam Smiths, which we kept in 36-gallon oak barrels.

'In 1971 Trumans bought Geoff out and the first thing they did was to reduce my salary. So I, together with my wife Anthea, carrying my son James in a papoose, walked around to the Watney Mann Brewery on King Street and asked what was available. They said: "What about the Adam & Eve?" And I said: "That will do". In the end myself and Anthea were there the best part of 12 years. In fact whilst we were there we had an addition to the family in the shape of our lovely daughter Joolia.

'We took over the Mischief in 1976 whilst we still had the Adam & Eve. I was one of the first landlords with multiple tenancies. Others were Douro Potter whose pubs included the Woolpack, the Rouen and the Pig & Whistle, whilst Frank Knight was running the George & Dragon, the Post Office Tavern and the Lion & Castle.

'At one time in the 80s we ran five pubs: the Adam & Eve, the Mischief, the Black Horse on Earlham

Road, the Garden House on Denbigh Road and the George & Dragon on Hay Hill. What was even more unusual was that four were tied to Watneys but the Black Horse was tied to Whitbread.

'When we lived in the Mischief we used to look across the river at the building which now houses the Ribs of Beef. In the early 1980s the owner, who ran a business called Spectrum Lighting from there, decided to sell up and we were able to buy it. My original intention was to open it as a boat club for small crafts, such as dinghies, but our plans were turned down. The suggestion was then made that we should put in for a pub. I really didn't think that we'd have a chance because along the street there was literally one every 100 yards or so. But at the time practically every City pub was tied to a big brewery which made it virtually impossible for small local brewers to sell their beers. We put forward the plan that we would support small independent breweries. In fact some of the local brewers came to court and told the licensing bench that they were really interested in getting the Ribs open as a means of opening up trade. After a day in court I was granted what was probably the first new City licence since WWII. It generated a lot of publicity.

'At the time décor in real ale pubs tended to be a bit spartan. We wanted to attract professionals who liked beer so we bought leather chairs and installed carpets to give it a bit of class. We also served wine, which helped develop the image.

Roger and Anthea Cawdron outside the Black Horse on Earlham Road, 1986

'When we opened in 1985 we sold six real ales including brews from Woodforde's, Rayments, Batemans and the Reepham Brewery. But after the first year we increased to nine after we realised it was good advertising to be able to say that we sold "one over the eight". Because we already ran a number of pubs Anthea and I were well-known publicans and we received a lot of support from old customers.

'We were well placed to serve professionals from the Close. We were also near to the Jarrolds' printworks and lots of customers came across from Norwich Union, as it was then, and the HMSO. However, since we opened many businesses in the City have either closed altogether or moved to the business parks on the outskirts.

'Over our time in the trade much has changed. In particular in the early 1960s most pubs would only have two or three beer pulls. The main brews available were Bullards' Mild and S&P Bitter although during winter they may have served a stronger beer such as nips or stingos. Lager was virtually unheard of and could only be found in bottles.

'When we used to close at night we often had lock-ins, whereby we locked the doors but continued to serve drinks. If the landlord got caught he had to pay a hefty fine. So it was an unwritten law that customers had to buy shorts which cost 2/6d as opposed to beer which cost a shilling to make it worth the risk of being caught. On the odd occasion we were raided everyone used to rush upstairs, leave by the back exits or hide in the toilets. When the police came in we'd tell them we were clearing up, and as long as there was no trouble they'd turn a blind eye.'

Tombland Stores (Edith Cavell)

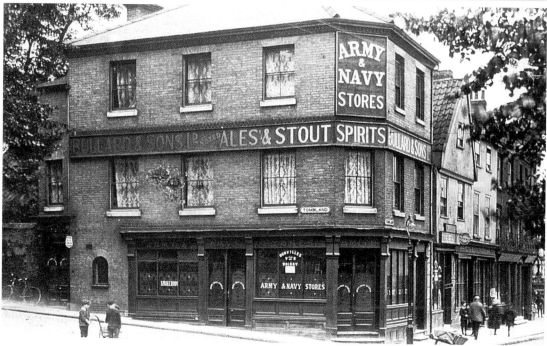

Army & Navy (Tombland) Stores, c1920

The Tombland Stores opened as a beerhouse on Tombland in 1870. In the early 20th century it was briefly converted into a clothing shop. When it opened again as a tavern it was rechristened as the Army & Navy stores. At this time it took its name from a home for soldiers and sailors on Queen Street.

In 1975 it was described by John Riddington Young as being: 'A tourist attraction in the summer for those foreigners who wanted to see "an English pub". The etched windows indicate where the original rooms used to be. The best example faces the Cathedral and bears the endearing epithet "Jug and Bottle". The back of the bar is a fine example of Victorian pub décor.'

Alas, following an extensive renovation the Victoriana is no more. Nevertheless it is still an attractive venue with an upstairs dining room. Another major difference has been the change of name to Edith Cavell, in memory of the heroine who is buried beside the Cathedral.

 Edith Cavell (1865-1915) grew up in the vicarage at Swardeston, a village just south of Norwich. In 1914 she was a nurse in Belgium. During the following year she helped over 200 Allied soldiers escape the German authorities. In 1915 she was captured and, despite efforts to save her, was executed by a firing squad.

The Allies acclaimed Edith as a martyr. Within eight weeks of her death recruitment into the British Army had doubled. After the War Edith's remains were returned to England for a state funeral at Westminster Abbey. On 15th May 1919 a special train transported her body back to Norwich. Once here a great procession accompanied her coffin to the east end of the Cathedral where she was finally laid to rest. Edith was a true British heroine who lived her life by the maxim 'patriotism is not enough'.

Edith Cavell's coffin, Norwich Cathedral, 1919

Turkey Cock

Turkey Cock, undated

The licence to the Turkey Cock can be traced back to the late 18th century. It traded from the same position on the corner of Elm Hill and Wensum Street until around 1964, when the licence was surrendered. Today the premises is occupied by Olive's café.

Over the 1940s Ann Redgrave's grandmother, Ellen Lebbell (later Beales) was landlady here:

'My grandmother was tiny. She was 5 feet 2 inches tall and wore size three shoes, with very high heels. She had very fair hair which was short and curly and took great pride in her dress, often wearing vivid colours.

'I spent many hours of my childhood at the pub. The bar was extremely small and always crowded. It was frequented during the War by both British and American servicemen as well as locals. Next to the bar was a tiny parlour, resembling an old-fashioned railway carriage, with high-backed red leather long pews facing each other. These were usually occupied by feisty old ladies in black, knocking back their Guinness or gin. I remember going to the cellar with Charlie the barman. It was pristine with whitewashed walls and well kept beer barrels. The smell of beer still reminds me of that cellar.

'My grandmother also did B&B. Her customers were often an overflow from the Maid's Head whose housekeeper was a friend. At Christmas my grandmother played the piano in the lovely large sitting room upstairs which had a roaring fire. She was very well supplied with eggs, and other scarce food, during the War by the farmers who were regulars. I believe she swapped them for the odd bottle of scotch. She was very kind hearted and I remember accompanying Charlie with baskets of food for elderly or ill neighbours. She loved flowers and used to trot up Elm Hill avoiding the cobbles on her high heels, down London Street and into the market where she was a regular customer at the flower stalls.'

Waggon & Horses (Take 5)

Waggon & Horses, c1895

The history of the Waggon & Horses (Tombland) can be traced back to the late 18th century. When the back yard had its own smithy. Just down the road goods would have been unloaded onto the quayside at the back of the Maid's Head. It is likely that the hostelry took its name from the carriers who served this quay.

 In 1976 it was renamed the Louis Marchesi after Eminio William Louis Marchesi (1898-1968) who founded the Round Table, an international fellowship and charitable organisation for young businessmen. The first group was formed in 1927 just up the road at Suckling House (now Cinema City).

It closed in 2004 and reopened as Take 5, a pub with a continental café bar atmosphere, where you can enjoy home-cooked food and real ales.

Louis Marchesi

White Lion (Wig & Pen)

Wig & Pen, 2011

Wild Man

Wild Man, 2005

The licence to the White Lion (Palace Plain) can be traced back to the 18th century. It occupies a 17th-century house which is reputed to have a tunnel from the cellar, now blocked up, which led to Whitefriars' Bridge.

 In 1985 Norwich's new Magistrates' Court opened down the road in Bishopgate. In the same year the pub was rechristened as the Wig & Pen. The name was adopted from the famous Wig and Pen Club on the Strand which served as a popular drinking den for both the lawyers from the neighbouring Royal Courts of Justice and the journalists of nearby Fleet Street.

Today the 'Wig' prides itself on the quality of its beers and food. It is especially popular in the summer months when customers spill onto the outside terrace overlooking the beautiful Cathedral.

Did You Know?

Tombland comes from Old English words meaning 'empty land or space'. It was here that the old Saxon market used to operate

The Wild Man (Bedford Street) was named to commemorate 'Peter the Wild Boy'.

 The story goes that whilst George I (1660 -1727) was hunting in a forest near Hamelin he discovered Peter who had been abandoned as a child. The King brought Peter back to England and left him in the care of Thomas Fenns of Berkhampsted from whom he escaped. Peter eventually made his way to Rackheath near Norwich. As he was unable to speak and was dressed in rags it was assumed that he was a vagrant and he was incarcerated in the Bridewell, a prison for minor offenders, tramps and beggars. In 1751, following a fire in the parish of St Andrew's, Peter was transferred to the City Gaol where he was recognised and returned to Thomas Fenns. He lived a further 34 years, eventually dying at the ripe old age of 73.

The pub has been trading here since the 18th century. At one time it had a special licence which allowed it to open at 4 a.m. for night-shift workers. It is reported that by 8 a.m. a pianist would be well through his repertoire and it wasn't unusual for whist drives to be well underway before breakfast.

In 1974 the Wild Man had the distinction of being the only Norwich pub featured in the first CAMRA Good Beer Guide. The entry read: 'Last Tolly house in Norwich serving beer by traditional methods.'

Wine Vaults (Mischief Tavern)

Mischief Tavern, 2011

The Wine Vaults on Fye Bridge Street was housed in a 16th-century merchant's house. In 1963 it was rechristened the Mischief, a name it still holds today.

 At one time a copy of Crome's version of Hogarth's sign of the 'Man Loaded with Mischief' hung outside. In today's politically correct world it has long since been removed.

In 1964 local jazz legend Albert Cooper, together with his brother Tony, launched a new folk club here: 'It was my brother Tony's idea to start the Jacquard

 Club. Folk music was becoming prevalent and he already had experience as he ran a trad jazz club called "Jazz at Studio 4" on Crown Road, We looked for a room and eventually found one at the back of the Mischief Tavern. It used to be the pub brewery and had a sloping floor and a gutter running through the middle. The landlord Leslie Izzard and his wife Billie agreed to let us use it every Thursday. He put in a bar that took up half of the room and then wanted to paint the panels various colours and call it the Harlequin Club. But we wanted a folk-oriented name with a bit of history to it. We came up with the Jacquard Club after Joseph Marie Jacquard who invented the first automated loom which was used to make Norwich shawls.

'You could fit in 80 people at a squeeze. Mind you it was then so packed you couldn't move. Performers included Judy Collins and Paul Simon. We paid them about £15 in those days, which was a fair bit but not a fortune. I performed as "Albert and the Jacquards" backed by Gerry Parish and Dave Keeley.

'Many club goers will remember the two golden cherubs that hung on the club wall which Tony and I rescued form the Old Hippodrome in St Giles. It was being demolished and we went to the site and asked the foreman if we could help ourselves. He gave us hard hats and said: "Take what you like, but be quick you only have ten minutes." They hung in the club until it closed on 17th October 1968 by which time membership had reached 900.'

Albert Cooper and Jacquards, Jacquard Club, c1965

Beehive, c1945
St Martin at Palace Plain
George Swain

Black Bull, undated
5-7 Magdalen Street
Derek McDonald's collection

City Arms, c1895
2 Princes Street
NCC Library & Info Service

Crown (left of Dog Market), 1936
29 Elm Hill
George Plunkett

Cupid & Bow, 1938
23 St Martin at Palace Plain
George Plunkett

Duke of Connaught, 1960
72 Prince of Wales Road
Derek McDonald's collection

Duke of Marlborough, 1936
29 Fishergate
George Plunkett

Evening Gun, c1910
7 Rosary Road
NCC Library & Info Service

Jack of Newbury, 1959
19 Fye Bridge Street
George Swain

Jolly Dyers, c1930
16 Fishergate
NCC Library & Info Service

King's Arms 1953
1 Rosary Road
George Plunkett

Lord Raglan c1990
30 Bishop Bridge Road
Derek McDonald collection

Masonic Tavern, 1905
24 Elm Hill
NCC Library & Info Service

New Star, 1958
8 Quay Side
Derek McDonald's collection

White Friars, c1890
13 Whitefriars' Street
NCC Library & Info Service

Sir Garnet, 2015

Market Place and Surrounding Area

Below is a list of the pubs, inns and taverns located in this area of Norwich. Those with a page reference have an entry or illustration. For further details see page 83.

Page	Pub Name	Location
	Adelphi	7 White Lion Street
	Albion	31 Market Place
	Baron of Beef	Market Place
156	Beaconsfield Arms	Pudding Lane
	Bear & Staff	14 Fishers Lane
172	Bedford Arms	13 Bedford Street
	Beehive	7 St Peter's Street
172	Black Horse Inn	23 St Giles' Street
172	Black Prince	4 Market Place
172	Blue Bell	21 Lower Goat Lane
156	Boar's Head	2 Surrey Street
	Bricklayers' Arms	2 Union Street
	British Lion	64 Coburg Street
172	Castle Hotel	3 Castle Meadow
	Club House Tavern	Old Post Office Court
	Coach & Horses	3 Red Lion Street
157	Coach & Horses	51 Bethel Street
	Coach & Horses	1 - 3 Coach & Horses St
172	Coachmakers' Arms	3 Bethel Street
	Cock	78 Upper St Giles' Street
	Corn Exchange Vaults	Exchange Street
	Cricketers' Arms	15 Red Lion Street
158	Curat House	2 - 4 Haymarket
	Curriers' Arms	16 St Giles' Street
	Edinburgh	11 Dove Street
	Eldon Stores	2 Bethel Street
	Farriers' Arms	7 - 9 Pottergate
172	Fishmongers' Arms	8 Market Place
172	Free Trade Tavern	35 St Peter's Street
	French Horn	7 Bedford Street
172	Fruiterers' Arms	2 - 4 White Lion Street
159	George & Dragon	18 Hay Hill
	Goldbeaters' Arms	20 Bethel Street
173	Goose & Gridiron	Little Orford Street
173	Grapes Hotel	1 Earlham Road
	Green Dragon	Little London Street
159	Guildhall Stores	2 Market Place
173	Half Moon	38 Market Place
	Ipswich Tavern	4 St Stephen's Plain
173	Ironmongers' Arms	1 Lobster Lane
160	Jenny Lind	11 Market Place
	King's Arms	5 Bethel Street
	King's Head	93 Upper St Giles' Street
160	King's Head	8 Castle Street
161	Lamb Inn	Old Haymarket
161	Light Horseman	20 Westlegate
173	London Restaurant	2 Brigg Street

Page	Pub Name	Location
	Market Stores	22 Haymarket
	Mitre Tavern	8 Brigg Street
173	Mortimer's Hotel	34 St Giles' Street
	Nelson Tavern	17 Bedford Street
162	Norfolk Hotel	25 St Giles' Street
	Oak Shades	11 Lower Goat Lane
173	Old Theatre Tavern	17 Bethel Street
163	Orford Arms	25 Red Lion Street
	Peacock	1 Red Lion Street
173	Pope's Head	St Peter's Street
173	Punch Bowl	37 Market Place
	Queen's Hotel	4 Exchange Street
174	Queen's Head	90 Upper St Giles' Street
166	Rampant Horse Hotel	Rampant Horse Street
166	Raven Stores	1 St Giles' Street
	Royal Exchange	38 Julian Street
174	Royal Exchange	44 Market Place
167	Royal Hotel	16 Gentleman's Walk
	Royal Standard	12 Chapel Street
174	St Giles' Gate Stores	100 Upper St Giles' Street
168	Sir Garnet Wolseley (Sir Garnet)	36 Market Place
	Spear In Hand	27 Vauxhall Street
	Stanley Arms	23 Bedford Street
169	Star Hotel	10 Haymarket
	Suffolk Hotel	33 Market Place
	Sun Stores	5 St Giles' Street
	Theatre Stores	Theatre Street
169	Tuns Inn (Temple Bar)	2 Unthank Road
174	Two Necked Swan	42 Market Place
	Unicorn Inn	28 St Stephen's Street
	Vauxhall Tavern	47 Vauxhall Street
	Victoria Tavern	2 Horace Street
170	Vine	7 Dove Street
	Vine Tavern	1 Upper St Giles' Street
174	Volunteer Stores	1 Chapel Field
170	Walnut Tree Shades	Old Post Office Court
174	Waterloo Tavern	43 Market Place
174	Wheatsheaf Inn	14 Bethel Street
	White Hart	39 St Peter's Street
174	White Horse	20 Haymarket
	White Lion	10 White Lion Street
	White Rose	10 Back of the Inns
170	White Swan	31 St Peter's Street
	William IV	26 Salford Street
171	Wounded Hart	17 St Peter's Street
174	York Tavern	2 Castle Meadow

Bear &
Staff

Holy
Apostle
R.C.
Church

Grapes
Hotel

Kings
Head

St Giles

Vine
Tavern

St Giles
Gate
Stores

Queens
Head

Cock

Mortimers
Hotel

Tuns
Inn

Volunteer
Stores

Coach &
Horses

Coachmakers
Arms

CHAPELFIELD GARDENS

Spear
in
Hand

Theatre
Stores

Victoria
Tavern

Congregational
Chapel
and
School

Vauxhall
Tavern

Royal
Exchange

Bricklayers
Arms

Coach
& Horses

Royal
Standard

British
Lion

William
IV

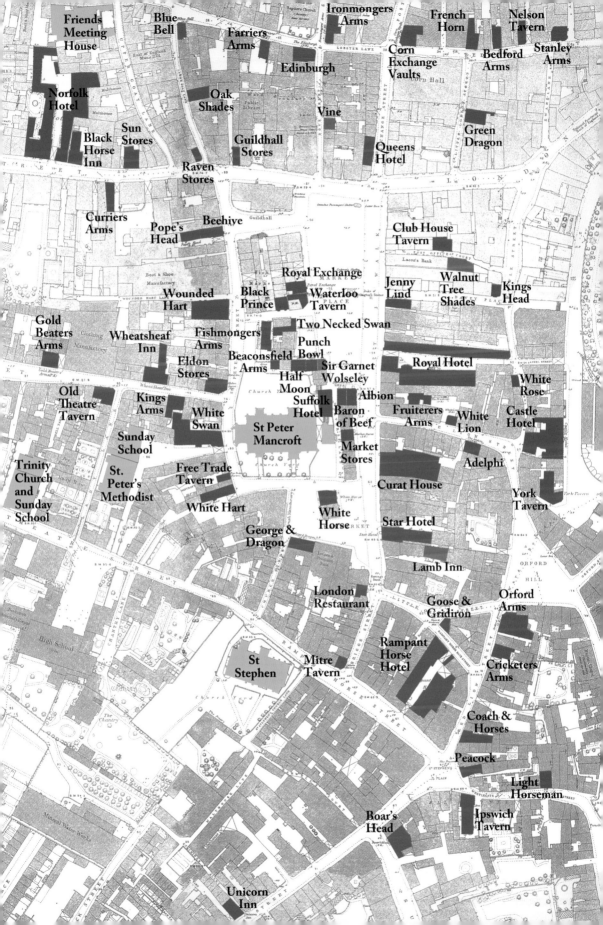

Market Place and Surrounding Area: Historical Background

Vegetable Market and Guildhall, David Hodgson, undated

This map covers Norwich's commercial centre. Where you have shops and trade you also need food, drink and lodging yet even by 19th-century standards the concentration of inns and taverns around the Market Place was phenomenal.

Norwich's provision market still trades on the same site that it occupied in the 11th century, when it was established by Norman merchants within the protective shadow of their new Castle. Additionally, in medieval times and beyond, a number of subsidiary markets operated within this area including the horse market outside St Stephen's Church, and the livestock market on the Haymarket.

In 1884 there were over 70 hostelries within the near vicinity of the Market Place. Not only did they serve as watering holes and long-distance coach stations they also provided business premises, salerooms and entertainment venues. Of particular importance were the coaching inns. At least four opened onto the Walk and were all of similar construction. Narrow gateways opened onto long yards which were overlooked by guest rooms on the first and second floors. Public

rooms were grouped around the ground floor and included warehouses used by itinerant dealers for the storage and sale of their stock. Other coaching inns covered in this section are the Norfolk Hotel (St Giles' Street) and the splendidly named Rampant Horse Hotel, which derived its name from the nearby horse market. The area was almost a coaching equivalent of a railway station. The thought of all those horse drawn vehicles making their way into a bustling city-centre almost defies imagination.

Some of the City's major buildings have been built around the Market Place. These include the Guildhall, St Peter Mancroft and in later years the City Hall.

In 1404 King Henry IV gave a new charter to the City whereby Norwich became a county in its own right and could elect a mayor, 24 aldermen and 80 councillors. Civic government had outgrown the Market Tollhouse and so in 1407 work was started on a new Guildhall. Although it cost around £500 to build, at a time when the City's income was £120, it proved to be money well spent as the building still survives today, albeit with a few Victorian embellishments.

154

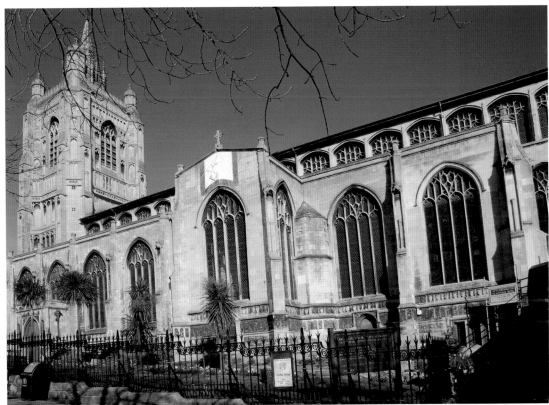

St Peter Mancroft , 2007

Less than 30 years after the building of the Guildhall the magnificent St Peter Mancroft Church was built adjacent to the Market Place. It was largely financed by the City's merchants who had amassed great wealth. Unlike the Guildhall, which was built from local flint and to a budget, this was a building designed to flaunt the wealth of its benefactors. Dedicated to St Peter and St Paul, it replaced the Norman church built by Ralph de Guader.

In the early 20th century many of the hostelries highlighted on the 1884/5 map ceased trading. Some were 'closed under compensation' and their licences were transferred to public houses in the newly built suburbs, others were demolished in the 1930s after the decision was made to erect a new City Hall.

In 1937 the foundation stone was laid to build the new City Hall as part of a £348,000 scheme which also incorporated the redevelopment of the Market, building the Garden of Remembrance and the widening of adjacent roads. Six years earlier Charles Holloway James and Stephen Rowland Pierce had beaten off more than 140 rivals to win a national competition to design the building. Despite this the scheme did not win universal approval. Indeed not only did it prompt two local enquiries but its rather Scandinavian style (likened to the Stockholm Town Hall) led some to dub it 'the marmalade factory' whilst the well-known artist John Piper rather scathingly wrote 'fog is its friend'. It was even suggested that Hitler entered into the debate promising to 'bomb it before it was paid for'. Notwithstanding such criticism the renowned architectural historian, Nikolaus Pevsner, describes it as 'the foremost English public building of between the wars'.

Although many of the hostelries covered in this section have now been demolished their stories and pictures live on.

Did You Know?

The 'Back of the Inns' is the name still given to the narrow lane which runs from Arcade Street to White Lion Street. It took its name from the old inns and taverns which literally backed onto it including the Royal and the King's Head.

Beaconsfield Arms

Church Stile, by Edwin Edwards, 1880

The Beaconsfield Arms stood to the north of St Peter Mancroft Church on Pudding Lane. Named after Benjamin Disraeli (the Earl of Beaconsfield), it took over the site of the Church Stile in 1881, the year its namesake died. It only survived for nine years which is in contrast to its rather colourful predecessor.

 The Church Stile took its name from the old custom of drinking beer at the church gate at the church's expense on certain holy days in the ecclesiastical calendar.

 The inn was a favourite with travelling showmen who seemed to specialise in wild animals, particularly reptiles. In the Norfolk Chronicle of 25th April 1801, 'lovers of natural curiosities' were invited to view 'the largest rattlesnake ever seen in England, 45 years old, near 9ft long, in full health and vigour'. A footnote that 'a quadruped is to be put in the rattlesnake's cage at 12 o'clock on Thursday next', no doubt provided further excitement.

Walter Wicks speculates that the feeding of reptiles with a live 'quadruped' was a big attraction, especially as it was customary to admit persons free of charge who produced live cats and rabbits at the pay box! Although the mind boggles at a visit from a rattlesnake, in August 1806 this feat was surpassed by the visit of 'a most surprising crocodile from the Nile ever seen in the kingdom. He is so remarkably tame that any lady or gentleman may touch him with safety.' It is rather interesting to speculate what the public reaction would be if such a spectacle were advertised today!

Boar's Head

Boar's Head, 1934

 The Boar's Head on Surrey Street was housed in a 15th-century building that at one time was the home of Richard Browne, sheriff in 1449 and mayor in 1454. It was originally called the Greyhound but by 1840 the premises, together with the adjoining property and yard, had been purchased by the Norgate family whose coat of arms incorporated a boar's head, hence the change of name.

In the early 19th century the Boar's Head was particularly popular with farmers and hence was extra busy on market days. Walter Wicks reports: 'The large dining room was well patronized and in the kitchen could always be seen on Saturdays three or four spits loaded with meat before a roaring fire.'

 In the mid 19th century the landlord, Fred Philips, tastefully fitted out a room capable of seating 200 visitors. Called 'The Shades', it was an attempt to introduce Norwich citizens to the delights of the Music Hall. In 1854 the Norfolk Chronicle explained: 'Every evening there is to be a vocal and instrumental concert by London professionals, who are almost weekly changed so as to secure as large an amount of novelty as possible.' Unfortunately it was not a success, in fact the old-fashioned music hall style of entertainment never really took off in Norwich.

 In 1902 Arthur Turner was appointed as Norwich City Football Club's secretary. Arthur was the manager of the Boar's Head from 1908 to 1916 and so the hostelry naturally became the HQ of City's first Supporters' Club. They met here until they outgrew the venue. Norwich City is believed to be the first team in the country to have a supporters' club, which means that the Boar's Head holds the accolade as being the first venue in the country to hold supporters' club meetings.

Coach & Horses

Coach & Horses with landlord Philip Beck, 1963

Boar's Head, 1942

The Boar's Head was badly damaged in the Baedeker Raids of April 1942. Visiting the ruin in 1946 Leonard Thompson describes standing '…in the midst of the somewhat insecure-looking ruin which presented bleak and blasted frontages to St Stephen's Street and Surrey Street. Tufts of grass were thrusting through the floor on which we stood, and above our head massive first-floor oak rafters were in much the same position in which they had rested for five centuries.' Eventually the original building was demolished rather than restored. Construction took place further back from the original site which conveniently allowed the road to be widened in line with a proposal that had been made in the 1930s but rejected as the historic building could not be destroyed. At this time the ancient hall behind, with its vaulted brickwork cellars, was also lost despite arguments that it was repairable.

The hostelry finally reopened c1952. In 1966 it was given a 'Flemish' makeover complete with a huge Flanders' tapestry and a Windmill Salon which incorporated a model Dutch windmill. Not surprisingly the look doesn't appear to have caught on and in 1972 all these decorations were removed.

 The premises were eventually converted into a large dimly lit room with no windows and it was reinvented as a music pub with a dais built at one end for groups and a large dancing area. As described by John Riddington Young: 'The music was loud; the atmosphere was smoky and tense; the clientele was young and bucolic; but the Boar's Head has a character all of its own.' Sadly very much like Fred Philips' earlier attempts to establish music at the Boar's Head, this venture was unsuccessful. The hostelry eventually closed in the autumn of 1974.

Parts of the Coach and Horses on Bethel Street are said to date back as far as 1200.

On the wall a rare stone parish boundary marker, dated 1710, marks the division of the St Peter Mancroft and St Giles parishes. This was the site of the once popular Ascension tide custom of 'beating the bounds' whereby choirboys were 'bumped and dusked' at their parish boundaries to ensure that they would not forget where the parish ended.

In 1987 the Coach & Horses was obtained by Greene King via a swap for a Cambridge pub, and continues to be owned by them today. For many years the pub sported a deep red carpet and dark-wood panelled walls. Following a refurbishment to give it a 'new lease of life' these are no more, but the beams and exposed brickwork remain, ensuring that the historic character of this ancient pub lives on.

Coach & Horses, Bethel Street 2003

Curat House, Vine Tavern and Backs

John Curat, a mercer and notary who held the title of sheriff in 1529, built his house in 1480 on the site of the old Jewry which had been destroyed by fire in 1286. There have been many stories of the spirits of departed Jews haunting the site, including a certain Rabbi Isaacs who murdered his wife there in the 13th century.

By the 1840s this house on the Haymarket was in the ownership of the Back family. In 1855 Messrs Back & Sons were described as 'grocers, tea dealers, wine, spirit and hop merchants'. However, they were best known as being the leading vintners in the City. This activity was very much facilitated by the huge labyrinth of cellars beneath the house where the firm did their own bottling. Unsurprisingly this ancient house became known as Backs. From 1840 the premises also incorporated the adjacent Vine Tavern. In 1952 the Back family sold out to Hennekeys who owned the premises until its closure in 1971.

In 1925 Walter Wicks reported: 'Upon entering, one feels suddenly transported from the bustle and din of a sternly commercial age to the rollicking days of Falstaff and the merrie England of Good Queen Bess.' At this time the large lounge on the first floor was panelled with oak on which were carved the arms of the Mercers' and Scrivners' Guilds together with John Curat's arms, trademark and rebus. The latter consisted of a 'Q' and a rat. Other woodwork, which was described as 'more renaissance than English', is said to have been completed by Italian workmen, who had been engaged to complete carving work at the near by St Peter Mancroft Church. Beneath this, on the ground floor, was the Wine Room, which had a handsome 16th-century ceiling and a glass whose contents included a cannonball, found in the old chimney of the Curat's room above, reportedly fired by Kett's followers at the the King's troops who were stationed in the Castle ditches. Here was also housed the Long Bar were one could enjoy Backs' famous Norwich Silk Sherry.

Bram Lowe remembers visiting in the early 1960s: 'A pal of mine, Bernard Skipper was the area director

"Elizabethan Wine Room"
BACKS LTD. Wine Merchants, HAYMARKET NORWICH.

for Hennekeys, he had the off-licence adjacent to the Curat House on the Haymarket. The cellar had its own "tramway system" for trolleys which went on and on. They even used to bottle beers down there. The old bars were something else. One was a Gentleman's Bar, where city shopkeepers and businessmen went to drink and talk. You always knew who would be there. The only place you saw ladies was in the Elizabethan Bar (pictured above), which was presided over by a lovely old gent called Alfred Parsons who was your classic aged retainer. All was very nice and "oldy worldy". He'd prepare hot toddies in a brightly burnished kettle on the bar which he'd religiously boil and bring over to your table to serve.'

In 1962 the 'Long Bar' was damaged by fire, though luckily the building survived, and by the mid 1960s the house was described as a 'scheduled ancient monument'. In the 1960s the house catered for a wide range of clientele at lunchtimes. However, towards the end of its life it became the favourite meeting place for students from the 'new' university, who eventually took it over. Unfortunately the students did not possess the spending powers to support a bar of this size. Takings declined and in the autumn of 1970 the management took the unprecedented step of banning students. This was followed by a series of protests culminating in a student sit-in. The following year in May 1971 Backs closed and the property was taken over by Hepworth's tailors, an event described by John Riddington Young as 'one of the greatest single losses to the Norwich drinker'.

Backs, c1970

Backs 'Long Bar', c1970

George & Dragon

The George & Dragon operated on Hay Hill. It was built on the site of an inn with the rather unusual name of 'Abraham offering up his son'. In 1619 it became known as Abraham's Hall.

In 1763 it was licensed as the George & Dragon although during its lifetime it was also known as the George and the St George & Dragon. In the late 1970s during renovation work many ancient timber beams were discovered. Unfortunately these were not deemed to look 'authentic' so were clad with more 'realistic' polystyrene replicas!

Roger Cawdron, owner of the Ribs of Beef, recalls: 'I took over the George & Dragon in 1977 from a wonderful landlord called Frank Knight. He was an amazing character. He used to be a warrant officer in the RAF and sported a magnificent handlebar moustache. He was reputed to have the authority to sign off the nuclear bombs on Vulcan aircraft.

'It was a really busy pub and for a time we were renowned for the Cornish pasties made by my cook Lucy. On Saturday mornings it became quite a tradition to buy one of "Lucy's pasties". It was a very busy pub attracting both the Market stallholders and the "Trawler Boys" who worked on the fishing fleets in Lowestoft. It could be very rough, in fact it's the only pub where I've ever had a knife pulled on me. Luckily I come from a boxing family, both my brothers Andrew and Brian were well-known Norwich Lads' Club amateur boxers, and my assailant wasn't expecting a left hook.

'When I was given the licence of the Ribs of Beef I stood in court and said that Watney Mann had done something that the German's had never achieved when they closed the brewery on King Street. As a result they took the tenancy away from me, which at the time I thought was fair enough. But after a year they asked me back.'

The George & Dragon ceased trading in 1988 and was converted into a building society. The property now houses a McDonald's.

George & Dragon just before it closed in 1988

Guildhall Stores

Located adjacent to the Market Place the Guildhall Stores shared a yard with the neighbouring hostelry: the Labour in Vain. Both establishments can be traced back to the 18th century. When the two pubs amalgamated in 1877 the Labour in Vain ceased to exist. Eventually in 1934 the Guildhall Stores was closed under compensation

 John Crome is believed to have painted the sign for the Labour in Vain which tastelessly showed 'two women engaged in the fruitless task of trying to scrub a little black boy white'. An errand boy is reputed to have chopped up the original pub sign for firewood.

John Riddington Young tells the story of a Navy press gang visiting Norwich at the beginning of the 19th century which set up its HQ at the Labour in Vain. In an attempt to prevent them using brutal methods, Norwich Corporation offered a bounty to each man who joined. Despite the offer of eight guineas for every able-bodied seaman and two for an ordinary seaman, naval life obviously did not appeal to Norwich citizens as only eight signed up.

The building at the rear of Labour in Vain Yard provided stables for the fire-station horses whilst the upper floor space housed the pulley wheel mechanism used for grinding mangels for feed. Since being renovated the Yard has been the home of various retail outlets (most notably the Rainbow wholefood shop) and restaurants.

Labour in Vain Yard, 2009

Jenny Lind

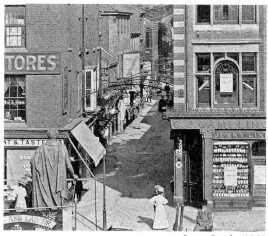

Jenny Lind, c1910

 The Jenny Lind (Market Place) was located on the corner of Davey Place and Gentleman's Walk. Licensed in the second half of the 19th century it took its name from the famous singer, also known as the 'Swedish Nightingale', who appeared in Norwich four times between 1847 and 1862. She was very popular and is still remembered for the money she bequeathed to a local children's hospital, since named after her. Before the Corruption and Illegal Practices Act of 1833 it was particularly busy during elections when candidates for Parliament threw money from the windows and bought voters beer and pies in a bid to gain popularity.

The house was closed under compensation in 1924. Today it is a coffee shop.

King's Head

King's Head, by Robert Dighton, 1799

The King's Head was originally located on the Market Place. It was a popular coaching inn particularly favoured by Parson Woodforde, the Rector of Weston Longville, who often stayed here and featured it in his 'Diary of a Country Parson'.

 It was also famed for offering outstanding entertainment, including prize fights, plays and natural curiosities. Thus it was here in 1729 that the Norwich Company of Comedians presented 'Macbeth with all the witches'

songs and dances'. In 1797 the major attraction was the 'greatest' man in the world, namely the Irish giant with the stage name O'Brien (real name Patrick Cotter) who was eight feet four inches tall (his skeleton is preserved in the museum of the Royal College of Surgeons in London). In 1807, 200 spectators witnessed a prize fight between the two noted pugilists of the day, Tom Cribb and John Gulley. It all goes to make today's pub entertainments a little tame!

 During this time the Norwich Mail Coach Office was located at the King's Head. In 1802 two mail coaches travelled from here to London daily, one running via Ipswich the other via Newmarket. The fare for either coach was 42 shillings for inside and 22 shillings for outside. In the same year a new service between the King's Head and the Globe in King's Lynn was being advertised. Potential customers would have been pleased to hear that the proprietor considered it his duty 'to treat the passengers with every attention and civility, and to take especial care in the conveyance and speedy delivery of all parcels and game'.

In 1813 the inn relocated to Castle Street when the original building was destroyed to make way for Davey Place. At the time Alderman Davey, a Baptist radical, found it amusing to announce that he would 'blow a hole in the king's head', which resulted in his house being put under guard. Thus proving that it is not a good idea to crack political jokes when there is danger of revolution! It continued trading through to 1981 after which the building became the home of the Body Shop.

Lamb Inn

Entrance to the Lamb Inn, 2015

 Following the Norman invasion in 1066 a Jewish Ghetto was established in the area between the Haymarket and White Lion Street. In 1296, four years before Edward I expelled all Jews from England, it was ravaged by fire. Subsequently part of the area, including that now occupied by the Lamb (Old Haymarket), was settled on the Church of the Mass of Jesus, in nearby St Peter's. When an inn was established it was given the suitably ecclesiastical name of the 'Holy Lamb' later abridged to the 'Lamb'.

Over the years the Lamb has developed a somewhat sinister reputation, the following event may go some way as to explaining why!

 In 1783 John Aggas was the landlord here. By all accounts he was a popular and friendly man. In later life he married a young lady called Alice Hardy. Alice's brother Timothy was a ne'er-do-well who not only moved in with the couple but also took to helping himself from the till and the cellar. This incensed John who ejected his brother-in-law from his premises. Timothy was much aggrieved and took his custom to the nearby Magpie on Orford Hill. Here he fell in with some ruffians who decided to visit the Lamb in the hope of getting a few free drinks. The rowdy group, led by Timothy, fell foul of John Aggas who forcibly evicted them. All was well for a while then on 5th November 1787 Timothy and his unwholesome friends were debating whether their evening's entertainment would be to attack the Watch or to rob the communion plate at St Peter Mancroft. At this point Timothy remembered the grudge he bore his brother-in-law and on the stroke of midnight the motley crew broke into the Lamb cellar, where they were heard by the landlord. An enraged John ran down to the cellar where he was stabbed in the belly by his brother-in-law. As Aggas fell his assailant ran into the arms of the Watch who took him to the City Gaol. It is said that Timothy had nightmares about the dreadful deed he had committed, but not for long, as soon afterwards he was publicly hanged under the shadow of Norwich Castle.

More recently, in 1979 the premises was renovated. It was decided that spreading sawdust on the floor would create an authentic and convivial atmosphere, a view not shared by the health and fire authorities who condemned the building as a fire hazard. It subsequently reopened with a brand new carpet! Then in 1996 there was much consternation in the City when it was rechristened the Rat & Parrot eventually becoming Henry's Cafe Bar. However, this popular venue has now reverted to its ancient name and once again invites customers to enjoy a 'traditional pub and dining' experience.

Light Horseman

'Barking Dickey', 1965

 From around 1830 to 1858 the Light Horseman on Westlegate, sometimes called the Light Dragoon, occupied an attractive 16th-century timber-framed cottage. However, it is still better known as the Barking Dickey. The name is believed to derive from the pub's badly painted sign which appeared to depict the soldier's mount as a donkey (or dickey) braying or 'barking'.

Norfolk Hotel

Hippodrome, 1966

The Norfolk Hotel (St Giles' Street) became one of Norwich's foremost inns during the 'Golden Age' of coach travel. By 1837 there were ten daily coach departures including the Phenomena, which traversed the route to London. It was drawn by six grey horses and driven by George Wiggins. In 1838 Wiggins was presented with a silver cup at the Norfolk Hotel 'in testimony of the respect for his general good conduct during his dragmanship of 11 years on the Norwich and Lynn road'. He eventually overturned the coach in a fog and died shortly after at the age of 38.

Another noted 'coachey' was Thomas Thoroughgood who was known to have a 'safe pair of hands'. Thomas drove the Times coach daily from the Norfolk Hotel to the Swan with Two Necks (London). During his career he drove in excess of 182,300 miles and never suffered an accident. His reputation contrasted somewhat with that of 'Mad' Windham, who was not given his nickname lightly!

Frederick William Windham's family owned the Felbrigg estate. He was something of an eccentric and lived a life of debauchery and excess. 'Mad' Windham set up a Norwich to Cromer coach, which became the terror of travellers along the country roads. Not only was Windham's driving suspect, but also his passengers could never be sure of reaching their destination as 'Mad' Windham had a tendency to divert to Yarmouth without giving notice. After squandering his fortune he eventually spent his final days living in a small room at the Norfolk.

On a different note the author George Borrow often visited the hostelry in the 1870s. When he came to his 'fine old city' he stayed in Lady Lane (which was located in the area now occupied by the Forum) and could often be seen passing along Bethel Street through Rigby's Court on his way to the Norfolk, where he met up with his friends.

The demise of coaches also brought about the end of the Norfolk Hotel. In 1898 its freehold was bought by a syndicate of investors for £9,500. In 1902 its vacant cleared site was sold to Fred Morgan, the manager of Norwich Theatre Royal, who employed the theatrical designer W G R Sprague to design the Hippodrome Theatre. This was opened in August 1903 as 'The Norwich Opera House and Theatre of Vanities'. Some of the greatest names in entertainment performed here between the wars including Charlie Chaplin, Marie Lloyd and Gracie Fields. It closed in 1966 and is now the site of a multi-storey car park.

Did You Know?

The White Horse pub, which stood on the Haymarket, didn't have an adjacent yard so one of its more intrepid landlords converted its underground cellar into a stable for customers' horses.

Orford Arms and the Orford Cellar

The licence of the Orford Arms (Red Lion Street) can be traced back to 1865. In 1925 it became very popular as it was the only hotel in Norwich with a silver grill. For the princely sum of 2/6d on Saturday nights 200 diners would be served with: soup, steak or chop, potatoes, vegetables 'in season', sweet, biscuits and cheese.

 In 1962 Douro Potter and his family returned to Norwich from Leicester, and took over the lease of the Orford Arms. Douro's original intention had been to run a traditional pub and supplement his income by providing B&B accommodation in the eight bedrooms that were included with the tenancy. However, this did not prove to be financially viable. As a result Douro was happy to allow local agents to book acts for the Cellar, a room located under the main pub. It was this decision which gave the premises a cult status and ensures that those who visited the Orford in the heady days of the 1960s still remember it today. At its peak the Cellar had the atmosphere of the famous Cavern Club in Liverpool. Its maximum capacity was 300 yet incredibly it played host to performers who became international stars such as: Eric Clapton, Rod Stewart, Ginger Baker and Gino Washington. Additionally many local groups performed here including: The Continentals, Lucas & the Emperors and Gary Freeman & The Contours.

Harvey Platt remembers the Orford in the 1960s:

'It had three bars on the ground floor. One was known as the Big Room which, on the back of the popularity of the Orford Cellar, became an entertainment venue in its own right. It had fluorescent lights picking up the vivid Day-Glo wall coverings, which included a big picture of Al Capone, and an extensive juke box. One night my brother Howard booked the Moody Blues to play there whilst the Continentals performed in the Cellar.

'For some reason the Big Room attracted a lot of local villains, who weren't always too subtle. Take the occasion when the milk company on the Larkman estate was robbed. There was a lot of money in the safe so it received extensive local publicity. Amazingly the boys who did it turned up two days later in brand new suits, which were a bit of a giveaway.'

In this era it really was a family business. The guest rooms were soon occupied by the many musicians who played at the venue and Lily Potter (landlady) became renowned for her large breakfasts and home cooking. Her sister, who was in her 70s, was recruited to serve in the cellar a couple of nights a week and was very popular with the customers.

Meanwhile Douro Potter's son, also called Douro (who subsequently took on the tenancy of many City-centre pubs including the Woolpack and the Gardeners' Arms), became the barman in the Cellar. It was here that he met his wife Jenny who used to socialise there before she eventually gave up her office work and started to work behind the bar full time. On one particularly busy Friday night she was pulling pints when she started having labour pains and had to be rushed to hospital where she gave birth to their son.

Andy Field (member of the group The Continentals) recalls that young Douro had a great sense of humour: 'We'd all grown up with the Goons who we loved. Harry Secombe, playing the part of Ned Seagoon used to ask for "a whisky and pronto" meaning give me a whisky quickly. However, the barman played by Spike Milligan always responded: "A whisky and pronto coming up immediately", as though pronto was an addition to the drink. This really tickled Douro so he made a little sign saying, "Pronto 3d Extra" and attached it to a gin bottle filled with water. I can remember some of the Jack the Lads of the day ordering a "gin and pronto" and being convinced they were getting something extra.'

By the end of the 1960s the Orford's popularity was waning. Around 1967 many had turned their backs on the traditional Rock & Roll and Rhythm & Blues bands which had made the Cellar such a popular venue. For the vast majority seeing a band was no longer the most important part of a night out and listening to records became a more popular form of entertainment. In 1970 the Potters gave up the tenancy of the Orford Arms and in 1974 the venue was closed. Today a building society occupies the premises.

Orford 'Big Room', c1965

Memories of the Orford Cellar

Andy Field was a member of the popular local group The Continentals which performed at the Orford Cellar in the 1960s:

'The group all came out of skiffle and at the time as young lads we all wanted to be guitarist. My pal Harvey Platt blagged his way into The Continentals by claiming that he could play bass. None of us could read music so we'd listen to the record, decide what key we'd do it in, sort out the chords and that was it. We steered clear of the songs everyone else played and tended to do the 'B' sides which we'd then make our own. We specialised in R&B and introduced Norwich people to material by artists such as Ben E King, the Drifters and Little Willy John. Over the years the line up of The Continentals changed quite a lot. Though we did sometimes have a guest singer in the Orford days we were a quartet made up of myself, Harvey Platt, Ivan Zagni and Denny Royal. Even now people tell us we had a 'sound' but I'm not sure how you'd have defined it.

'The Cellar held about 300 people in those pre Health and Safety days. The only way in and out was one little staircase. It was so narrow people couldn't pass on it. It was hot, it was black, it had condensation dripping off the walls. It really was Norwich's "Cavern".

'In 1966 we joined the Decca record label who renamed the group the News. I left in 1967 but the band continued to play in the Cellar as the News. Over the following years they had many different line-ups and eventually went on a tour of the Far East. If anyone had told me then that in the 21st century people would still remember The Continentals I wouldn't have believed them. It's great that they do.'

Ray Lince, recalls: 'Douro contacted Brian Epstein, manager of the Beatles, as he wanted to book the Fab Four. He received a letter back in confirmation that they would perform for an evening at a fee of £75.00. There was, however, a proviso that if their new release, "Please Please Me", reached the Top Ten, the fee would treble to £225.00. Douro couldn't risk this outlay and cancelled the booking. He always regretted the decision and kept Epstein's letter for many years!'

Harvey Platt a fellow member of The Continentals remembers:

'My brother Howard was a local promoter, his strength was working with pop artists. From 1962 Howard organised pop events in the Cellar. Performers he brought to Norwich included Rod Stewart and Cream. In the early 60s promoters had clubs where all their bands played, so Howard thought it would be a good idea to do the same with the acts he managed which included my group The Continentals.

'At one time Douro Potter and I got involved with Scalectrix racing and we built a huge track around the beer barrels in the pub cellar, which was located behind the bar of the Orford Cellar. All the visiting acts wanted to join in. I remember playing there with Long John Baldry, Andy Summers from the Police and even with Rod Stewart.'

Andy Field, c1966

Harvey Platt, c1966

Gary Freeman and The Contours in the Cellar, 1965

Orford Arms, c1960

Gary Freeman recalls: 'We first performed in the Cellar in 1962 and subsequently played there another 75 times. In the early years we tended to play tunes made popular by groups such as the Beatles but later, when we started to meet and mix with the black Americans, we sang more soul music.

'It was always a fantastic evening at the Cellar. There was a certain amount of kudos attached to playing there. You knew that if you were invited to perform that you weren't a bad band.'

Bram Lowe, who was both sales director of Woodforde's and local Chairman of CAMRA, was also closely linked with the Cellar:

'In the 50s I was a brass musician based in London where I played in clubs and got to know a lot of people "on the scene". From 1960 through to 1967 I booked acts for the Cellar. I started by holding a modern jazz evening on Tuesdays. I was than approached by a friend called Howard Platt who'd been playing banjo in a trad-jazz band called the Collegians. He wanted to put on some Rock & Roll on a Sunday night. I said "yes" and he packed out the Cellar. Howard was always very much in tune with the pop scene.

'I then started R&B on a Wednesday night. We had people like Georgie Fame and Graham Bond. They were great characters. In fact my best nights at the Orford were when the Graham Bond Organisation performed. Graham played the organ, Ginger Baker was on drums, Jack Bruce on bass and Dick Heckstall Smith on the tenor sax. It was fantastic.

'You could get 300 people in the Cellar but then it was packed. It wasn't worth trying to smoke a cigarette because you were unable to lift your hand. The only place you could drink a beer was by standing at the bar. The dressing room consisted of a broken piece of mirror that hung behind the bar.

'In 1967 I was contacted by Charles Chandler, who was bass player with The Animals. He'd met this guitarist called Jimi Hendrix and asked if we could put him on. I'm not a fan of loud zingy guitars so I wasn't keen but Howard thought we should book him. It was one of the last evenings I was involved in at the Cellar. We didn't pay him much, I think it was about £40. I'm often asked about that evening. We were full, but not packed, and Jimi was high as a kite. The only time I heard him say anything was when he stood in front of the mirror behind the bar, patted down his dreadlocks and said "Yeah man, yeah" than wandered off. Later I learned that his bass player didn't like the venue because it wasn't big enough to accommodate their equipment… well to be fair it probably wasn't.'

Bram Lowe (right) with Ray Ashworth, 1993

Rampant Horse Hotel

 The Rampant Horse Hotel (Rampant Horse Street) replaced a 13th-century inn that stood a little nearer St Stephen's Church. The somewhat unusual name is said to derive from the horse market that took place outside St Stephen's churchyard.

 As with so many of Norwich's inns the Rampant Horse was a venue for entertainments, which today seem a little bizarre. Thus it was here in 1784 that Dr Katterfelto, a notorious quack, astonished his audiences with his performances of 'perpetual motion and occult secrets'. His audiences watched in awe as he raised his daughter to the ceiling, they might have been less astonished if they had known that he was using a huge hidden magnet! It was also here, a year later, that Parson Woodforde observed 'the sagacity of the learned pigg', a black boar with a magic collar that could spell and add.

 During the late 18th and early 19th centuries the Rampant Horse became one of the City's premier coaching inns and provided a terminus for both local and national travel. In 1782 the first coach service to Ipswich was launched here. Additionally the Comet headed off for Great Yarmouth daily at 8am via Loddon, Haddiscoe and Southtown. By 1830 if you wanted to travel to London you had the choice of two daily coaches namely the Magnet that departed at 4.30am or the Telegraph, that left at 7am.

 Around the same time the Rampant Horse was the meeting place of the local medical fraternity. This was not a problem until a number of parcels, that looked like long boxes, were left here to be carried to London. Once suspicion was aroused one of the packages was opened and found to contain the body of a man recently deceased which had been dug up from the Old Lakenham churchyard. The cadaver was en route to the dissecting rooms of the London medical schools.

In the 1880s the Rampant Horse fell into decline and by 1900 it was demolished and the site became part of Messrs. Curl Brothers' drapery establishment which in turn was bombed in April 1942. Today it is the location of Debenham's store.

Raven Stores

Raven Stores, 1936

  In the years before WWII the Raven Stores (St Giles' Street) was a fashionable hostelry where gentleman would meet to play billiards in the upstairs room. Unless you were a barmaid or the landlady it was a definite men only zone! During much of this time (1928-1940) Albert Gosnell, NCFC's manager in the early 1920s, was licensee.

It is rumoured that the cellars link with a labyrinth of underground tunnels which lead to St Giles' Gate. Although this is unsubstantiated draymen had to bring special ropes, 50% longer than the norm, to lower the barrels into the tavern's vaults.

The pre-war photograph, taken by George Plunkett in 1936, shows the Raven before it was severely damaged during the Norwich Blitz in April 1942. Interestingly following the bombing a beautiful gable believed to date from c1450 was revealed. The building was closed for less than two years and recommenced trading on 11th April 1944. They continued to operate in the remnants of the building until c1955 when the premises was rebuilt. It continued to trade as the Raven until 1985 when it reopened as Refreshers. In 2009 it was reincarnated as an Italian restaurant.

Royal Hotel

The Royal Hotel was situated on Gentleman's Walk where it was first licensed c1840. It was located on the site of the Angel, an Elizabethan inn. Over the years this ancient hostelry was the scene of many events, some more outlandish than others!

 The Angel was the terminus for a number of coaches. From here you could travel daily to Yarmouth taking the Day post coach, which took three hours, or the Norwich and Yarmouth Telegraph which took half an hour less. From August 1814 the Telegraph which was 'a new and light day coach', departed from here for London at 8am every Monday, Wednesday and Friday. Inside seats cost 25 shillings and outside ones 15 shillings. The journey terminated at the Three Nuns in Whitechapel and took 13 hours.

 Like so many inns, the Angel was host to many entertainments and peep shows. These included a visit by a pair of elephants in 1685, followed by a series of 'monsters freaks and marvels'. Culture was introduced in 1696 when 'The Little Opera' played here, whilst in 1825 Monsieur du Pain provided the entertainment when he dipped his feet in boiling lead!

On a more serious note it played a part in events of civil unrest. Thus in 1648 it was mentioned in the trial of the Royalist rioters when a witness, Robert Haddon, stated that he 'had had a mug of beer at the Angel'.

In 1815 Lord Albemarle and TW Cooke (MP) were chased into the Angel by an anti-Corn Law mob that they had upset earlier at the Jolly Farmers, whence they had escaped after an enterprising butcher had freed a bull and twisted its tail so it had charged the crowd. The two fugitives remained trapped in the Angel until the military were called out and they were able to leave by the back door.

In the 1830s the Royal became the HQ of the Norwich Whigs who entered into a pitched battle, from here, against the Tories. Various missiles, reported to include bags of flour, were hurled from the Angel's windows and polling booths were torn down and set on fire. Throughout the proceedings, bands performed 'stirring tunes' until the fighting was eventually stopped following the intervention of the 7th Hussars.

Detail from the Market Place, unknown artist, c1850

On 18th July 1840 the demise of this colourful establishment was announced in the Norfolk Chronicle when it was reported 'The public are respectfully informed that the Angel Inn, Market Place, Norwich, having recently been disposed of, is now refurnishing and fitting up with every convenience for the reception of families and commercial gentlemen, and will in future be know as the Royal Hotel.'

Following the refurbishment it became one of Norwich's principal hostelries and was the venue for many sumptuous parties. Even when it was only six months old it was the venue for a banquet given by the Mayor to celebrate the christening of the Princess Royal, Queen Victoria's eldest daughter. 16 years later it hosted the celebrations for her wedding. Despite its popularity c1897 it moved to a new venue on Bank Plain and the hotel was converted into the beautiful Royal Arcade.

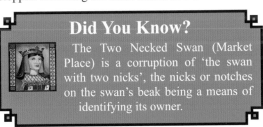

Did You Know?

The Two Necked Swan (Market Place) is a corruption of 'the swan with two nicks', the nicks or notches on the swan's beak being a means of identifying its owner.

The 'new' Royal Hotel on Bank Plain, postcard, c1920

167

Royal Hotel (cont.)

Royal Arcade, 2010

The Royal Arcade was designed by architect George Skipper in an Art Nouveau style. Glazed Doulton tiles depict peacocks whilst the flooring came from Italy and was laid by Italian craftsmen. When it opened in 1899 a local newspaper said: 'it's as if a fragment of the Arabian Nights had been dropped into the heart of the old City'. Nikolaus Pevsner, the renowned architectural historian, said it was 'innocent from the front, but very naughty once its back is turned'. Langley's Toy Shop is the only original business remaining in the Arcade.

When the Arcade was built it incorporated a new pub, the Arcade Stores, located on the corner with the Back of the Inns. In keeping with the rest of his masterpiece Skipper designed it in an Art Nouveau style complete with stained glass windows, bunches of grapes and William Morris designs. In 1962 it was sold and the premises were divided between a dress shop and a butcher's shop. Today the space is occupied by a Jamie Oliver Italian restaurant.

Arcade Stores, 1955

Sir Garnet Wolseley (Sir Garnet)

Sir Garnet, 2015

The Sir Garnet Wolseley (Market Place) started trading as a public house c1861. It was originally called the Baron of Beef, possibly because the premises used to be a butcher's shop.

 In 1874 it adopted the name Sir Garnet Wolseley. It was named after Field Marshal Garnet Joseph Wolseley, 1st Viscount Wolseley, who in the same year received accolades for his brilliantly executed Ashanti campaign. The Field Marshal's reputation for efficiency led to the late 19th-century phrase 'everything's all Sir Garnet', meaning 'all is in order'. The sign depicting the Viscount on his horse and resplendent in his uniform (see below) was designed and painted by Peter Burrows.

In the 20th century the pub extended in size when it took over 37 Market Place, which had previously traded as the Punch Bowl. In July 2012, after a major refurbishment, it was renamed the Sir Garnet. Today, as it has been through its long history, the building is distinguished by its curved facade overlooking the Market.

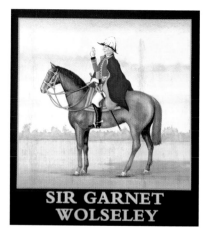

168

Star Hotel

The Haymarket, David Hodgson, 1825

The Star Hotel (Haymarket) was a coaching inn. As early as 1684, in the early days of stage wagons, conveyances travelled from here to Diss. At the height of the coaching era coaches ran from the Star to both London and across East Anglia. For example, if you wanted to travel to London overnight the Phoenix coach left at 4pm and arrived at the Bull Inn, Aldgate at 8am the next morning. Alternatively if you only wanted to travel as far as Bungay you could catch the Eclipse.

The Star put on a selection of shows to entertain its customers. It particularly seems to have excelled itself on 27th December 1783 when it advertised the arrival of 'a capital collection of wild beasts' to the premises. Ladies and gentlemen were charged 6d whilst tradesmen and children paid 3d and servants 2d to view a selection of curiosities including: 'A beautiful lion from Algiers, being the only one alive that travels . . . an amazing large black wolf from Siberia . . . the female satyr . . . an Ethiopian savage from the Island of Madagascar . . . and a curious night walker from the Island of Borneo.' Visitors would have been pleased to know that: 'The Collection is well secured and kept clean!'

After the end of the coaching era it was unable to survive and finally closed in 1894. The Star features above in David Hodgson' painting of the Haymarket.

Tuns Inn (Temple Bar)

Tuns, 1937

The Tuns Inn (Unthank Road), now rechristened the Temple Bar, survived when many of its immediate neighbours were demolished to make way for the inner ring road.

It used to be thought that the house was as old as the Adam & Eve (Bishopgate), however, this listed building is now known to date back only as far as the17th century. Its age has been 'disguised' by a 19th century facade.

In the 1860s, when election fever ran high, the Tuns espoused the cause of the 'Orange and Purples' (the Tories) whilst the nearby Grapes Hotel (Earlham Road) was a 'Blue and White' (the Whigs) stronghold. During the elections each house would put a placard announcing the 'state of the poll' on an hourly basis which led to many lively altercations on the plain separating the two establishments.

From 1892 to 1911 the Tuns was presided over by landlord 'Bob' Booty who, as a sideline, drove the Judges' carriage. Booty built a reputation for putting on convivial evenings remembered nostalgically by Walter Wicks who recalls him providing 'tradesmen's suppers of rabbit and neat's cheek, sumptuously served, invariably followed by an excellent smoking concert, when some of the best amateur talent in the county contributed to the harmony of the evening'.

Did You Know?

The Volunteer Stores (Chapel Field) was named to attract custom from the nearby drill hall that was used by the City of Norwich Rifle Volunteer Regiment. It was here in 1879 that the Norwich Amateur Bicycle Club was formed.

Vine

The Vine (Dove Street) is possibly best described as 'small but perfectly formed', but this has not always been the case.

The licence can be traced back to 1842 but when it closed in 2006 the end seemed nigh. Subsequently in 2008 it was rescued and reinvented. Today, despite being hailed as Norwich's smallest pub, the owners have also managed to integrate a Thai restaurant. This has been achieved by combining two miniscule rooms downstairs into an area containing four small tables and a tiny bar whilst the dining room is upstairs. Even more remarkable, given the size of the pub, they hold beer festivals and feature in the Good Beer Guide.

Vine, 2003

Walnut Tree Shades

The licence of the Walnut Tree Shades (Old Post Office Court) can be traced back to 1841.

John Riddington Young speculates that although the name was one frequently adopted by publicans who were also cabinetmakers, there is no evidence that this was the case here. In the past the premises were used by the Norwich Brewery as an outlet for trial brews and it is alleged that Starlight was first sampled here!

For many years the premises has successfully traded as an American bar and diner. It offers its clientele live bands, good food and a selection of ales.

Walnut Tree Shades, 2011

White Swan

 The White Swan (St Peter's Street) flourished as an inn as far back as 1648. Not only was it one of the City's premier coaching inns but it was also famous as a playhouse, indeed it was sometimes called the 'Metropolis of the East'. It was the HQ of the Norwich Company of Comedians from c1730 until 1758 when it was superseded by the first Theatre Royal. Undeterred by its loss of status it still put on passing shows. Thus in 1762 visitors could view an ox weighing more than 100 stone whilst in 1811 Napoleon's coach (allegedly!) was on show. It also continued to put on variety shows in its Little Theatre sometimes called the Large Room.

 In the early 19th century it was one of Norwich's principal centres for cockfighting. Matches normally lasted three days and would typically see the 'Gentlemen' of Norwich or Norfolk pitch their birds against the 'Gentlemen' of another East Anglian county or city. A fairly typical advertisement appeared in the Norfolk Chronicle of 5th April 1823 which announced: 'The annual great main [match] of cocks between the gentlemen of Norwich and Northamptonshire for £5 a battle and £200 the odd, will be fought at the White Swan Inn . . . on Tuesday 22nd April and the two following days. A silver tankard will be fought for by 16 subscribers. No cock to exceed four pounds ten ounces. The above to be fought in fair silver spurs.'

 The Large Room also proved a perfect venue for pugilistic pursuits. Thus for example if you had visited the inn on 4th July 1818 you would have been treated to a display of prize fighting by noted boxers of the day including Sprigg, Scroggins and Purcell. Then on 22nd July 1820 a huge party was held here to celebrate Ned Painter's historic victory over Tom Oliver after 12 rounds of boxing. The fight, which had taken place in a field near North Walsham, was said to have attracted a crowd of 20,000 people including the young George Borrow, who featured it in his acclaimed novel 'Lavengro'. The party was a benefit for Ned and was attended by many of the county's most noted boxers.

 The White Swan was the terminus for many coaching routes. In May 1780 the 'new and commodious' Flying Post coach departed from here on the 17-hour journey to London accommodating six inside passengers for the sum of 21 shillings each. As roads and vehicle design improved journeys quickened and by 1821 a coach was travelling between here and London in just 12½ hours. At the time this was the quickest advertised time for the journey.

At the height of the coaching age in the early 19th century the White Swan was one of Norwich's principal inns. Regretfully as coach travel declined so did the White Swan and it eventually closed in 1895. In 1947 Leonard Thompson describes what was the Large Room: 'It is a storeroom now, but there is still moulded plaster on its ceiling and walls, and the raised platform at one end is still proudly surmounted by a plaster shield bearing a faded coat of arms. It seems a pity that this room, which knew so much life and gaiety, should perforce suffer disintegration.'

In 1961 what remained of the building and the undercroft were pulled down to make way for a library and car park. At the time it was observed that one room used as a dining room in the Regency period had 13 wallpapers!

Wounded Hart (Heart)

Wounded Hart, 1934

 This ancient hostelry was located behind the Fish Market on St Peter's Street. Between 1823 and 1825 Ned Painter, the boxer whose benefit dinner was held at the White Swan, was the landlord here.

 In Whites Directory of 1836 it was noted for its religious sign which depicted a representation of the 'Sorrowful Mysteries of the Rosary' i.e. the Virgin Mary's heart pierced with five swords. In the same year the Oddfellows were introduced to the City and the first annual dinner of the Norwich Lodge was hosted here. By the end of the century the name had been changed to the Wounded Hart and the sign depicted a hart or stag wounded by an arrow. In 1915, in a fit of patriotism, the hostelry was rechristened as the Kitchener's Arms. It ceased trading in 1928.

In 1934 the building was one of many demolished to make way for the new City Hall.

Courtyard of the White Swan, c1960

Bedford Arms, 1968
13 Bedford Street
George Plunkett

Black Horse Inn, c1960
23 St Giles' Street
George Swain

Black Prince, 1938
4 Market Place
George Plunkett

Blue Bell, 1935
21 Lower Goat Lane
George Plunkett

Castle Hotel, 1984
3 Castle Meadow
George Plunkett

Coachmakers' Arms, 1924
3 Bethel Street
Jarrold & Sons

Fishmongers' Arms, 1925
8 Market Place
NCC Library & Info Service

Free Trade Tavern, 1936
35 St Peter's Street
George Plunkett

Fruiterers' Arms, 1967
2-4 White Lion Street
George Plunkett

Goose & Gridiron, 1890
Little Orford Street
NCC Library & Info Service

Grapes Hotel, 1937
1 Earlham Road
George Plunkett

Half Moon, c1890
38 Market Place
NCC Library & Info Service

Ironmongers' Arms, 1936
1 Lobster Lane
George Plunkett

London Restaurant, 1898
2 Brigg Street
NCC Library & Info Service

Mortimer's Hotel, 1969
34 St Giles' Street
George Plunkett

Old Theatre Tavern, 1959
17 Bethel Street
George Swain

Pope's Head, c1930
St Peter's Street
NCC Library & Info Service

Punch Bowl, 1934
37 Market Place
George Plunkett

Queeen's Head, 1938
90 Upper St Giles' Street
George Plunkett

Royal Exchange, 1875
44 Market Place
NCC Library & Info Service

St Giles' Gate Stores, 1964
100 Upper St Giles' Street
George Plunkett

Two Necked Swan, c1890
42 Market Place
NCC Library & Info Service

Volunteer Stores, 1964
1 Chapel Field
George Plunkett

Waterloo Tavern, 1900
43 Market Place
NCC Library & Info Service

Wheatsheaf Inn, 1934
14 Bethel Street
George Plunkett

White Horse, c1900
20 Haymarket
NCC Library & Info Service

York Tavern, 1895
2 Castle Meadow
NCC Library & Info Service

Below is a list of the pubs, inns and taverns located in this area of Norwich. Those with a page reference have an entry or illustration. For further details see page 83.

Page	Pub Name	Location
	Albert Tavern	36 Ber Street
193	Anchor	21 Rising Sun Lane
	Bakers' Arms	9 Ber Street
193	Bartholomew Tavern	27 Thorn Lane
181	Bell Hotel	Orford Hill
	Bird in Hand	75 King Street
193	Boilermakers' Arms	57 King Street
	Bricklayers' Arms	9 Farmers' Avenue
193	Buff Coat Inn	21 Cattle Market Street
	Builders' Arms	52 - 54 Cattle Market St
	Carpenters' Arms	33 Thorn Lane
	Cattle Market Inn	2 Farmers' Avenue
193	Cellar House	109 King Street
182	Cock Tavern	34 Crown Road
	Eagle & Child	3 Market Avenue
	Elephant & Castle	120 King Street
	Engineers' Tavern	17 St Julian Street
	Exhibition Tavern	20 Ber Street
193	Express Train	63 Rose Lane
180	Foundry Bridge Tavern	69 Rose Lane
194	Free Trade Tavern	41 Rose Lane
183	Gardeners' Arms	2 - 4 Timberhill
194	Globe	17 Globe Lane
194	Golden Ball	18 - 19 Cattle Market St
194	Great Eastern (Nelson)	111 Prince of Wales Road
194	Green Man	131 King Street
	Hop Pole Gardens	St Faith's Lane
	Jolly Farmers' Inn	5 Farmers' Avenue
	Jubilee Inn	21 Ber Street
	King's Arms	8 Ber Street
	Lion Inn	31 Cattle Market Street

Page	Pub Name	Location
	Lion & Castle	27 Timberhill
184	Nag's Head	33 Crown Road
	Napier Tavern	1 Farmers' Avenue
	Nelson	45 Timberhill
194	Nelson's Monument	66 King Street
185	Norfolk Railway House (Compleat Angler)	Prince of Wales Road
186	Old Barge	123 King Street
188	Orchard Tavern	38 Mountergate
189	Plough Inn (number 12)	1 Market Avenue
180	Princess of Wales	25 Rose Lane
190	Queen of Iceni	6 Riverside Development
	Red House	33 Timberhill
	Rose Tavern	25 Thorn Lane
	Rose Tavern	2 Rose Lane
	Royal Oak	46 King Street
	Royal Standard	12 Ber Street
190	Shirehall Tavern (Owl Sanctuary)	25 Cattle Market Street
	Sons of Commerce	30 Thorn Lane
	Star & Crown	20 Timberhill
	Steam Packet	92 King Street
191	Steam Packet	39 Crown Road
	Thorn Tavern	25 Ber Street
	Three Tuns	60 King Street
	Toper's Tavern	2 Thorn Lane
191	Tuns Inn (Pig & Whistle)	2 All Saints Green
191	Waterman	142 King Street
	White Hart	6 Ber Street
	Windmill	24 Ber Street
192	Woolpack Inn	9 Golden Ball Street

175

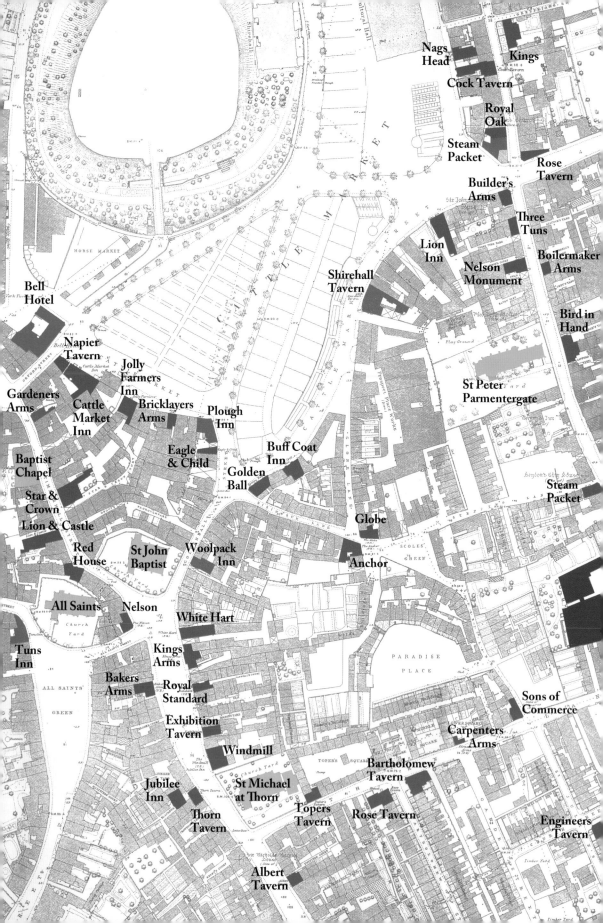

Nags Head

Kings

Cock Tavern

Royal Oak

Steam Packet

Rose Tavern

Builder's Arms

Three Tuns

Lion Inn

Nelson Monument

Boilermaker Arms

Bird in Hand

Bell Hotel

Napier Tavern

Jolly Farmers Inn

Shirehall Tavern

St Peter Parmentergate

Gardeners Arms

Cattle Market Inn

Bricklayers Arms

Plough Inn

Steam Packet

Baptist Chapel

Eagle & Child

Buff Coat Inn

Golden Ball

Star & Crown

Globe

Lion & Castle

Red House

St John Baptist

Woolpack Inn

Anchor

All Saints

Nelson

White Hart

Tuns Inn

Kings Arms

PARADISE PLACE

Bakers Arms

Royal Standard

Sons of Commerce

Exhibition Tavern

Carpenters Arms

Windmill

Bartholomew Tavern

Jubilee Inn

St Michael at Thorn

Thorn Tavern

Topers Tavern

Rose Tavern

Engineers Tavern

Albert Tavern

Free
Trade
Tavern

Express
Train

Foundry
Bridge
Tavern

Norfolk
Railway
House

Princess
of Wales

Great
Eastern
Hotel

Orchard
Tavern

Hop Pole
Tavern

King St.
Old Brewery

Malthouse

(Home of
Morgans Brewery)

Cellar
House

Elephant
& Castle

Malthouse

Queen
of Iceni

Old Barge

Green
Man

St Julian

Malthouse

Waterman

Malthouse

South-East Central Norwich: Historical Background

River Wensum, view from Carrow Bridge, undated

This area of Norwich contains two of the City's most important historic buildings, namely the Castle and Dragon Hall. It also features the river Wensum and numerous yards and additionally played host to the Cattle Market. All of these have had an impact on the development of its numerous drinking establishments.

Robert Toppes (1405-1467) built his magnificent trading hall on King Street c1403. Being a rich merchant the main hall, on the first floor, was built to impress. It was 88ft long. Its crown-post roof was made using expensive oak timbers and incorporated 14 carvings of dragons. Although only one of these mythical creatures survives the building is now known as Dragon Hall. In the 100 years after Toppes' death the building served as the town house of wealthy citizens. Subsequently as trade and industry spread along King Street the elite moved out and the hall was divided up to provide much needed living space. Extra floors, staircases, windows and chimney stacks

filled the Great Hall and the yard at the rear (Old Barge Yard) was filled with poor-quality housing. The ground-floor rooms had many uses, in particular they played host to three alehouses namely: the Black Horse, which had closed by 1880, the Two Merry Wherrymen and the Old Barge.

The Normans built Norwich Castle between 1067 to 1121. Today only the mound and keep survive, but the original earthworks once covered 23 acres and included stone gatehouses, stables and grazing meadows. As the City grew, the south bailey became the Cattle Market. From about 1300 the Castle was used as a prison and was host to numerous public hangings. In 1883 the county jail moved to Mousehold Heath in Norwich. In 1884, when the map was produced, local architect Edward Boardman would have been in the process of drawing up plans to convert the Castle keep into a museum, a role it still has today.

Norwich Cattle Market, c1890

The Cattle Market was held on the same site in the centre of Norwich from at least the 17th century. At this time it was decreed that it should be held in the castle dykes. To accommodate it banks were removed, ditches filled in and rows of houses were demolished. The market took place here on Saturdays until 1960, after which the site was converted into a car park, and later the Castle Mall shopping centre opened in 1993.

Ber Street became an adjunct to the Cattle Market. Every Saturday morning, and at the great Christmas and Easter fairs, animals were driven up the thoroughfare. On these occasions the sheer number of animals led Alfred Mottram to describe the street as: 'A "parking" place for drove after drove of frightened,

fidgeting, lowing beasts, rounded up and kept together by drovers and dogs until a place could be found for them in the iron fenced pens in the Cattle Market.'

Ber Street also provided parking for the carriers' wagons and private gigs driven into the City by the thousands who travelled from across the county to attend the market. They all had a horse to stable and of course they all needed sustenance, both of which were provided by the numerous public houses that populated the adjacent streets. Not surprisingly in the area we see a number of establishments whose names were influenced by their proximity to the Market including : the Plough Inn, the Jolly Farmers' Inn and of course the Cattle Market Inn.

Did You Know?

Norwich Castle had the largest castle mound (motte) in the country.

Did You Know?

On the Thursday before Easter the 'Hogget Fair' was held on the Cattle Market when upwards of 20,000 sheep and 2,000 cattle descended on the area.

Chris and Ruby Baker recall visiting pubs around Rose Lane in the 1930s

Chris and Ruby Baker, 2009

Princess of Wales, c1900

'Most of the pubs on Rose Lane were little corner places, they were like the front room of a house. The only food would be crisps and nuts. They were a meeting place for locals, a bit like community centres today. You knew that your friends would be there on a Saturday night and that's where we'd all meet up. In most pubs you'd have bar games such as cribbage, shove ha'penny and darts. We mostly went out at weekends, you couldn't afford more than that. If you went out midweek, you'd have one drink and that would be that.

'Most pubs had a bar and a smoke room. Many had a snug. If you saw a chap skulking in there you thought they had gone there to get away from their wife. You could always get sweets in the snugs, they were like little shops.'

Chris often visited the Foundry Bridge (Rose Lane): 'George Cousins and his wife kept it in the late 1930s till he was called up. I went in the forces then as well so I don't know what happened to him. It was very basic. There was a fairly big corner bar with a small smoke room and they had living accommodation upstairs. Customers were mainly locals.'

Moving up Rose Lane Chris would have arrived at the Express Train: 'It was on the corner of Bloomsbury place. It was just like a part of a house. There wasn't much to it just a bar and a smoke room. There was a piano in the corner but customers made their own entertainment. Mr Potter was the landlord, I don't remember much about him, he seemed old to me but I was just a young lad then.'

Further along Rose Lane was the Free Trade Tavern: 'I lived practically next door when I was a boy so I knew the landlady Polly Horstead even though I was just a lad. Her husband was the landlord, but she ran it on her own. She ran a good house, but was very strict. She was a bit of tartar and very blunt.'

After Chris met Ruby they visited some of the pubs together, but there were a few to avoid. So for example: 'In the 1930s we all steered clear of the Princess of Wales (Rose Lane), because it was used by "ladies of the night". The others were more family places where you'd go to meet your neighbours.'

It was different at the Cock Tavern (Crown Road): 'We used to go to the Cock Tavern just before the War when we were courting. The landlady was a proper bar lady, she had big dangly earrings. It was a lot bigger than the places on Rose Lane. You used to go in on King Street and work your way through and come out on Crown Road. It was really friendly. As soon as you went in you were included. You didn't sit there like wallflowers. You'd soon all be playing darts.'

Finally: 'One of our favourite pubs before the War was the Builders' Arms on the Corner of King Street and Cattle Market Street. We really liked the landlord Jim Barber and his wife. They always played Bing Crosby records. We used to stand at the bar and give requests. Whenever we hear a Bing Crosby record now we always think of old Jim.'

Foundry Bridge Tavern, 1962

Bell Hotel

Bell Hotel (Castle Hotel in foreground) c1930

The Bell on Orford Hill (known as the Blue Bell from c1763 to c1822) was likely to have been in existence in the late 15th century. By the early 18th century it was an established hostelry and a renowned venue for cockfights. Thus it was in 1725 that the landlord advertised that '…there will be a great cock match at the Blue Bell…to show 31 cocks…Gentlemen shall be accommodated with a glass of excellent wine and care taken to prevent disturbance by the mob'.

In 1759 Samuel Barker, landlord, claimed erroneously that his establishment was the first house at which porter (a malt liquor) was sold in Norwich. He also advertised that he would keep 'a large quantity [of porter] always bottled and fit to drink' which he sold at 'five shillings the dozen [13 bottles to the dozen] or three shillings and bottle returned', so launching the sale of bottled beer in Norwich.

The Bell has been the home of a number of organisations including the notorious 'Hell Fire Club'. Formed in the mid 18th century it consisted of ruffians who described themselves as 'gentlemen of principles inimical to government and with a determination to crush the Methodists'. The Bell was only one of the clubs where the gang met to plan their vicious attacks on this religious group. Others included the White Lion (White Lion Street) and the Castle Inn (Castle Meadow). The group are particularly remembered for disrupting meetings led by John and Charles Wesley, who first visited Norwich in 1754.

In 1764 the Bell Corporation (governed by the mayor, sheriffs and various civic officers) was founded. Originally it was considered to be highly respectable but in 1793 the French Revolution created a rift in the membership. As a result the anti-revolutionaries moved down the road to the Castle Inn (Castle Meadow). The remaining members, consisting of 'a considerable number of inferior tradesmen and three or four merchant manufacturers', formed themselves into the Bell Revolution Club whose maxims were mainly those of the French Revolutionists. Although their activities were closely monitored there are no reports of them being involved in violent activities.

In the 19th century the Bell continued to be linked with a variety of clubs and societies. In 1858 it hosted the first annual dinner of the Norfolk and Norwich Anglers' Society. In October 1881 it was the venue selected to celebrate the golden jubilee celebration of the Eldon Club, which also held meetings here. Club members included the Duke of Wellington.

Although not a leading coaching inn, the Bell was a terminus for some of the more important local coach journeys. For instance the Norwich and Yarmouth Volunteer made regular runs from here to the Wrestler in Yarmouth.

Around 1890 parts of the Bell which fronted the present main road from Castle Meadow were pulled down. Luckily the main part of building survived.

During the 20th century its fortunes were mixed. In WWII it played its part in the war effort when it was used as headquarters and billets for the American Women's Army Corps. Then, following a period of closure, on 12th December 1993 the J.D. Wetherspoon group opened their first pub in the City in part of the building. This popular venue continues to thrive.

Cock Tavern and Studio 4

Bell Hotel, c1890

The pictures above and below show the Bell before and after buildings were demolished to make way for trams in the 1890s.

Cock Tavern after closure, 1982

Bell Hotel, 1936

The Cock Tavern had entrances from both King Street and Crown Road. Around 1960 the premises was effectively split into two venues, the second being Studio 4. Both served under one licence.

 In 1958 the Agricultural Hall became the Headquarters of Anglia Television. It had three studios so 'Studio 4' seemed an appropriate name for the 'new tavern' which opened opposite.

 In the 1960s a trad jazz club called 'Jazz at Studio 4' was run here by Tony Cooper. In the mid 1960s Tony, together with his brother Albert Cooper, went on to set up the Jacquard Club at the Mischief Tavern (Fye Bridge Street).

Visiting it in 1975, John Riddington Young noted that the picture rail in the smoke room 'boasts of the many celebrities who have visited the pub whilst appearing on Anglia Television'.

Gardeners' Arms (The Murderers)

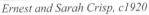

Ernest and Sarah Crisp, c1920

The Murderers' pub sign

The licence of the Gardeners' Arms on Timber Hill can be traced back to 1841 but the building itself dates back to 1696. It has a fascinating history.

 Since the early 20th century it has been better known as the Murderers. For many years it was believed that it received its somewhat sinister nickname after a prostitute was murdered there by a client. However, following research by Philip Cutter, who has worked at the pub for over 20 years and is now the landlord, this was not the case. Philip discovered that in 1895 the landlady's daughter, Milly, was separated from her husband Frank and living at the pub. Frank, an ex-cavalryman, who worked for Morgans, wanted to be reconciled with his wife but suspected that she was seeing another man. One night he attacked Milly after which he immediately turned himself over to the police. Three days later she died and Frank faced a sentence of death by hanging. However, there was a huge outpouring of public sympathy which resulted in 16,000 people signing a petition and Frank's sentence was commuted to life imprisonment.

Ernest and Sarah Crisp (pictured above outside the Gardeners' Arms) ran the pub from 1915 to 1926. When they started in the trade Ernest was 29 and Sarah 24 and they already had four small children. Sarah managed the pub, which was also a lodging house, whilst Ernest continued to work as a carrier and horse dealer. In 1916 Ernest joined the Army Veterinary Corps. Although he survived and was awarded the British and Victory Medals he suffered the long-term effects of mustard gas. They gave up the licence c1926.

 In 1970 the pub was closed by Watneys and for a time it was used for a charity shop. Then in 1976 it was reported that Douro Potter the 'uncrowned king of the City-centre pub trade', working with partner Ray Lince, was about to spend £20,000 on renovating the premises. At the time they wanted to officially change the name to the Murderers but tentative enquiries at City Hall were not encouraging. Undeterred a new sign was painted portraying 'The Murderers' on one side (see above) and the 'Gardeners' Arms' on the other. An arrangement which carries on to this day.

Gardeners' Arms (cont.)

Nag's Head

Gardeners' Arms landlord Philip Cutter, 2011

In 1991 the pub took over the adjacent property and now also incorporates the Murderers' Cafe Bar. It is very popular and not only features in the Good Beer Guide but has also been listed in the Lonely Planet travel guide as a 'must visit' attraction.

The landlord, Philip Cutter, is well known as the co-chair of Norwich's City of Ale Festival which was first held in 2011. This popular event celebrates and promotes Norwich's vast selection of quality pubs and fine ales.

Nag's Head, August 1938

By 1900 the Nag's Head, originally on Crown Road, had relocated to King Street. At one time it held an early morning licence for the benefit of the employees at the nearby Post Office.

 Not surprisingly photos of the pub in 1938, 1957 and 1990 all show it had a sign picturing the head of a horse. The name, however, does have three possible origins. Firstly the word nag is believed to have evolved from the Dutch word negge, meaning a small horse. The word now usually applies to a horse that is old and decrepit but it originally meant a horse for riding as opposed to one for pulling a carriage. Whilst on a long trip travellers often needed to change horses which they could hire from wayside inns and taverns. Such places were likely to have advertised this service by displaying a sign outside depicting a nag's head. The second explanation dates back to around 1700 when pirates returning from the Caribbean waited offshore under cover of darkness for a sign that it was safe to land. Onshore an accomplice would fix a lantern around the neck of an old horse and walk the 'nag' along the cliff top as a signal to the ship that the coast was clear. The bobbing lantern was known as the 'nag's head'. The final explanation relates to the other meaning of nag, i.e. someone who carps and criticises.

Visiting the house in 1975 John Riddington Young reported that the house was very popular with 'the prosperous television crowd from nearby Anglia House'. It has since traded as Tusks, Barrio and Kings, before closing in 2014.

Gardeners' Arms, 2011

Norfolk Railway House (Compleat Angler)

Compleat Angler, 2015

In 1844 the original Thorpe Railway Station was opened in the area now occupied by the Riverside car park. The station and adjacent buildings were described in the Norwich Mercury as being: 'Situated on the meadow about 60 yards from the Foundry Bridge. They consist of a terminus 360ft long, in two compartments 50ft wide, each roof covering two lines of rail. To the north is the booking office, with a room for ladies. At each end of this side is a large door for third-class passengers to enter and retire, the first and second passing through the booking offices. The south side is open, the roof being supported by iron pillars and on arches, forming a very light and elegant appearance.' In 1886 it was replaced by the current building.

 In January 1851 seeing the opportunity to provide refreshments for travellers, Richard Bullard bought the Foundry Bridge toll house (Prince of Wales Road) from the Norwich Corporation. He subsequently converted it into the aptly named Norfolk Railway House, sometimes called the Toll House.

The pub contained an annexe called the Blue Room. Built practically on the bridge you could walk through it onto the river walk. In the 1950s there were still many American airmen stationed in Norfolk and, sadly, some pubs refused entry to black Americans. Not so at the Blue Room. Despite the risk of losing trade, black airmen were welcomed in and it became one of their main meeting spots in Norwich.

Compleat Angler sign, 2011

 In the 1960s it featured many local groups. Bob Cossey recalls playing there with his group Exhibit A: 'One of our first City-centre bookings was in the Blue Room, which could be a bit rough. We always set ourselves up in a corner so that we were able to jump over the amplifiers. They acted as our barricade in the event of trouble!'

 From 1958 to 1967 the landlord was Harry Proctor. Harry played briefly for Norwich City in both the 1930s and 1940s and also had a spell as their trainer.

 In 1973 it was closed for refurbishment, reopening in 1974 as the Compleat Angler. The 'Compleat Angler' in question is a book by Isaac Walton. First published in 1653 it is a celebration of the art and spirit of fishing.

The pub continues to be very popular today. Here customers can enjoy sitting on the patio overlooking the river and of course it's still very handy for the railway station!

Did You Know?

Following a visit to the Broads in the 1930s children's author Arthur Ransome set the opening paragraph of Coot Club (1934) at Norwich Railway Station.

Old Barge Yard, by Thomas Lound, c1850

Numbers 113 to 123 King Street, now known as Dragon Hall, 1935

The Old Barge, called the Two Jolly Wherrymen in the 18th century, owes its name to the proximity of the River Wensum. It in turn gave its name to the yard that is located behind which during the 19th century was filled with low quality housing.

Inhabitants of Old Barge Yard included cowmen, who grazed cattle over the river, and brewery workers. The yard and their buildings were demolished in 1937 as part of the City Council's slum clearance programme. One cottage survived and today this forms part of the Dragon Hall complex.

In 1948 Fred Hall began a three year stint as landlord. Fred was Norwich City's goalkeeper in the 1930s and throughout the War. The pub continued to trade until 1969 when Watney Mann closed it although they continued to use it as a training centre .

As noted previously, the Old Barge was part of the medieval building known as Dragon Hall. In 1979 Norwich City Council bought the Old Barge, together with its neighbours, which enabled essential repair works to be completed. Following an extensive renovation the Dragon Hall has been returned to its former medieval glory and is now acknowledged to be one of the most important historic buildings in Norfolk.

Medieval entrance to Dragon Hall, 1978

187

Orchard Tavern

The licence of the Orchard Tavern (Mountergate Street) can be traced back to the mid 19th century. Andy Field, member of the 1960s group The Continentals, recalls how his family had a lucky escape from there during WWII:

'Before I was born my parents kept the Orchard Tavern which they took on at the end of 1937. At the time you couldn't live on the income generated from keeping a pub and so, during the day, my dad worked at Laurence and Scott's. We had a cellar under the pub with an entrance on the street outside where barrels were lowered in. After the start of the War, when he left for work, dad always told mum that if we had an air raid she was to get herself and my brother and sisters into the cellar at all cost.

'Early evening on Monday 2nd December 1940, whilst dad was still at work, there was a raid. It was so sudden that mum didn't have time to get down into the cellar so she just grabbed the kids and they all dived under the kitchen table. This was a very good thing because a bomb dropped through the cellar hatch, in the pavement outside, and exploded in the cellar itself. The force took off the front of the pub. Meanwhile, by an amazing stroke of luck, a large beam remained in position just over the table where my family were sheltering and they all scrambled out. There wasn't a scratch on them!'

Later that month Lacons informed the magistrates that the house would be demolished. It was never rebuilt.

Orchard Tavern, December 1940

Orchard Tavern, December 1940

188

Plough Inn (number 12)

Plough Inn, 1967

number 12, 2011

 The Plough Inn (Market Avenue), sometimes called the Plough & Horses, would have received its name because of its proximity to the Cattle Market.

After being bombed in 1943 it was closed as a public house and was used by the American Army as headquarters for the Military Police. In 1973 it was taken over by Douro Potter and renamed La Rouen.

After trading for over 150 years it was temporarily closed c1995 after it was discovered that the Castle Mall development had undermined the building. However, it did reopen during the construction and became a favourite with the site workers for good food and a welcome pint or two.

Today it trades as the number 12 bar and restaurant where customers can relax in rooms full of charm and character.

Plough sign visible on photograph above

number 12 signage, 2015

Queen of Iceni

Queen of Iceni, 2011

In 2001 Wetherspoons opened the Queen of Iceni on the City's new Riverside development. The site, which covers around 42 acres, had previously been used for industrial purposes. It now incorporates a range of ventures and activities including both retail and leisure.

 The premises take its name from Queen Boadicea who ruled the Iceni tribe of East Anglia, alongside her husband King Prasutagus, during the 1st century AD. Following the King's death Boadicea led her tribes in an ultimately unsuccessful, but heroic, revolt against the Romans. Although not slain in battle, she killed herself with poison rather than suffer the ignominy of being taken prisoner.

The rather wonderful sign (pictured below) shows an image of the statue of Boadicea, designed by Thomas Thornycoat in 1902, which overlooks the River Thames in London.

Shirehall Tavern (Owl Sanctuary)

Shirehall, 1989

The Shirehall Tavern (Cattle Market Street) was located very close to the Cattle Market. As a result it was very popular with farmers and dealers who could use the large yard at the rear to store pigs and cattle.

 It is reputed to have once provided lodgings for judges sitting at the nearby Shirehall, the building which gave the establishment its name. Historically the Shirehall was the centre of jurisdiction and administration for the county. As early as 1270 a Shirehouse was located next to the Castle and was subsequently rebuilt in 1579 on the castle mound. In 1821 it was relocated to the base of the mound, where it stands today. It is still linked to the Castle by a tunnel which was originally used to take prisoners between the courts and the prison (which was located in the Castle). In 1988 the courts moved to a new site by the Cathedral and the building now houses the Regimental Museum and Norwich Castle Study Centre.

 In July 1840 the renowned pedestrian John Mountjoy set off from here to complete a twice daily return walk to Symonds Gardens in Great Yarmouth for six consecutive days, a daily distance of 76 miles. On the final day there was much jollification at the tavern when he successfully completed his challenge.

 In the latter part of the 20th century the pub has enjoyed mixed fortunes and a number of name changes. Today it is called the Owl Sanctuary, the name deriving from the comedy show 'I'm Alan Partridge' (Season 1 Episode 2). It is a popular music and arts venue.

Steam Packet

Market Tavern, 1987

 There were three Steam Packets open within the City-centre in 1884. The definition of a steam packet is 'a ship that sails a regular route between two ports'. In the late 1800s such a steam ship travelled from Norwich to Bramerton Woods End, Coldham Hall and other riverside resorts.

The Steam Packet on Crown Road has undergone many name changes since it opened c1840. Not surprisingly, in view of its vicinity to the Cattle Market, for most of the 20th century it was called the Market Tavern. It was here that farmers would have come to make many transactions.

Pub historian, Derek McDonald, knows the Tavern well: 'I lived in the Market Tavern from 1958 to 1962. In those days we still had the Cattle Market and on market days the pub was always full of farmers. I quite enjoyed it. In fact I even got a job on the Market. Every Saturday morning I used to work for a couple of blokes from Yorkshire. They bought around 100 head of cattle and we had to walk them up Cattle Market Hill and down Ber Street to Trowse station. I earned five bob for a days work.'

In 1993 the premises was again christened the Steam Packet, a name it still holds today.

Did You Know?
The Cellar House (King Street) was once home of the 18 Stone Club, Membership being conditional on minimum weight.

Tuns Inn (Pig & Whistle)

Tuns, 1938

 Although the licence to the Tuns can be traced back to the early 19th century, the present building dates from 1937. In 1971 it was extensively modernised by Douro Potter and was also first christened the Pig & Whistle. At this time it sported a sign showing a pig playing a whistle, which is the modern interpretation of the pub's name. In fact pig comes from the Saxon word 'piggin' which means a milking pail and whistle comes from 'wassail' which means to be in good health.

Since 1991 it has undergone many name changes, but in 2013 it reverted back to being the Pig & Whistle.

Waterman

 A Waterman was a person who managed or worked on a boat. The Waterman (King Street) would have received such a name because of its proximity to the river. Open from at least 1802 many of its landlords had alternative occupations. One of them was a barber who put up a notice outside saying: '*Roam not from pole to pole but step in here, where nought excels the shaving but the beer.*'

Waterman, sign

Woolpack Inn

The licence of the Woolpack (Golden Ball Street) can be traced back to the late 18th century. The original building (pictured right) was demolished when a new building was erected in 1938.

 At the time of the rebuild Morgans' brewery (who owned the premises) commissioned John Moray-Smith to produce six plaster bas-relief panels depicting aspects of Norwich's medieval wool trade, from which the pub gets is name.

The pub's heyday was in the late 1960s and 1970s when Douro Potter was landlord. Ray Lince, who began his licensed trade career working here with Douro explains why the Inn became so popular: 'Douro made sure that there were pretty girls behind the bar (always good for business) and brought in what were then thought to be very trendy ideas, like putting an "ice and a slice" in the vodka and gin and serving wine as an alternative to beer and spirits. The wine was supplied by the Norwich Brewery, based in King Street, and was called "Tarafino". This was, apparently, a bit of an acquired taste and wouldn't have suited today's sophisticated wine quaffers. It wasn't realised that white wine should be served chilled, and it was known at the Woolpack not as "Tarafino" but as "Parafino".'

Fellow landlord Roger Cawdron, a good friend of Douro remembers: 'He had a great advertising gimmick whereby he did a deal with a couple of car salesmen and persuaded them to park their more prestigious cars alongside the Woolpack. Having a Ferrari or an E-type parked outside was a good way of attracting customers in.'

 Harvey Platt, local businessman and friend also recalls how Douro recognised the importance of attracting local celebs: 'At the time footballers were starting to be fashionable and Kevin Keelan, who played in goal for Norwich City from 1963 to 1980, became Douro's good friend and the Woolpack's number one fan. Kevin bought in the footballers, who attracted the girls who in turn attracted the boys.'

Harvey sums up the position: 'Douro made the Woolpack successful because he paid attention to all aspects of the business, from the music to how the girls who served looked and from the ambience to the food he served.'

The Woolpack remains open today and you can still see five of the Moray-Smith panels behind the bar.

Woolpack, 1936

Douro Potter (right) with friends, c1975

Woolpack, 1939

Anchor, 1936

21 Rising Sun Lane
George Plunkett

Bartholomew Tavern, c1940

27 Thorn Lane
NCC Library & Info Service

Boilermakers' Arms, c1900

57 King Street
NCC Library & Info Service

Buff Coat Inn, c1950

21 Cattle Market Street
NCC Library & Info Service

Cellar House, c1900

109 King Street
NCC Library & Info Service

Express Train, c1950

63 Rose Lane
www.norfolkpubs.co.uk

Free Trade Tavern, c1960
41 Rose Lane
George Swain

Globe, c1900
17 Globe Lane
NCC Library & Info Service

Golden Ball, 1961
18-19 Cattle Market Street
George Plunkett

Great Eastern Hotel, 1962
111 Prince of Wales Road
George Swain

Green Man, 1936
131 King Street
George Plunkett

Nelson's Monument, c1905
66 King Street
NCC Library & Info Service

King Street
Drawing by Edward Pococke c1890
Philip Armes collection

South-West Norwich

Below is a list of the pubs, inns and taverns located in this area of Norwich. Those with a page reference have an entry or illustration. For further details see page 83.

Page	Pub Name	Location
	Anchor	16 Surrey Street
205	Bull Inn	69 St Stephen's Street
200	Champion	101 Chapel Field Road
200	Coachmakers' Arms	3 St Stephen's Road
	Crown	1 Goldwell Road
205	Crown & Angel	41 - 43 St Stephen's St
	Curriers' Arms	114 Essex Street
	Curriers' Arms	12 St Stephen's Back St
	Duke of Wellington	42 St Stephen's Street
	Eastern Union Railway Tavern	1 St Stephen's Road
	George Inn	66 St Stephen's Street
	George IV	Chapel Street
	Globe	21 Globe Street
	Grapes	9 Howard Street
205	Great Eastern	75 St Stephen's Street
	Hoop	35 St Stephen's Road
205	King William IV	15 Coburg Street

Page	Pub Name	Location
201	Lame Dog	68 Queen's Road
	New City	70 Shadwell Street
202	Nursery Tavern (Trafford Arms)	Grove Road
	Queen Victoria	67 Queen Street
	Rose	59 St Stephen's Street
	Royal Oak	221 Essex Street
	Royal Victoria Tavern	2 Horace Street
	Sardinian Tavern	34 St Stephen's Street
	Shoulder of Mutton	53 St Stephen's Street
205	Surrey Grove Inn	74 Grove Road
201	Surrey Tavern	46 Surrey Street
204	Trowel & Hammer	25 St. Stephen's Road
204	Trumpet	72 St Stephen's Street
	White Horse	Crook's Place
	William IV	King Street
	Windham Arms	36 Trory Street
	Wine Vaults	1 Queen Street

Globe

King
William IV

Curriers
Arms

Methodist
Chapel

George
Inn

New City
Sunday
School

Champion

Trumpet

White Horse

Bull Inn

Curriers
Arms

Eastern
Union
Railway
Tavern

Great
Eastern

George IV

Royal
Oak

Malthouse

Coachmakers
Arms

Royal
Victoria
Tavern

William
IV

New
City

Queen
Victoria

Wine
Vaults

Trowel &
Hammer

Mission
Room

Hospital
Chapel

Hoop

NORFOLK & NORWICH

HOSPITAL

Windham
Arms

Grapes

Sardinian Tavern

Duke of Wellington

Crown & Angel

Shoulder of Mutton

Rose

Anchor

Baptist Chapel

Surrey Tavern

Lame Dog

Methodist Chapel

Surrey Grove Inn

Malthouses

Nursery Tavern

Crown

Napier Tavern

South-West Norwich: Historical Background

St Stephen's Street looking north, c1955

In 1885, in contrast to other areas of Norwich, this area of the City had relatively few pubs. Here were neat rows of terrace houses, substantial residences on Newmarket Road, the Victoria Railway Station and large tracts of market gardens.

The exception to this was the area either side of St Stephen's Gate. Here, as elsewhere, inns would have provided succour and accommodation to travellers who were stranded in, or out of, the City when the gates were locked. St Stephen's Gate, also known as Needham or Nedeham Gate, was on the south-west side of the City and was the principal entrance into Norwich. It was on the road from London and the street now known as St Stephen's ran straight down from the gate to the Castle. In fact, in 1578, it was through this richly decorated portal that Queen Elizabeth I entered the City on a state visit.

In the 18th century the gates and walls were no longer considered necessary for defensive purposes and merchants considered them restrictive to trade. Therefore in 1793 they were destroyed. The site of the gate is now completely occupied by a large roundabout which was built in 1964 at the junction of St Stephen's Street, Chapel Field Road, St Stephen's Road and Queen's Road. On the outside wall of the Coachmakers' Arms (St Stephen's Road), Moray-Smith's interpretation of John Ninham's image of the gate can still be viewed.

All of the pubs leading from the gates into the City-centre have been demolished. Most were destroyed when the street was widened and developed in the 1960s. It still remains one of the major shopping areas of the City.

Further around Queen's Road, next to the Lame Dog, was the location of the Brazen Gate (sometimes referred to as the Brazen Doors). It was very narrow and more of a postern than a gate. It was originally knows as the Iron Door, but in later years became known as the Gate of the Swine Market, since it led along All Saints' Green to Hog Hill, now Orford Hill, where pigs were sold until the end of the 18th century. The gate arch was rebuilt in 1726, when it was made wide enough for coaches and carts to pass through, at which time it was renamed New Gate. It was removed in 1792.

In 1885 the area was home to the Norwich Victoria Railway Station. It would be easy to assume that the Royal Victoria Tavern was named after the station, but this was far from the case. The tavern took its name from the Raneleagh or Victoria Pleasure Gardens. Before cheap rail travel was available it was here that many families spent their holidays promenading around the grounds, roller skating, listening to live orchestras, visiting the Adelphi theatre or even see a balloon ascent.

The highlight of any trip would undoubtedly have been a visit to the pantheon, a large arena which staged extravagant firework displays and circuses at Christmas. Sadly the gardens were destroyed in 1849 when the Eastern Union Railway built the Victoria Railway Station here. They even went so far as to convert the pantheon into the railway booking hall (pictured above). The terminus was never as important as Thorpe station and by 1914 it was only being used for freight travel. By the 1980s all of the railway buildings were destroyed. The Eastern Union Railway Tavern and the Great Eastern both served the station. In fact the Great Eastern, previously called the Beehive, held an extended early morning licence 'for the benefit of employees at the Carrow Works and Victoria Station'.

The area outside the City walls was the location of the Norfolk and Norwich Hospital (N & N). Behind it were neatly laid out terrace houses together with their corner pubs such as the Royal Oak (Essex Street) or the New City (Shadwell Street). The N & N was founded in 1771 as a charitable institution for the care of 'the poor and the sick'. The original building, designed by Thomas Ivory, had around 100 beds. In 1875 the hospital became a training centre for nurses and eight years later a new expanded hospital was open with 220 beds. Its site can be seen on the map. Despite being damaged during the Baedeker Raids of 1942 the hospital remained on the same site until

Eastern Union Railway booking hall, c1910

2003 when the last departments vacated the building. Expansion of the hospital and the development of new road systems led to much of the housing behind the hospital being demolished. Today the area is home to the Fellowes Plain residential development.

Norfolk & Norwich Hospital, 1955

Champion

The Champion (Chapel Field Road) was named after the boxer Daniel Mendoza (1764-1836) who was a renowned English prizefighter.

Before Mendoza, boxers generally stood still and merely swapped punches. Mendoza introduced a new 'scientific style' which incorporated defensive strategies to avoid punches. As a result Mendoza was able to overcome much heavier adversaries. Despite standing at only 5 feet 7 inches and weighing 160 pounds, from 1792 to 1795 Mendoza was England's Heavyweight Champion. He is also the only middleweight to ever win the Heavyweight Championship of the World. In 1789 he opened his own boxing academy and published the book 'The Art of Boxing'. After retiring from the prize ring he toured England's theatres, which included a visit to Norwich, with an act which depicted the various 'heroic styles of great boxers'.

The premises, now owned by Batemans, is a traditional pub offering its customers a selection of real ales.

Did You Know?

In June 1814 the author George Borrow and his family stayed at the 'Crown & Angel' (St Stephen's Street). This was Borrow's first visit to Norwich which he later famously described as a 'fine old city'.

Champion, 2011

Coachmakers' Arms

Coachmakers' Arms, 2015

The licence to the Coachmakers' Arms can be traced back to 1802, though it may have been trading before this date.

On the outside wall hangs Moray-Smith's bas-relief of St Stephen's Gate, based on a 1792 Ninham print. Made c1937 it is said to weigh a little under a ton and be the heaviest 'inn sign' in Norwich. The panel was made and modelled on site. The artist is still remembered standing on the scaffolding outside the pub, wearing jodhpurs and bright red stockings, putting the finishing touches to his work. In 2013 the Norwich Society paid for the renovation and repainting of the panel. Before the work was completed by the Fairhurst Gallery the image was looking very drab. The new bright colours are true to the original, ensuring that Moray-Smith's striking image once again captures the attention of all who see it.

St Stephen's Gate, bas-relief by Moray-Smith, 2015

Lame Dog

Lame Dog, c1970

The Lame Dog originally stood on Queen's Road halfway between St Stephen's Gate and the Brazen Doors where it did a flourishing trade in the days of the Victoria Gardens. In 1871 it moved down to 68 Queen's Road, to a site previously occupied by the Brazen Door pub, where it traded until around 1976 when it was demolished as part of a road widening scheme.

Michael Holmes has fond memories of the Lame Dog being the first pub that he visited for an illicit drink as a teenager: 'Before discotheques Norman's School of Dancing played pop music records on Friday and Saturday evenings. Entrance was 2 shillings (10p) hence it was a very popular venue for teenagers in the early 1960s. A few yards along the road the Lame Dog would happily serve a glass of mild and lime for 7d (3p) without worrying too much about proof of age. So needless to say it was a great favourite with youngsters.'

 John Crome painted a sign for the tavern in 1803, for which he charged the fee of one guinea. The name is said to come from the idiom to 'help a lame dog over a stile' i.e. to help someone in difficulty or in trouble.

 In 1934 Herbert Skermer, Norwich City goalkeeper from 1919 to 1922, became licensee, a post he held until the 1950s.

Surrey Tavern

Surrey Tavern, 2004

 The Surrey Tavern took its name from the street it stands on. In turn, Surrey Street was thus named in Tudor times, when the Earl of Surrey lived there. His mansion has long since disappeared. It was replaced in 1905 by the opulent Surrey House, designed by George Skipper as the new headquarters of the Norwich Union Life Insurance Society, now Aviva.

The hostelry is very popular with Aviva staff whose offices are located nearby.

Did You Know?
Surrey House contains the stunning Marble Hall (pictured below) which is decorated with marble originally destined for Westminster Cathedral.

Surrey House, Marble Hall, 2006

Nursery Tavern (Trafford Arms)

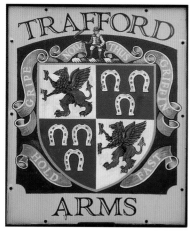

Trafford Arms after bomb damage, 1942

The licence of the Nursery Tavern can be traced back to 1865. It is possible that the first landlord, Robert Allen, continued his horticultural activities as well as being a publican, hence the name. In 1886 the Nursery Tavern was demolished and the licence was transferred to a new building that was erected on what is today 61 Grove Road. The new premises, the Trafford Arms, continues to trade on the same site today.

 The Trafford Arms was built on the Trafford estate from which it takes its name. The pub's sign (above) has always been the Trafford family coat of arms. Intriguingly this is topped by a peasant holding a scythe and carries the motto 'now thus hold fast'. Chris Higgins, the current landlord, discovered the story behind the figure: 'After the Norman Conquest English lands were being distributed to French noblemen. When the owner of the Trafford farmland found out that the French were coming to take his land he dressed himself as a peasant, took up a scythe and met the warriors. He explained to them that he was forced to dress and live poorly because the land did not generate a living. He then kindly suggested that they should return to William and request more valuable booty, which they duly did. So he kept his land.'

In March 1895 disaster struck the Trafford Arms when a three-hour cyclone blew two large chimney stacks through the roof of the pub. Although it survived this catastrophe the end seemed nigh on the 27th May 1942 when the pub was severely damaged by bombing. As a result on 15th October 1942 the licence was suspended because of 'war circumstances'. There was some concern that if the pub did not reopen within a short timescale that the licence may be forfeited.

To prevent this happening from August 1943 to 17th November 1955 the Trafford was run by the landlord and his wife, Cecil and Doris Clarke, in a temporary wooden building converted from a large broiler house which was nicknamed the 'Chicken House'. In autumn 1955 the first half of the present building was completed. The pub closed one evening in the Chicken House and reopened the next morning in the new wing which later became the bar. Later the Chicken House was pulled down and the second wing which fronts onto Trafford Road was built. Finally the two halves were joined with an ornamental doorway and the resultant passage became the snug. Unfortunately the two halves did not quite match, but with a little ingenuity and a change in the roofline it was eventually completed. In 2007 an anniversary party was held to mark the 65th anniversary of the bombing when the guest of honour was the lead fire-fighter who had attended the wartime blaze.

Chris Higgins first became joint licensee in 1993. The following year he bought the premises which he now runs with his wife Glynis. When he took over the freehold Chris relished the freedom it gave him, particularly to work with cask beers, which were his forte. He has very clear ideas on what makes a successful pub and good beer:

'Despite what is said about beer before the 1960s some beer was undrinkable. When people talk about the time as almost a golden era I tend to think: "Nostalgia's not what it used to be."

'On the other hand, I would suggest that today you're drinking in an era of the finest quality of cask beer that you'll ever have in your life. The reality of now, compared to earlier periods, is that hygiene standards are impeccable and there's been a massive improvement in production skills. But of course the real revelation that has occurred in the last 30 years is the growth of small breweries producing beers with stunningly different flavours, which give customers a wealth of options that they've never had before.

Half the Trafford Arms, 1955

'One of my big learning points is that you need a changing portfolio of beers. I have three house beers which are currently Woodforde's Wherry, Adnams and Tetleys. My other seven pumps are constantly changing. Customers don't know what treats we have on offer, so they come in to find out. They quite rightly have high expectations of service, choice and quality. It keeps pubs on their toes.

'I spend hours in the cellar. I want to make sure everything is perfect. So I'm fanatical about hygiene and also conditioning and nurturing the brews. Looking after beers is an art form. When they arrive here it can take a week to condition and prepare beers before they're ready to serve.

'There are still some issues around how some landlords look after their beers. In 1997 the industry started the Cask Marque, which is a sign that appears outside pubs guaranteeing that inside you will get a great pint of cask ale. We were the first pub in the City to get it and are proud to say that we still hold it.'

'I think in the future pubs that put themselves out, and go the extra mile for their customers, are the ones that will survive one of the worst periods in our history.

'With a few notable exceptions, such as Colin Keatley's Fat Cat, pubs won't last if they don't serve hot food. People now have greater expectations, which is why I think pubs will become more cafe related than they are at the moment.

'Pubs have a lot of negative press. We seem to have become the whipping boys of the health brigade who hold us responsible for binge drinking despite the fact that, quite rightly, pubs operate in a strict regulatory environment which encourages sensible drinking. In practice people who abuse alcohol are much more likely to buy from supermarkets and off-licences and consume the alcohol at home. Many of the youngsters are known to pre-load, that is drink alcohol at home, before they go to nightclubs.

'Supermarkets are able to sell alcohol much cheaper than pubs. There are a number of reasons for this including the fact that their rateable value is lower than ours and that they buy such massive volumes they get huge discounts. The way we compete with the supermarkets is to offer things they can't including: cask beers, atmosphere and extra levels of service. I like to think of the Trafford as a theatre. When people visit we want to give them a performance so that when they leave they think: "That was great. I'll go back there." '

 From the first, Chris and Glynis have practised what they preach. The Trafford is renowned as a community pub that offers quality real ale and food. During their time here they have raised thousands of pounds for charity. According to Chris: 'When Glynis and I first came here we spent a lot of time building our relationship with the neighbourhood, so that the people who live in the area know that they have somewhere that is theirs. We also do a lot of work for charity. Each year we select a new charity to support which has links with the neighbourhood. Recently we've helped the Hamlet Centre, the Magdalen Group and St Martins Housing Trust.'

In recognition of his work in the community, over 2011/12 Chris served as the City's Sheriff. Since then both he and Glynis have continued to be involved in numerous local events. As Chris says: 'We are proud to be a pub at the hub of the community, which is what all pubs should be.'

Trowel & Hammer

Trowel & Hammer, 2015

Around 1700 the building on St Stephen's Road was known as the 'Spittle House'. The name was believed to be a corruption of the word hospital, as it is documented that it was frequented by 'lepers, lame and decrepit persons'. Around 1755 it was known as the 'Lazar House', 'lazar' being an old term for leper.

 By 1811 the premises was licensed as a tavern. It is assumed that the name relates to a trade guild. However, it is also possible that an early landlord was a Freemason.

 In 1829 the artist William Martin (1753-1831) was lodging here in very poor circumstances. Martin had painted two large pictures, namely 'The Death of Lady Jane Grey' and 'Queen Eleanor, Consort to Edward I', both of which hung for some time in St Andrew's Hall. Around the same time he was voted a grant of 100 guineas by a sympathetic Norwich Corporation.

For many years the Trowel & Hammer was the closest pub to the Norfolk & Norwich Hospital and enjoyed the patronage of many of its medical staff, who often went there for an after work drink. Not wishing to draw attention to their activities they referred to their visits as 'going to see the vicar'.

Trumpet

Trumpet, March 1962

The Trumpet originally stood on the corner of St Stephen's Street and Coburg Street. In the 18th century it was renowned for bitter electioneering clashes between the Whigs and the Tories which took place here.

The original house was demolished in the 1960s, when St Stephen's Street was redeveloped. It was rebuilt in 1963. At this time its off-sales department was located on the site where the original tavern stood.

 The name was linked with the army and according to John Riddington Young in the 1970s 'a beautiful etched mirror... showing a regimental trumpeter of the Household Cavalry' stood in the foyer of the new establishment. At this time it was well known for hosting music groups who appeared there almost nightly. In 1983 it was renamed Swifts and closed six years later.

Bull Inn, 1936

69 St Stephen's Street
George Plunkett

Crown & Angel, 1936

41-43 St Stephen's Street
George Plunkett

Great Eastern, 1961

75 St Stephen's Street
George Plunkett

King William IV, 1954

15 Coburg Street
George Plunkett

Surrey Grove Inn, 1939

74 Grove Road
George Plunkett

St Stephen's Gate, c1725

Drawing by Edward Pococke c1890
Philip Armes collection

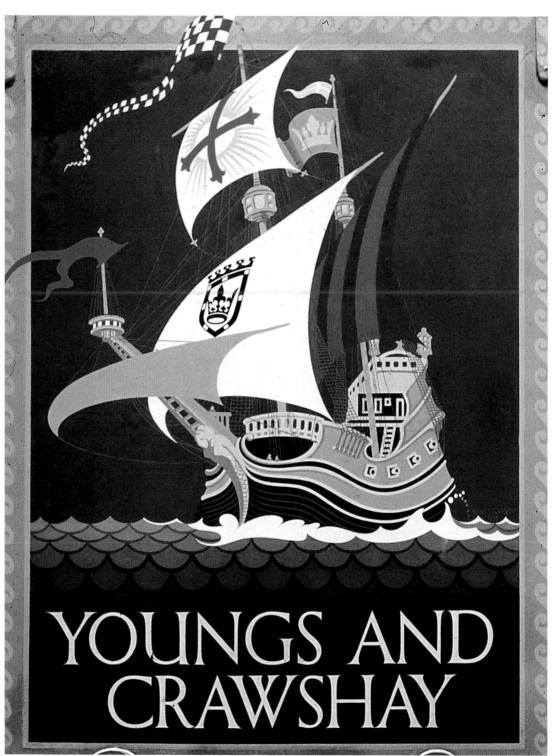

Ship Inn sign, King Street

South-East Norwich

Below is a list of the pubs, inns and taverns located in this area of Norwich. Those with a page reference have an entry or illustration. For further details see page 83.

Page	Pub Name	Location
	British Queen	258 King Street
219	Bull's Head	135 - 137 Ber Street
	Butchers' Arms	88 Ber Street
219	Cinder Ovens	257 King Street
	Cricketers' Rest	207 Queen's Road
219	Fox & Hounds	153 Ber Street
211	Freemasons' Arms	27 Hall Road
219	George IV	72 Ber Street
	Golden Lion	280 King Street
	Half Moon	240 King Street
212	Jolly Butchers	125 Ber Street
219	Jolly Maltsters	255 King Street
215	Keel & Wherry	214 King Street
215	King's Arms	22 Hall Road
216	King's Arms (Berstrete Gates)	174 Ber Street
219	Lily Tavern	152 Ber Street

Page	Pub Name	Location
	Lock & Key	89 Ber Street
219	Mariners' Tavern	39 Mariners' Lane
216	Music House	167 King Street
219	New Inn	194 Queen's Road
	Norwich Arms	103 Ber Street
	Old Friends	119 Ber Street
	Old Friends	136 Ber Street
220	Pheasant Cock	244 Queen's Road
217	Rainbow	185 King Street
220	Recruiting Sergeant	120 Ber Street
220	Richmond Hill Tavern	1 Ber Street Gates
217	Rose	233 - 235 Queen's Road
	Rose Tavern	22 Mariners' Lane
	Royal Oak	64 Ber Street
220	Ship Inn	168 King Street
218	Steam Packet	191 King Street

207

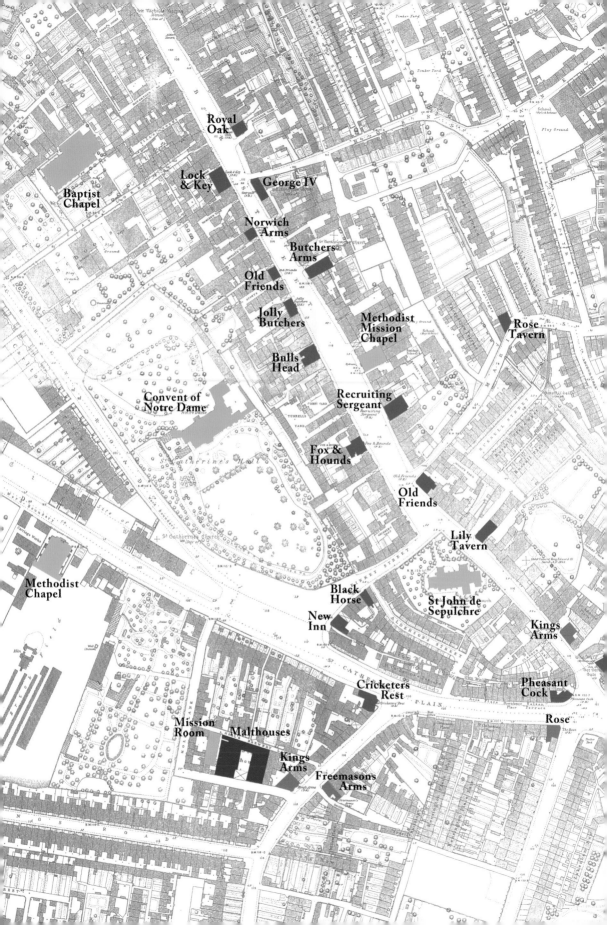

Royal Oak

Lock & Key

Baptist Chapel

George IV

Norwich Arms

Butchers Arms

Old Friends

Jolly Butchers

Methodist Mission Chapel

Rose Tavern

Bulls Head

Convent of Notre Dame

Recruiting Sergeant

Fox & Hounds

Old Friends

Lily Tavern

Methodist Chapel

Black Horse

New Inn

St John de Sepulchre

Kings Arms

Cricketers Rest

Pheasant Cock

Rose

Mission Room

Malthouses

Kings Arms

Freemasons Arms

Music
House

Ship Inn

Mission
Room

Crown
Brewery

Malthouses

Malthouses

Malthouses

St Etheldreda

Mariners
Tavern

Rainbow

Malthouse

Steam
Packet

Malthouses

Keel &
Wherry

St Peter Southgate

Richmond
Hill Tavern

Half
Moon

Malthouse

Jolly
Maltsters

Cinder
Ovens

British
Queen

Golden
Lion

South-East Norwich: Historical Background

Ber Street looking south, c1920

So we come to our final map. Although by Norwich standards it doesn't have a high concentration of hostelries, or a surfeit of buildings of great historical importance, other cities would rightly consider this to be an area of great interest.

It does of course encompass Youngs, Crawshay & Youngs' Crown Brewery (King Street) together with the ancient Music House. Although most of the brewery has been demolished the Music House, together with some of the brewery buildings, have survived and been incorporated into the Wensum Lodge Adult Education Centre.

Of the three medieval churches both St Etheldreda (King Street) and St John de Sepulchre (Finkelgate) still exist and are now in the care of the Norwich Historic Churches Trust. However, in 1884/5 when this map was produced the parish of St Peter Southgate was united with St Etheldreda and subsequently St Peter's (Southgate Lane) was demolished. Today the remnants of a tower are all that survive.

The River Wensum played a large part in the development of this district. In medieval times it made it attractive to rich merchants who built their grand houses here. As time progressed the wealthy moved out of the City in search of the clean air and open spaces beyond and the number of industrial sites grew. Labourers moved into the area. Demand for housing escalated. This was met by cramming ramshackle dwellings into the yards adjacent to the pubs and derelict mansions which proliferated here. For example, we had Fox & Hounds Yard (Ber Street) and Half Moon Yard (King Street). The river also influenced the names of many pubs on King Street, including the Ship, the Keel & Wherry and the Steam Packet.

Finally there are a handful of pubs in Norwich that everyone would expect to be included in this book. One of these is the Jolly Butchers on Ber Street. Unlike other establishments this isn't because of ancient history but it is because of a landlady who gave this quirky pub a character all of its own. I refer of course to Antoinette Hannent who died in 1976, a colourful lady who is still referred to today with much affection as 'Black Anna'.

Freemasons' Arms

Freemasons' Arms, 2005

The original Freemasons' Arms (Hall Road) was a much smaller alehouse than the pub which still trades today. It expanded when the brewery took over the adjacent post office.

 From 1885 to 1912 the landlord was the well known local sportsman George Rye. In his day George was one of Norfolk County Cricket Club's best medium-paced bowlers. He subsequently umpired many matches at the Lakenham ground. After they finished he just managed to sprint back to the pub and be ready for the crowd who would call in to discuss the contest over again. During George's reign the pub naturally became very popular with many local sportsmen including cricketer 'Bones' Howlett and boxer 'Cock' Blyth.

In 1966 Harry and Ethel Lambert took over the pub where they spent many happy years as remembered by their son Barry:

'Mum and Dad first moved into the Freemasons in November 1966. It was the realisation of Dad's dream of having his own pub. When they arrived it was a bit run down and, being on the fringe of the Ber Street red-light district, it had become a favourite haunt of several 'ladies of the night'. It took several months to persuade them to move elsewhere, but after this the pub once more became a recognised family venue.

'The general clientele consisted of men who popped in for a quick pint on the way home from work and those who dropped in and stayed all night drinking and playing the "fruit machines". Wives and partners often accompanied them. The pub also became a regular venue for "the boys" as Dad called them. These were a bunch of around 12 young men who were in local football clubs etc who got together on Friday and Saturday nights to visit all pubs within walking or, more accurately, staggering distance of each other. Depending upon what pub they started

in, the Freemasons was either used as a one or two drinks pop-in venue, or they ended up staying until closing time. We rarely had trouble but Mum was always ready to grab an ex-police truncheon, that she kept behind the bar, should the need arise. I can only remember her going for it once in all the time they had the pub.

 'Dad developed a couple of darts teams in the Lakenham and District League, a cribbage team and a strong social club. Members paid a small weekly sum so that one Sunday in September, we could have the pub annual outing with a coach taking all members to a day on the coast. We'd set out early in the morning to somewhere like Yarmouth or Lowestoft and then would have the obligatory "stop off" en-route, when everyone consumed the large amounts of bottled beer, sandwiches, crisps etc that had been loaded onto the coach prior to departure. The day usually culminated in a meal at a pub or hotel on the way home. A couple of times a Broads' boat trip was organised with all food and beer being provided. These developed into very boozy days out indeed. The community spirit was also very strong at Christmas and the New Year, when we were often so busy we ran out of glasses and had to sell shorts in beer mugs!

'Mum and Dad retired from the pub in 1983 after 16 really great years.'

 Between 1994 and 2005 the premises were taken over by Woodforde's Brewery who asked for suggestions for a new name and couldn't resist calling it after Norwich character Billy Bluelight (c1860-1949).

Harry and Ethel Lambert, 1970

Billy's real name was William Cullum and he would have been turning in his grave at the thought of having a pub named after him, because he was a Temperance campaigner. Some think Billy's nickname came from the blue light of the matches that he sold but it is more likely to be because 'Bluelight' was the popular Victorian nickname for an enthusiastic Temperance worker . . . and Billy was very enthusiastic.

He was famed for standing outside pubs and factories extolling the virtues of abstention. The super fit Billy also advertised the merits of an alcohol free life by racing the Norwich steamboat from Bramerton to the old Carrow Bridge. When the boat passed he would announce to its passengers: 'My name is Billy Bluelight, my age is 45. I hope to get to Carrow Bridge, before the boat arrive.' He would then run off and invariably be at the bridge in time to greet the day trippers, who would shower him with pennies. He was also famed for selling his own cough medicine which he offered as a substitute for the popular domestic remedy of the day, which was hot rum and butter.

It is a surprise to many that Billy did not return to haunt the place when Woodforde's took the opportunity of brewing a new beer to celebrate the opening of their new acquisition, which they called Bluelight Bitter! When Woodforde's sold the pub the name reverted to the Freemasons' Arms, and Billy could rest easily again.

Jolly Butchers

The licence of the Jolly Butchers (Ber Street) can be traced back to the early 19th century.

During WWI it was kept by a William Day, who had been head cellarman for Morgans. William's son, Corporal Sidney Day, went to St Mark's School on Hall Road. In August 1917, when serving in the Suffolk Regiment, Sidney faced the German Hindenberg line at Hargicourt. On 26th August, whilst in command of a bombing section, he was ordered to clear a maze of German trenches between two British advance points. After destroying a machine gun and taking several prisoners, he went on alone to bomb his way forward and link up with one of the advance positions. Subsequently he returned to his section where he saved the lives of five comrades by ejecting a stick bomb from their trench, which immediately exploded. After clearing the trench he established himself in an advanced position which he held for 66 hours under intense hostile fire. His inspirational heroic actions deservedly won him the Victoria Cross (above). Miraculously he survived the War, eventually dying in 1959.

It was in 1935 that landlady Antoinette Hannent (née Carrara) took over the helm of the pub and steered it on to become part of Norwich folklore.

Antoinette, better known as Anna, was the daughter of one of the Italian families who migrated to Norwich around 1880 and until WWI formed a lively community in Ber Street. There is no doubt

Billy Bluelight, c1910

Antoinette Hannent, c1960

Jolly Butchers, 1936

that they were distinctive. The men sported big black moustaches and had little gold rings in their ears whilst olive-skinned women with fiery temperaments had raven black hair that they piled on their heads. Anna's mother, Elizabetta, hired out piano organs from a depot in Newman's Yard, and earned the soubriquet 'queen of the organs'. Anna inherited both her mother's good looks and her fine singing voice. Even as a girl she sang the same Italian operatic airs that rang out from the piano organs. However, jazz became her real love, and she became known as Norwich's Sophie Tucker.

 During WWII Anna was exceptionally popular with US airman who admired her talent and enthusiasm. After the War locals flocked to the Jolly Butchers to hear her, and others, perform. Although she sang on the stage and at jazz festivals she will always be associated with the pub where she reigned supreme for over 40 years.

Out at the back of the Jolly Butchers was a long brick building believed to have been built around 1850 specifically as a lodging house. By the 1920s it was known as Day's Lodging House after William Day. The ground floor contained one huge, tiled kitchen with a big cooking range that used to be kept alive both day and night. Upstairs were dormitories. It was rumoured that at one time the Jolly Butchers had 76 beds. By Anna's time it was basically a doss house. When Anna died in 1976 the brewery closed the lodging house and social services met with residents

who needed to be rehoused. A social worker at the time remembers: 'There were two men still living there and one chap was close to tears. He told us "this is my home". At the end of WWII he'd returned from fighting and found his wife with another man. He walked out and got himself a bed in the Jolly Butchers and had been there ever since, which would be about 30 years. I always found that very moving.'

Albert Cooper, well known for setting up the Jacquard Club, has fond memories of Anna and the Jolly Butchers:

 'After completing National Service I joined the Norwich Philharmonic Choir, which at the time practiced at the Lads' Club on King Street. After rehearsals I walked home along Ber Street where I heard Anna singing at the Jolly Butchers. I used to go in just for a drink. At the time I knew a lot of jazzy type songs and could do simple things like "Baby Won't You Please Come Home". I hit it off immediately with Anna and one night in about 1954 she said: "Why don't you give us a number?" So I did "Hello Central Gimme Doctor Jazz" and things went on from there. She offered me a gig and before I knew where I was, I was performing two to three nights at the Butchers. She started promoting me as part of the bill, always introducing me as "My boy Albert". We formed a partnership and played hundreds of engagements between 1955 and 1964.

'The pub itself was made up of a lounge and bar separated by a narrow hallway. Neither room was more than 12 by 15 feet. Anna sang in the lounge. When I first went there she'd hung some plastic butchers' meat together with a mannequin's head from the ceiling. It could get really smoky and hot in the main bar so on busy nights she'd take the doors off the hinges to let the smoke out and also to let people in the passageway hear.

'The top floor was the lodging house. There was a big room with a row of beds. I always remember that the police had a couple of beds reserved for vagrants who arrived in the City. We'd be half way through a chorus and a police sergeant would arrive and we'd have to stop and Anna'd take them upstairs. You'd find the old boys who stayed there in the bar, they were never allowed in the lounge. Anna's living quarters were on the middle floor and at the back of the pub in another big room was the kitchen and dining hall where she served her lodgers with food. She was hard but also fair and generous. She had a copper stick to stir the laundry and if anyone got out of line she'd use it to shepherd them out of the door. It appears great now, the atmosphere and all, but it was also quite rough. I think one of the attractions was the diverse range of people who came. They ranged from the landed gentry to the down and outs.

'Anna never wanted fame but always had the show biz thing of wanting to be number one in the pub. She never drank, she was teetotal, but she knew I liked a tipple and before we went to perform she always gave me a big whisky in a bone china tea cup. She always had a bottle with her, everyone thought it was gin, but it was tonic water. Her thing was to sing songs with a double entendre such as "Lovely Water Melon". She also did lots of calypsos.

'At that time I picked up songs where I could. I sang anything from folk to gospel to jazz and blues, especially numbers that would be seen as a bit exotic compared to the English style.

'Around 1956, along with friends, I started the Jolly Butcher's skiffle band. Dave Keeley was on the tea chest, Bernard Rudden on the guitar and a chap called Vernon on the washboard. We hardly ever played alone. When she wasn't touring, Beryl Bryden would turn up which was always fun. She'd duet with Anna and play washboard with the skiffle group. By 1961 the group evolved into the Albert Cooper Folk Group, which contained the same musicians, but our set had evolved. We were better musicians and tastes had changed. I stopped playing with Anna regularly in 1964 when my brother Tony and I started the Jacquard Club. She continued to sing in the pub and elsewhere for many successful years after I left. I owe her a lot, she taught me how to entertain an audience.'

Anna enjoying a night out with her barmaids, undated

Keel & Wherry

The Keel & Wherry (King Street) took its name form its proximity to the river. It traded there for almost 200 years before being demolished in 1964. Ray Lince remembers it in the late 1950s: 'The coal wherries used to unload along the river. Opposite the coal yards was the Keel & Wherry pub, whose clientele were mostly drawn from the wherry men. One of them, a colourful character who was "too big to argue with" had a special party trick. When he'd drunk too much at the bar, which happened fairly often, he'd cut the neckties off unsuspecting visitors to the pub!'

Working ships on the River Wensum, undated

King's Arms

The King's Arms (Hall Road) was built in 1824 and first licensed in 1830. Around 1855 Thomas Cott, a pawnbroker, sold it to local brewers Charles Crawshay and John Youngs for £545.

From 1951 to 1973 the pub was presided over by popular landlord Charlie Drake who became so well known that the pub was just referred to as 'Charlie Drake's'. After being a tied house for a number of years in 1998 it was purchased by John Craft and Nicky Howard who ran it as a free house selling a wide range of well-kept cask ales.

In 2004 it was bought by Batemans' Brewery of Wainfleet who carried on John's and Nicky's good work. In fact the King's Arms has gone from strength to strength and has the accolade of being listed in all CAMRA Good Beer Guides this century!

The King's Arms is a traditional City pub that takes pride in offering a great selection of drinks including real ales, imported draught lagers and bottled Belgian beers. It considers itself to be a 'proper local' and is well set up, having both a beer garden and conservatory. It is a favourite with Norwich City fans before and after games but always welcomes away fans, as long as they appreciate real ale! The only food served is a Sunday roast, at other times customers are encouraged to bring in their own food. The landlord then supplies plates, cutlery and condiments enabling diners to enjoy their meals in comfort.

King's Arms, 2011

King's Arms (Berstrete Gates)

The King's Arms (Ber Sreet) could trace its licence back to the 18th century. In 1937 it was renamed the Berstrete Gates, after the nearby portal in the City Wall. The Ber Street Gate was one of the first gates built giving entrance to the City. It consisted of a strong arch with a chamber over it and was placed between two lofty towers. In 1727 it was rebuilt with red brick, but around 80 years later it was demolished, to allow easier movement of traffic.

 On the wall of the premises is Moray-Smith's wall panel depicting the gate. The panel is one of two in the City based on a series of engravings made by Henry Ninham of the City Gates c1792.

Berstrete Gates, 2004

Music House

Parts of the Music House, including the vaults and the northern gable of the current building, are believed to be Norman. It is thought that they were built by Isaac the Jew, a financier, who constructed the cellars as a semi-fortress to store his supply of coin and bullion. The mason's marks on some of the stonework indicate that its builder also worked on the Cathedral Priory. The fact that Isaac was allowed to live outside the Jewry, which was located in the area between the Haymarket and White Lion Street, clearly indicates that he was a privileged person.

Although the early history of the house is hazy it is known that it came into the hands of Henry III. After this it belonged to a string of noble families until it was eventually passed to the Paston family who lived here c1488. From them it was conveyed to Sir Edward Coke (1552-1634), who was Chief Justice for both Elizabeth I and James I.

 It was christened the Music House after it became the home of the Norwich Waits, a famous band of five musicians, each of whom had a residence in King Street. They were presented with their instruments by Queen Elizabeth I, in whose reign they were constituted.

By the late 18th century it had been licensed as a pub. In 1865 Youngs, Crawshay & Youngs bought the Music House, which was adjacent to their Crown Brewery. The cellars' vaulting, which would not discredit the vault of a cathedral, were perfect for storing their brews. The main building not only housed the Music House Inn, where the brewery sold their fine ales, but was also used as offices and was the home of the chief brewer. In 1932 the renewal of the Music House's licence was refused because 'its defects are beyond question'. In the following year it was closed.

After WWII the brewery gave the Music House to the City Corporation and it is now part of the Wensum Lodge Adult Education Centre. Jurnet's Bar, named after the Jewish family who settled here in the 12th century, is located in the Music House cellars.

Music House, 1936

216

Rainbow

YOUNGS AND CRAWSHAY

Rainbow sign, King Street

The licence of the Rainbow (King Street) can be traced back to 1770 when its landlord also worked as a worsted weaver.

 The name could be a reference to the biblical story of the flood and Noah's Ark. However, in view of the importance of the textile trade in Norwich it is more likely to derive from the sign of the Dyers' Company which consisted of a dove and rainbow.

 The rather splendid sign (above) was painted by Arthur Pank in 1957, two years before the tavern was delicensed. Here the rainbow arcs over some of the City's most splendid buildings, including the Cathedral and the Guildhall. In the background large industrial chimneys, which could belong to the breweries, billow picturesque smoke. All in all it is a real reminder of Norwich's heritage.

Rose

Dawn Hopkins, 2015

The Rose (Queen's Road) was first licensed in the mid 19th century. Since then it has also been known as the Rose Tavern and the White Rose.

Since 2003 Dawn Hopkins has run a friendly, welcoming pub complete with a pool table, dartboard and a selection of board games. Being near to Carrow Road, the Rose is always busy on match days with Norwich City fans although 'jolly away fans' are also welcome.

Dawn is a well-known campaigner for pubs, both locally and nationally, often acting as an ambassador for the industry. She believes that local pubs should work together, and so unsurprisingly is a firm supporter of the City's annual City of Ale event.

Rose, 2011

Did You Know?

 In the mid 19th century a pub called the Tumble Down Dick was located on Ber Street. The name is thought to be a derisory reference to Richard Cromwell, who in the 17th century unsuccessfully succeeded his father Oliver as Protector. The words 'tumble down' were frequently used to allude to a 'fall from power' in Restoration satires.

Steam Packet

 In 1884 there were three Steam Packets open within the City-centre including two on King Street. A steam packet is 'a ship that sails a regular route between two ports'. In the late 1800s such a steam ship travelled from Norwich to Bramerton Woods End, Coldham Hall and other riverside resorts.

Ferry Boat, c2000

 The licence of this Steam Packet (King Street) can be traced back to the 1820s. In 1925 it was rechristened as the Ferry Boat Inn. Its name derives from the activity of a former landlord, William Thompson, who set up a ferry service across the Wensum.

The pub was memorable in the early 1970s for having well worn seats in the front bar which were the same shape and had the same covering as then used by the Eastern Counties Omnibus Company! At this time the landlady was Mrs 'Mottie' Warminger, who ran the house for 30 years from 1945. She was considered by John Riddington Young as being a real character who presided over the bar 'with queenly grace at the ripe old age of 84'. She was much cherished and missed after her death, following which the pub was closed for a short period. When it reopened as a free house regulars found that a stuffed cat had been introduced to guard the chimney breast!

In 2006 the Ferry Boat was 'closed for refurbishments' and has never reopened.

Steam Packet next to Thompson's Ferry, c1890

Bull's Head, 1936
135-137 Ber Street
George Plunkett

Cinder Ovens, undated
257 King Street
David Hodgson

Fox & Hounds, 1936
153 Ber Street
George Plunkett

George IV, 1936
72 Ber Street
George Plunkett

Jolly Maltsters, 1983
255 King Street
George Plunkett

Lily Tavern, undated
152 Ber Street
Derek McDonald's collection

Mariners' Tavern, undated
39 Mariners' Lane
NCC Library & Info Service

New Inn, undated
194 Queen's Road
Derek McDonald's collection

Pheasant Cock, 1912
244 Queen's Road
NCC Library & Info Service

Recruiting Sergeant, 1936
120 Ber Street
George Plunkett

Richmond Hill Tavern, 1913
1 Ber Street Gates
NCC Library & Info Service

Ship Inn, 1939
168 King Street
George Plunkett

The Fat Cat

Bar of the Fat Cat, 2011

Few would dispute the fact that the Fat Cat (West End Street) is one of Norwich's most successful pubs of modern times. As we write it has twice been named the CAMRA National Pub of the Year whilst the Good Pub Guide has awarded it the title of Beer Pub of the Year, no fewer than four times. So although it is located outside the 1884/5 City-centre map, we decided that it had to be included.

Going back to 1868 the hostelry was owned by Steward & Patteson and it traded as the New Inn. During 1972, whilst owned by Watneys, it was one of 42 pubs in the City swapped with Courage as part of a government-enforced scheme aimed at bringing more competition to the market. In 1991, when it was bought by Colin and Marjory Keatley, it was sold by Courage as a failing 'bottom end' pub.

Following his tenure at other City hostelries, including the White Lion (Oak Street), Colin was already building up a reputation for selling real ales. When he bought the New Inn he was particularly inspired by the ethos of the Fat Cat pub in Sheffield and decided to rechristen the New Inn accordingly. Subsequently it was closed for five months during which time the premises were refurbished. It reopened with a new décor and, more importantly, four hand pumps.

Today the décor remains simple. On the walls is a superb selection of pub memorabilia, including wonderful old pub signs, indeed its worth visiting just to see these. The Fat Cat is one of the few, successful hostelries which doesn't sell cooked food instead clientele are offered an extensive range of beverages including real ales from no fewer than 12 hand pumps.

Amongst the ales on sale are those produced by the Fat Cat Brewery on Lawson Road (Norwich) which was opened in 2005. Located behind the Brewery Tap (previously the Shed) its opening was the realisation of Colin's dream to operate a brewery. Its brews have included: Marmalade, Cougar and Cat & Canary (the latter in support of Norwich City Football Club aka The Canaries).

Colin believes that the Fat Cat is successful because: 'Our customers always know what they're going to get. Our prices are reasonable and there's always a bargain to be had. We not only sell a huge range of well-kept drinks from across Britain but also from around the world. We even have visits from customers who have come to Norwich specifically to come to the Fat Cat. When I bought the New Inn it was a bit of a gamble . . . but I think that the gamble has paid off!'

221

In Conclusion

Norwich is a lovely city. The pubs and breweries have contributed greatly to both its character and its rich heritage. Rather than mourn their closure we should rejoice in what survives today.

Although we have lost our large breweries and their beers, we must not forget that these have been replaced by many small breweries who take great pride in producing high-quality brews giving drinkers a huge choice.

Similarly few other cities contain the diverse range of pubs that are found in Norwich. There is truly something for everyone. But we cannot afford to be complacent. Although we did have too many drinking establishments in the 19th century, and inevitably some had to close, over the years we have lost superb venues. If we are not to lose more it is essential that licensees are supported.

The very clear message is that Norwich should be proud of its pubs and breweries. A fact very much celebrated in the 'Norwich City of Ale' festival that was launched in May 2011.

Finally we hope that this book has illustrated that pubs and breweries are not only about drinking. They both contribute to, and reflect, our social and economic history. Over time they change but it is essential that we do not forget the stories that surround them and how they have moulded our lives.

Dawn Hopkins, landlady of the Rose and national ambassador for the pub industry, 2015

Acknowledgements

We are very grateful to all our contributors without whom this book could not have been written.

Thanks must be given to Jude Sayer, Olwyn Venn, Paul Venn, Mike Dixon and John Watt, all of whom assisted in preparing the book.

We are exceptionally grateful to Derek McDonald and Richard Bristow (www.norfolkpubs. co.uk) who have both shared their materials and knowledge with us.

Martin Ward and colleagues at Norwich & Norfolk CAMRA have been very supportive throughout as have the team, past and present, at Woodforde's.

Thanks must be given to all of those who shared their own, or their relative's, memories of working in the breweries including: John Hutson, Barry Berwick, John Beaumont, Arthur Houlston, Gloria King and Pauline Smith. In this respect we must also thank modern-day drayman Derek Spanton.

Many landlords, current and former, have also shared their stories including: Peter and Carol Turner, Roger and Anthea Cawdron, Chris and Glynis Higgins, Colin Keatley, Ray Lince and Philip Cutter. Also thanks to Janet Hope, Barry Lambert, Ann Redgrave and Ollie Potter for passing on information about other family members.

We received much help and information in our sign section. Here we need to especially thank Arthur Pank's family, who shared images of his extensive collection of signs with us. Additionally we are very grateful to: Pat Burrows, Cass and Dave Devlin, Philippa and Tony Sims and Antony Murray.

Entertainment has always been very closely linked with the pubs and the following have kindly shared their memories with us: Albert Cooper, Bram Lowe, Bob Cossey, Andy Field, Harvey Platt and Gary Freeman.

We are indebted to the following for sharing ideas and information: Arthur Anderson, Chris and Ruby Baker, John Curson, James Woodrow and Ted Williams.

The book contains many images. Special thanks must be given to the following who have kindly allowed us to reproduce them: Jonathan Plunkett for his permission to reproduce his father's photographs, the Norfolk County Council Library and Information Service, Norfolk Museums and Archaeology Service (Norwich Castle Museum & Art Gallery and the Bridewell Museum), Dick Hudson, Mary Standley (who gave us access Philip Standley's collection of postcards), Philip Armes and Basil Gowen. Details of all contributors can be found at the front of the book.

We have made much use of printed works especially those by John Riddington Young and Walter Wicks. A list of publications can be found in the Bibliography.

A special thank you must be given to Penny Clarke for her guidance and help in preparing this book.

Finally we apologise if we have inadvertently failed to acknowledge any of our sources. Anyone who has not been contacted is invited to write to the publisher so that full recognition can be given in subsequent editions of this book.

Bibliography

Anderson A.P. & Storey N.R. 'Norwich, eighty years of the Norwich Society', Sutton Publishing.

Archant Publications including the Eastern Daily Press and the Eastern Evening News.

Ayers, Brian 'Norwich, A Fine City', Tempus Publishing Inc, 2003.

Brooks, Pamela 'Norwich Street by Street', Breedon Books Publishing, 2006.

Burke, John 'The English Inn', B. T. Batsford, 1981.

Burn,Richard 'The Justice of the Peace and Parish Officer', Cadell, 1797.

CAMRA 'Good Beer Guide', John Waddington of Kirstall Ltd, 1974.

Chapman, Kenneth 'The Breweries of Norwich', (no publisher recorded), 1986.

Clark, Roy 'Black Sailed Traders', Putnam & Company Ltd, 1961.

Coates, Robert 'Pulling Pints: Brewery Vehicles, Past ,Present, Future', Ryburn Publishing Services, 1993.

Cozens-Hardy, Basil & Kent, Ernest 'The Mayors of Norwich 1403 to 1835', Jarrold and Sons Ltd, 1938.

Glover, Brian 'New Beer Guide, A Guide to Britain's Small Brewery Revolution', David & Charles Publishers plc, 1988.

Goreham, Geoffrey 'Yards and Courts of Old Norwich', (no publisher recorded), undated.

Gourvish, Terry 'Norfolk Beers from English Barley: A History of Steward & Patteson', Centre of East Anglian Studies', 1987.

Gurney Read, Joyce 'Trades & Industries of Norwich', Crowes of Norwich, 1988.

Gurney Read, Joyce Miscellaneous collection of information retained in the Local Studies Section, Norfolk & Norwich Millennium Library.

Harris, Kinglsey 'Albert Cooper, A Chronicle of Norwich's King of the Blues', Hannah Publications, 2003.

Hawkins, C.B. 'Norwich: A Social Study', P.L.Warner, 1910.

Haydon, Peter 'The English Pub, A History', Robert Hale Ltd, 1994.

Holmes, Frances and Michael 'The Courts and Yards of Norwich', Norwich Heritage Projects, 2015

Hooton, Cass 'Pubs and People of Norwich', Running Angel, 1987.

Jack, Albert 'The Old Dog and Duck', Penguin Books Ltd, 2009.

Jenkins, Simon 'England's Thousand Best Churches', Penguin Books Ltd, 2000.

Jennings, Paul 'The Local', Tempus Publishing Ltd, 2007.

Livock, J.S. & Dent J.I. 'Wensum Lodge', Wensum Lodge, 1990.

McDonald, Derek 'A Pub Walk With A Difference in 1883', (Big C), 2000.

McDonald, Derek 'Pubs Over the City Walls in 1883', (Big C), 2001.

Meeres, Frank 'A History of Norwich', Phillimore, 1998.

Mottram R.H 'If Stones Could Speak', Richard Clay and Company Ltd, 1953.

Munnings, Sir Alfred 'An Artist's Life', Museum Press Ltd, 1950.

Norwich CAMRA '33rd Norwich Beer Festival Programme' (no publisher recorded), 2010.

Norwich HEART 'Norwich 12', Norwich HEART, 2008.

Norwich Heritage Projects 'A Market For Our Times', Norwich Heritage Projects, 2010.

Norwich Society 'John Moray-Smith', Norwich Society, 2007.

Protz, Roger 'The Little Book of Beer', Campaign for Real Ale Ltd, 2007.

Protz, Roger 'Good Beer Guide, 2011', Campaign for Real Ale Ltd, 2010.

Rawcliffe, Carole and Wilson, Richard 'Medieval Norwich', Hambledon and London, 2004.

Rawcliffe, Carole and Wilson, Richard 'Norwich Since 1550', Hambledon and London, 2004.

Saunders, Pat 'Giants, Evolution and Over Regulation in Brewing', The Journal of the Brewery History Society, 2005.

Smith, Gavin D 'British Brewing', Sutton Publishing, 2004.

Standley, Philip 'Norwich, Volume 1, A Portrait in Old Picture Postcards', S.B. Publications,1988.

Standley, Philip 'Norwich, Volume 2, A Portrait in Old Picture Postcards', S.B. Publications,1989.

Thompson, Leonard 'Norwich Inns', W.E. Harrison & Sons, Ltd, 1947.

Tooke, Colin 'Time Gentlemen Please' Blackwell Print, Great Yarmouth, 2006.

Wicks, Walter 'Inns and Taverns of Old Norwich', (no publisher recorded), 1925.

Youngs, Crawshay & Youngs 'A Coronation Souvenir Brochure of the Crown Brewery, King Street, Norwich', Home Publishing Co, 1937.

Young, John Riddingtom 'The Inns and Taverns of Old Norwich', Wensum Books (Norwich) Ltd, 1975.

Web Sites

www.breweryhistory.com	Owned by the Brewery Society 'for all who are interested in the history of British breweries'.
www.georgeplunkett.co.uk	An outstanding collection of 20th century photographs of 'old Norwich'.
www.archives.norfolk.gov.uk	Information about the archives relating to the history of Norfolk held at the Norfolk Record Office.
www.norwichcamra.org.uk	The web site of the local branch of CAMRA provides a range of information including details of the annual Beer Festival.
www.norfolkpubs.co.uk	An excellent web site which we used extensively. It provides information on all Norfolk's pubs and a selection of breweries.
www.norridge.me.uk	The site incorporates a huge amount of information on both pubs and breweries.
www.picture.norfolk.gov.uk	A superb site operated by the Norfolk County Council Library and Information Service which contains over 16,000 fascinating images of people, places and events from across the county.

Norwich Heritage Projects

Norwich Heritage Projects is a voluntary organisation which is self funding. We are a small group of volunteers who to promote Norwich's rich past. Additional information, including audio and visual recordings can be found on our various websites:

www.norwich-heritage.co.uk
www.norwich-market.org.uk
www.norwichshoes.co.uk

www.norwich-pubs-breweries.co.uk
www.norfolkstainedglass.co.uk
www.norwich-yards.co.uk

Index

226